# The Girls' Life

## Guide to

# Growing Up

ISBN 0-439-27264-5

The information contained in this book is intended to be educational and not for diagnosis, prescription, or treatment of mental and/or physical health disorders, whatsoever. This information should not replace competent medical and/or psychological care. The authors and publisher are in no way liable for any use or misuse of the information.

12  11  10  9  8  7  6  5  4  3  2  1          1  2  3  4  5  6/0

Printed in the U.S.A.                          23

First Scholastic printing, February 2001

Edited by Michelle Roehm
Designed by Andrea L. Boven
Proofread by Laura Carlsmith

# The Girls' Life Guide to Growing Up

**COMPILED & EDITED BY KAREN BOKRAM
AND ALEXIS SINEX**

**ILLUSTRATED BY DEBBIE PALEN**

SCHOLASTIC INC.
New York  Toronto  London  Auckland  Sydney
Mexico City  New Delhi  Hong Kong

# Contents

## THE GIRLS' LIFE GUIDE TO CRUSHES

## THE GIRLS' LIFE GUIDE TO SCHOOL

## THE GIRLS' LIFE GUIDE TO YOU

## THE GIRLS' LIFE GUIDE TO YOUR BODY

## THE GIRLS' LIFE GUIDE TO THE TOUGH STUFF

# Karen's Page

We at *Girls' Life* always get letters asking for advice. Snail mail, e-mail, phone calls, you name it. While the concerns have changed a lot even since we started the magazine ("How do I know my on-line crush isn't some pervert?" "Could a shooting happen at my school?"), it always amazes me how much most of the problems are the same. ("My BFF dumped me." "This guy won't pay attention to me." "My mom doesn't get me.").

The best part of this job has always been meeting with girls one-on-one and hearing what is going on in their lives. Often, I am asked for some great life lesson or word of advice. I hardly know what to answer. We each go through such a unique process growing up, so how could I ever come up with one universal truth? But after giving it much thought, here goes: Never, ever leave frosted, fruit-filled PopTarts unattended in the toaster. Especially *my* toaster.

Conveniently located under a wooden kitchen cabinet, my toaster loosely interprets the "light" setting as something just shy of nuclear meltdown. I shudder to tell you about the morning I ran upstairs to blow-dry, only to come back down to find my breakfast flambée-ing nicely, flames nearly touching the tinderbox that houses my priceless collection of Smurf glasses (and to think they started out life at just 99 cents, while supplies lasted).

PopTarts, I've decided, could possibly serve as the world's next wonder fuel. While other breakfast foods, like toast and English muffins, merely disintegrate into crumbs, you could have a barbecue over a PopTart.

And you have to admire the tenacity and downright bravado of a burning PopTart. Unplug the toaster and your frosted cherry with red sugar sprinkles will only continue to roast in bold defiance. You cannot tame the beast.

I panicked at first, thinking I'd be burning down a national forest by lunchtime. (I live 300 miles from anything vaguely resembling Smokey the Bear territory, but this is a PopTart!) Then I discovered the ancient Chinese secret of PopTart removal—chopsticks. Grab a pair, gingerly grasp the offending PopTart and in one clean motion fling into sink (spring, summer, fall) or snow pile (winter only, and don't forget to open the kitchen window first). So there you have it. My one great truth—a watched PopTart never burns.

I know some people may feel cheated by this, but fact is, I have advice on a million things—and none at all. Why? Truthfully, for as much advice as someone else can give girls, they often already have the best answers. Sometimes it takes hearing it from a trusted person (or their favorite magazine). Sometimes it takes talking over the problem. But most of the time, we girls just need someone else to say what that little voice in our heads and heart already is telling us to do.

There is no crime in asking for advice. And there is even less crime in asking for help. Girls need to know that they are not alone in this journey. It's my hope that after reading this book, girls will feel confident in dealing with the tough stuff. Girls just need to weigh their options, listen to people who genuinely care about them, and then use their best judgment and do what they believe is right. So maybe that's my best advice. That and to get a toaster oven.

When we first had the idea for *The Girls' Life Guide to Growing Up*, I don't think we had a clue what we were getting ourselves into. It all started innocently enough. *Girls' Life* readers would write us and ask for advice on things. Sometimes normal things like guys, family, puberty, friends, school. Sometimes oddball questions like, "Does getting your period stunt your growth?" (No, not unless you smoke your tampons. Oh, just kidding).

Anyway, after six-plus years of doing Girls' Life, we sure had some answers. Why not, we thought, put them all in one place so girls could reference them over and over as the need arose? And with that, a book was born. And by the time we delivered it, it was about twice the size of the one you are holding. Literally.

Our intrepid, patient, wonderful, talented book editor Michelle gave us the bad news. Time to trim. What a buzz kill. We could barely spare a word. After lots of debate and late nights, we got the book down to a meager 300+ pages. What you are holding in your hands is, we think, the best of the best. While we do credit each author in the back of this book, I would like to give a major hearty thanks to those whose talents make *The* Girls' Life *Guide to Growing Up* and *Girls' Life* magazine great.

Here's to my fabulous and foxy regular contributors—writer Roni Cohen-Sandler and senior contributing editor Michelle Silver. Where would Girls' Life be without your wise words?

And I could never thank enough our favorite advice guru, Carol Weston, our own Dear Carol. Be sure to check out her books *Private and Personal*, *For Girls Only*, and *Girltalk* for more great girl guidance. Many thanks also to Bill and Dave, who bravely answer the question, "Why are guys so clueless?" a hundred different ways. You two are the best.

As they say, behind every great magazine is a super talented team of editors and writers (really, they do say that). For the past seven years, Girls' Life has been lucky enough to have some of the best.

Thanks a million to executive editor Kelly White, who makes every sentence come alive. Thanks to art king Chun Kim, who dazzles us, issue in and issue out, with his amazing design skills. (How do you put up with all of us? Remember, we love you.) Thanks to copy babes Georgia Wilson and Debbie Chaillou, who make sure all our text is, well, English. And thanks to all the awesome editors who have made *Girls' Life* the best mag around—Jennifer Lawrence, Kerstin Czarra, Kristen Kemp, Miki Hicks, Molly Dougherty, and Sarah Cordi.

And thank you, Eric and Jack, for not only having faith in *Girls' Life* when no one else did, but also for never once wondering aloud what the heck we're writing about this issue.

Okay, nobody but my mom must still be reading at this point, but I am saving the best for last. We could never have done this book without Michelle Roehm and all of the great folks at Beyond Words. Thanks, Debbie Palen, for the adorable illustrations.

And, finally, mucho thanks and big kisses to my co-editor on this book, Lucky Sinex—you are up to any challenge. I never could have done this without your talent. Hey Luck, anything you want to add? "Thanks to my mom for inspiration, for being there throughout all the stages—you know?" She knows. Suzi, you rock.

Phew, am I done yet? Almost. Thanks most of all to you, our readers. Not only are you the biggest contributors to this book, but you are the reason we did it in the first place.

You can start reading now.

# Letter from Lucky

As recently as a couple of years ago (I'm 17 now), dinner at my house consisted of a few meaningless exchanges of words but mostly just stony silence. The kind of silence that made chewing noises seem annoyingly exaggerated.

Then one night, my mom, in a sincere attempt to have a real conversation with me, asked, "So... what do girls your age like to do?" I answered in a terse, stubborn tone, "I dunno—go to parties, hang out...." My mom smiled and said, "That's nice!"

But I looked down at my plate, frustrated. All I could think was how much she didn't know and how much I wished she did. There were confusing things in my life. But as much as I wanted my mom to understand, I had no interest in sharing everything with her.

Why? Well, my mom and I were at an awkward stage. It's not that she didn't have good advice. I just felt my life was way more complicated and a lot different than when she was growing up. I had issues with boys and dating, school pressure and grades, peer pressure, and all that stuff. Things I sure wasn't comfortable discussing with my mom, of all people.

No way would she understand how things are now, how much more complicated things are than when she was a girl. She couldn't possibly tune in to the whole popularity thing. Nobody asked boys out in her generation. And she never had to deal with her parents getting a divorce.

I needed someone to talk to, someone who had faced the same stuff and totally got what I was going through. My friends were just as lost as I was. We were facing mixed-up feelings about crushes on boys who didn't know we were alive, friendship fights that seemed like the end of the world, and family situations that made our lives ten times harder.

I remember spending hours with my friends, spread out on the bedroom floor, flipping through pages and pages of YM, Seventeen, and Cosmo. We hoped we'd find the magic answers to all our questions. Of course, article after article was about sex and men, things that were only funny to us and held absolutely no relevance. I needed help with my dilemmas.

One time, a boy I had a huge crush on told the whole school I was a lousy kisser and not worth dating. I was devastated and certain my whole life was ruined. Worse yet, my friends started talking about it behind my back. I was convinced no boy would ever talk to me again and that I didn't have a friend in the world.

My mom knew from the way I was acting that something was wrong, but pigs would have to grow wings before I'd tell her what was going on. I kept wishing I had someone to turn to for advice, someone outside my little world who could help without being too involved.

So many things are changing—your body, your thoughts, your emotions, your world—and it's normal to feel lost in what seems like a nightmare with no end. But trust me, it gets easier. A book like this, with good advice from girls who know what they're talking about, sure could have helped me. This book is honest—no cutesy, pretend stuff—and gets to the heart of growing up and coping with real life. It doesn't preach and tell you what to do but instead guides you to make informed decisions and to better understand things.

Take it from me, girls, a little extra advice for all your questions—the serious ones and even the silly ones—will help clear up some of the confusion, even when you're positively convinced nothing will ever make sense!

Love Always,

Lucky (Alexis)

# The Girls' Life Guide to

## Friends

# F-R-I-E-N-D-S

## How To Spell True-Blue Buds

Who just by listening to your good news makes it seem a million times more exciting? Who makes you feel like rejoining the human race after you've been thoroughly humiliated? If we posed these questions to every girl from Boston to Baja, we'd hear a chorus of "Friends!" So why aren't we taught how to find these majorly important people? True, you know a good bud when you've got one, but it's harder to describe just exactly what makes a friend a friend. So letter by letter, we've spelled out exactly what it is to have a bud who's true-blue.

### DOES SHE MAKE YOU FEEL VALUED?

How can you tell if your friend truly likes you? Some girls are naturally affectionate—always throwing arms around shoulders. Others are more comfy showing they care by what they say or do. As Janet, 14, describes, "My best friend isn't the huggy type. Nobody in her family is. But she always makes time to call me, even when she's busy." Waiting for friends, saving seats, and offering to share your very last blue M&M are other ways girls show buds they're important.

With words, however, things sometimes get complicated. Eve, 10, says, "My friends always say sweet things, like how I'm an awesome soccer player and great friend. I love that." But other girls question whether compliments guarantee friendship. "No way," says Megan, 13. "Some girls try to flatter you, and it's not real." Beware of the hyper-complimenter—she may want to use you.

Unlike a user, a true bud values your qualities more than your DVD, pool or hunky big brother. She also lets you know she's lucky to have you as a friend. A real friend makes you feel like a million bucks.

### DO YOU RESPECT HER?

It may be tempting to be friends with the girl whose whispered critiques of classmates provoke rounds of giggles from the others (there's one in every school). Maybe the target of their laughter had the "wrong" shoes, a bad-call haircut or a snort for a laugh. Girls say these "victim bashings" happen all the time and without mercy. Nikki, 12, confides, "I know it's not fair, but the girls who live in the smallest houses or can't afford expensive clothes are ignored by the popular girls. It's like they're not good enough."

Some girls are squirming guiltily—it can be hard to resist being one of the popular's chosen few. But when picking friends, it's important to consider whether you respect how she judges and treats others. Picking a potential friend on the basis of wealth (how many bathrooms are in her house?), clothes (how much Calvin is in her closet?) or possessions (where is her cell phone?) may sound ridiculous, but it happens all the time. You've heard it a million times, but we'll say it again: It's what's on the inside that counts.

There's another, more immediate (and potentially harmful) risk in befriending someone who thinks it's her job to cut on everyone: If she does it to others, is your turn coming?

## IS SHE INTERESTING?

Your friend doesn't have to win an electrophysics scholarship or tour the world by junior high, but she needn't be an ignoramus. If she's got nothing but empty space in her attic, exploring together will be pretty boring. You can only discuss the merits of Kate Spade bags for so long.

Having a friend who knows what's going on in the world, who has interests of her own and can appreciate yours, can spark lively debates and provide food for thought. Don't agree on everything? Even better. Hearing other points of view helps you figure out where you stand.

Amanda, 12, says, "My friend and her family are into politics. Even though my parents vote for the other side, I love to have dinner at her house 'cause they have awesome arguments." Despite not sharing her friend's interest, Suze, 11, also learns from her friend. "Katie's been into riding her whole life," she says. "I've never been on a horse, and I don't plan to either. But it's fun hearing about the competitions, her biggest rivals, and all the places she goes." Whether your friend is an environmental crusader, a collector of awesome stamps, a master of lanyards, or an authority on gerbils, she knows stuff you don't. She brings different ideas and experiences to the friendship.

Also, you don't have to be identical twins. A good bud is comfy with each of you being your own person. Unlike some friends who are all smiles as long as you're doing things their way, your true bud doesn't require you to hate rap, like French pastries or try smoking. A good friend understands that each of you has to make her own personal decisions. And she knows that having your own thoughts, interests and even mannerisms keeps your brains—and the friendship—much more exciting.

## IS SHE EXCEPTIONALLY TRUSTWORTHY?

There's the obvious sort of trust. You wouldn't want a friend to double-cross you, rat on you or spread rumors about you. But we're also talking about the more subtle kind of trust which, when earned, makes a friend amazing.

If you can't count on your good friend to tell you when your zipper's open or your bra strap's making an appearance, who can you trust? When the subject's more personal, it gets even trickier. Ali, 13, confesses that at first it wasn't easy to hear what her best friend had to say. "She basically told me I was too flirty with guys and was getting a bad rep. I was ticked off at first! But later I realized what courage it must have taken for her to tell me. It's not like she wanted me to feel bad. She knew I'd be better off knowing."

On the other hand, there's a fine line here: *How* your friend tells you is part of the trust. Melanie, 13, found out the hard way. "My friend told me I had a huge zit while we were standing in the middle of the lunch line," she says. "She said it loudly, too. And it wasn't like I didn't know!" Afterward, Melanie wondered, "How could she have said it in front of everyone? It was so mean!"

When friends feel close enough to mention the unmentionable, saving you from embarrassment, that's trust. When they humiliate you, that's betrayal.

## IS SHE A NOTCH ABOVE?

We'd rather mention these qualities last because they're bonuses—but then we'd be spelling FRIEDSN. First, if your friend has a sense of humor, cool. You know those moments when you're on the verge of tears or losing it? Then you catch your bud's smirk, and the next thing you know you're both cracking up.

While laughter is great medicine, not all ailments can be cured by a session of giggles. That's when you need a friend who's "a notch above"—willing to go above and beyond the call of duty. Lots of friends can be sweet, kind, and thoughtful. But it's the rare friend who will do these things even when it's totally not convenient for her.

For example, Tracy, 14, says, "When a rumor was going all around school about me, my friend did not ignore it. She marched right up to the kids who started it and blasted 'em. She couldn't have cared less if they got mad."

## IS SHE DEPENDABLE?

Your friend might be reliable in showing up when she says she will, or doing her share of a group project. Then again, Holly, 12, says not all good friends can even pull this off. "My friend," she says, "is a total flake. But she's got lots of good qualities too. So I've learned not to let her borrow my best stuff." Living with friends who are late or forgetful isn't the worst thing. If you can stand it, great. But another kind of dependability test often makes or breaks a friendship: Is your friend loyal?

If, for example, your group decides this week you're the one they'll be mad at, what will your friend do? Will she go along, saying, "Sorry, no choice!"? Or will she stick by you? If you've been left out of weekend plans, accidentally or otherwise, will she remind others that you exist? Tara, 12, has a good example: "On a field trip, we were split into groups, and I was put on a bus all by myself. When Julie saw what had happened, she got right off that bus and went with me."

Let's face it, the social scene can be nerve-wracking. Having a friend's loyalty is like carrying around a good-luck charm.

## IS SHE A GIRL OF SUBSTANCE?

Not every friend can—or should be expected to—fulfill all your needs. But a great friend is someone you can turn to when something big is on your mind. We're not talking gym socks here—your gym teacher's dorky knee-highs can be hashed with anybody (except the gym teacher). But some things are too important—saved strictly for confidantes.

Aimee, 12, says, "Last year when my grandmother died, I was confused and upset. There was only one friend I could talk to. I definitely felt lucky to have her." A friend of substance doesn't ignore you when something bad happens in your life.

You want to share your most personal thoughts with a friend who's comfortable with feelings. She should be a good listener, understand the seriousness of what you're telling her, and be able to imagine herself in your shoes. When you tell a girl of substance something that matters, she's there for you.

While not all friends need to have every quality, really good friends should. And double-check yourself every once in a while. That's what F-R-I-E-N-D-S are for.

# 25 Reasons Why Girlfriends Rock

1. She can lift your spirits when you're in the dumps.
2. She's always on the lookout for the perfect guy.
3. She'll guard the bathroom door.
4. She'll pick up your homework when you're sick.
5. She buys you the silliest souvenirs when she's on vacation.
6. She keeps a lookout for your crush.
7. She makes time after school to help you study.
8. She knows all the dirt from your past...and keeps it to herself.
9. She never laughs when you trip in public.
10. She never tells you to shut up when you are crooning your favorite tunes, even though your voice is bad.
11. After reading her horoscope, she checks out yours and clues you in.
12. She takes your back when you slip in late for class.
13. She makes up the sweetest white lies.
14. She thinks you look great without makeup.
15. She lets you moan about your problems...for hours.
16. She brings out the silly side in you.
17. She always has good advice to give you.
18. She shares your embarrassing moments.
19. She lends you a shoulder to cry on.
20. She gets along with your parents.
21. She lets you borrow her clothes on a weekly basis.
22. She lends you $5 when you forget your lunch money.
23. She makes you number one on her speed dial.
24. She knows what you are thinking before you even say it.
25. She think you rock and lets you know it.

**—KRISTEL BOE, 15**

# Best Bud Challenge

"We're like two peas in a pod," you claim. "I know her better than she knows herself." But do you really know your BFF as well as you think? There's one way to find out. Grab a pen and your best bud. Take turns answering the following questions. Give each other a point for every right answer, and then check your score to see if you two really are of the same pod.

## WOULD SHE OR WOULDN'T SHE?
*Write true or false in the blanks as to how you think your BFF would behave.*

If the school bully was being nasty and calling a second grader "Shrimp," your BFF would be the first to stand up for her. ____

She'd be honest and tell you if your mini was too mini before you showed your undies to the entire middle school.____

If she found a twenty-dollar bill on the sidewalk, she'd stuff it in her pocket and swear she had dropped it. ____

She'd lie to your parents and hers if it meant you wouldn't be grounded for a month. ____

The dog has definitely eaten her homework more than once. ____

If your mom asked for help washing the dishes after you and your BFF cooked dinner, she'd be out the door before you could blink an eye. ____

If you two were crushing over the same guy, she'd be happy for you if he called. ____

## PICK HER FAVORITES
*Circle the item in each category that your BFF likes the most.*

**Clothes**: embroidered jeans, Adidas sweats, a black tube top, Gap cargos, anything clean

**Shoes**: flip flops, Doc Martens, Nikes, platform knee-hi boots, red sling back wedges

**Food**: veggie burger, pizza, burrito, sushi, peanut butter and jelly sandwich

**CD**: Fiona Apple, Mariah Carey, LeAnne Rimes, BSB, Busta Rhymes

**Accessory**: Yankees hat, cat-eye sunglasses, a shrug, Kate Spade bag, Hello Kitty book-bag

**Subject**: American history, English, photography, chemistry, lunch

**Cause**: PETA, Greenpeace, Young Republicans, Habitat for Humanity, herself

## HER DREAMS
*Circle the letter of the option that best fits your friend.*

Twenty years from now, you'd most likely hear her say…
a) "I plan to open a seventh homeless shelter."
b) "I accept my nomination to be President of the U.S."
c) "I want to thank the Academy."
d) "Would you like fries with that?"

She'd choose to live:
a) in the mountains of Colorado
b) in New York City
c) in a country you need an atlas to find
d) exactly where she is

Her first car will be:
a) a Jeep Wrangler
b) a BMW convertible
c) an oversized pick-up
d) a Cannondale

If she could redo her bedroom, she would definitely include:
a) a four poster canopy, lots of lacey pillows, and frilly sheets
b) a futon, lava lamp, and her Phish CDs
c) a blow-up arm chair and wall-to-wall BSB posters
d) a walk-in closet with a computerized outfit selection system

Her idea of a perfect night is:
a) hanging with a group of guys and girls at a party complete with a DJ and dance floor
b) renting *Now and Then*—just the two of you
c) packing a dinner picnic and heading for a sunset hike with a small group
d) spending the evening with her boyfriend at a major league baseball game

Her dream guy will:
a) hike mountains, save whales, recycle
b) drive an Audi, have a gold card, invest wisely
c) hop on his Harley, wear leather, ride on the wild side
d) call back

She'll name her first daughter:
a) after her mom
b) after her favorite literary heroine
c) after you
d) after she gets back from the business trip she just couldn't miss

**IT COULD HAPPEN...**
*Circle the appropriate celebs for the following questions.*

If she could trade places with one of the following, she'd choose:
Hillary Clinton, Oprah Winfrey, Cindy Crawford, Britney Spears

Her dream date is:
Justin Timberlake, Brad Pitt, Chris O'Donnell, Derek Jeter

She would most like to raid the closet of:
Marilyn Manson, the Olsen twins, Sara Michelle Gellar, Jennifer Aniston

If she could switch her mom with a TV mom for a week it would be:
Roseanne, Annie Camden, Marge Simpson, Gail Leary

**LOVES AND HATES**
*Fill in the following blanks.*

Her favorite TV show of all time is _____.

She is most likely to spend her allowance on _____.

Her biggest pet peeve is _____.

Her dream vacation is to visit _____.

She'd most like to meet _____.

The beauty product she can't live without is _____.

The quality she loves about you is _____.

**IN A NUTSHELL**
*Circle one description in each line that best fits your BFF.*

1. info seeker/info giver
2. life of the party/couch potato
3. secret keeper/secret blabber
4. fashion diva/fashion disaster
5. it's always "on her"/splits tax down the middle
6. always early/"Oh boy, look at the time."
7. class clown/classy
8. adventurous/adventure-less

## ADD IT UP

*Give each other one point for each correct answer, add up the total, and locate your score.*

### 31 - 40 Siamese Twins

You two aren't just of the same pod. You're practically the same pea. It's awesome that you've found her; you're truest of buds. Knowing each other so well means you can really help each other in times of need and social planning. Instead of guessing what's best for each other, you rely on strong vibes. Still, don't forget there are lots of other great girls out there, so don't tune yourselves out completely to the world.

### 21 - 30 Closest of Companions

Just because you're not attached at the hip doesn't mean you're not the best of friends. You're obviously in sync with each other and enjoy talking about stuff that's important to you. You may be happiest exactly where you are in your friendship. If so, enjoy. If you aspire to know more about each other, find out—that's what having friends is for.

### 11 - 20 Room for Improvement

You might want to clue in a bit. But that doesn't mean you have to trash the friendship. If you like and trust each other, make more one-on-one time. Go for a hike, hang in your backyard, or just crash on the couch and chat. You don't have to force bonding by spilling your guts, but try to open up. Share some of your thoughts, goals and experiences. If you're having trouble, use this quiz to get started.

### 1 - 10 Missing the Boat

Yikes! Did you take this quiz with a stranger? Put simply, friendship takes effort. Try following the advice in "Room for Improvement" (above). When listening, pay close attention, ask questions and make an effort to truly understand her. Be sure she's doing the same for you. You may have to remind each other, but, hey, the friendship can only grow. If it doesn't, you may have to say adios and find new friends who are willing to put forth the effort it takes to make a friendship grow.

# SINGIN' THE U-HAUL BLUES

*How To Deal When Your Best Bud Moves*

Is your best bud moving? It's sad, I know. Here are some tips on dealing with it, staying close, and, gulp, finding new friends.

**Getting the news.** When your BFF tells you the sad news, don't start mourning right away. More than likely, she feels as bad as you do. Be supportive and take advantage of the time you have left. Spend your last weeks together having fun, not crying over the move.

**The big day.** The moving trucks are loaded, and you and your BFF are sitting on her porch. You haven't said much—you want your good-bye to be short, sweet and sincere. Finding the right words is the hardest part. There is no perfect phrase. Just let her know you'll miss her, and that you'll e-mail and call lots. Let her know she'll always be important to you even though she may be ten states away.

**Hitting the new school year...without her.** You meet your friends at the normal spot to catch up on gossip. But something's not right. You sit solo on the bus while your other friends have someone to sit with. It's obvious what's missing here. But now that school is going again, you can meet a world of new people!

**Where to begin?** Start by being the first person to say "hi" to the new kids at your school who left their BFFs behind. Be polite, tell the new girl about yourself and ask about her. Just make sure every other word out of your mouth is not about how great your old BFF is.

**Make new friends and keep the old.** You're back on your feet and feeling good. You have new friends and things are going great. But don't get so caught up in your new social whirl that you forget your old friend. E-mail is a totally cheap, cool way to stay in touch. When you write, tell your old BFF what's up with you and everyone she knew. And call, if your parents say it is okay (long distance costs money, ya know). Send cute postcards of places you two hung out in your town. Go down to the beach you two used to hang out at and send her some sand, or pick a leaf from the tree you two used to climb. Little reminders mean a lot.

—APRIL A. MAAS, 11

17

# Peace on Planet Friendship

They're your two closest friends in the world—so why do they insist on disliking one another? Maybe they won't give each other the time of day; or worse, they bicker and talk behind each other's back. It makes no sense. You adore them *both*.

By mathematical standards, shouldn't they get along? If A likes B and A likes C, then B and C should like each other. Unfortunately, relationships can defy logic—mathematical theory just does not apply to anything as finicky as friendship.

Take Jennifer, 12. She loves hanging out with Debbie because the girl keeps her in side-splitting laughter. "You should see Deb's Britney Spears impression," Jennifer says. Jennifer's new friend, Meg from ballet school, is a class clown who will also do anything for a laugh, including pirouetting herself straight into the nearest wall. "It was obvious Deb and Meg would be crazy about each other," says Jennifer. "I couldn't wait to introduce them."

They all agreed to meet at a park one afternoon, go skateboarding and hang out for a while. Unfortunately, things didn't go as well as Jennifer predicted.

"I had been telling them they would love each other because they were both so funny," Jennifer says. "They couldn't wait to meet. But when the three of us got together, they just didn't get each other's sense of humor. When one made a joke, the other sat there, and I was the only one laughing." Jennifer didn't laugh long. The afternoon was cut short when Meg abruptly said she had to get home for dinner—at like 3:00. The rest of the day, Debbie talked about how obnoxious Meg was. Jennifer never got the two together again and can barely mention one of their names to the other without getting an eye roll.

The sad truth is that this happens all the time. One friend tries to set up two friends who she feels will be a natural fit. Only the fit is about as natural as cramming a tape cassette into a CD player. It's a bummer when your hopes for a fun-loving trio are dashed. What really stinks, though, is when both girls clearly disapprove of your friendship with the other. As the friend in the middle, you get pulled in both directions, defending yourself and apologizing after incidentally mentioning to one friend that the other just won the talent show at the rec center. ("Hello? Do I look like I care?")

It may be sheer jealousy—two friends vying for your attention, intent on disliking "the enemy" who steals too much of your time. Whatever the case, you can't force people to like each other. But you can arrange things so you don't feel guilty for being friends with both of them. After all, it's not your fault your friends dislike (read: can't stand) each other. Here's our six-step program for dealing with dueling buds.

**STEP 1: Face facts.** If your buds meet, don't hit it off, and choose not to hang out together, that's their call. There's nothing you can do about it, so why try? Just because you adore someone doesn't mean your bud has to.

Often, friends are drawn to each other because they appreciate each other's different qualities and personality traits. When you mix two buds who are alike—same outlook, humor, smarts—they sometimes clash. Whatever the reason, respect your friends' decisions to steer clear of each other. Pushing them together could make them more intent on disliking each other and resentful of you for not understanding. So, yes, you can feel bummed the threesome isn't happening, but don't take your disappointment out on them.

**STEP 2: Find out the real deal.** It's one thing if your friends choose not to acknowledge each other. It's quite another if you feel shunned for spending time with either of them. If they constantly make negative remarks about the other, find out what's causing the hostility. Don't guess. Ask.

★ Talk to each friend separately. Don't arrange a meeting for all of you to sit around and discuss the problem. They're likely to clam up and resent you for forcing them into an awkward situation.

★ Don't accuse ("You obviously hate her!") or demand ("You'd better be nicer to her!"). This only makes people defensive.

★ Ask straight out what the deal is: "I can see you dislike Meg, but why do you get mad when I bring up her name?" Let her talk without interruption.

**STEP 3: Listen, and decide for yourself.** Often, there's no good reason for one friend disliking another. Your bud just doesn't get good vibes, end of story. But on occasion, a bud will have a valid point as to why she thinks your other friend is bad news. She may believe this new bud uses you, lies to you, or is a bad influence. Hear her out. It's worth considering that your friend *may* have a good point. Then decide for yourself whether there might be an inkling of truth in what she says.

**STEP 4: Dish out a few kind words.** If this is not about a friend being territorial or protective, and she has no valid reason for disliking the other friend, face it, it may boil down to jealousy. She may be upset because you took your other friend to a concert,instead of her. Or you put your sleeping bag next to your other friend at the sleepover. If so, your friend may need reassurance that you still value her as much as ever. Sure, it's obvious to you, but don't assume it is for her. This is especially true when the angry one is an old friend feeling threatened by a new one.

Try a little empathy:

★ You don't have to mention that you suspect there is jealousy. It would probably just make your bud feel foolish.

★ Try, "I just want you to know that I love hanging out with you."

★ Plan fun things for the two of you.

★ Be sensitive. Is it really necessary to talk about how fantastic the other friend is—or even mention her name?

**STEP 5: Set boundaries.** It's good to keep your buds' feelings in mind, but you also have to stand up for yourself if you feel uncomfortable. You have the right to be friends with whomever you wish—without getting flack from any other friends. Fine—your buds want nothing to do with each other. But you don't have to listen to them tear into each other. If a bud makes jokes at the other's expense, spews nasty comments, or tries to convince you how horrible the other is, you need to set limits:

• Say, "It's okay that you don't want to be friends with Debbie, but it hurts my feelings when you make fun of her."

• If she continues to diss your bud even after you've asked her not to, you might have to take it a step further: "It really bothers me when you say nasty things about Meg. Let's change the subject."

**STEP 6: Keep a little faith.** Unfortunately, chances are your two buds will never like each other. But you never know—they may come to tolerate each other if you leave them alone. If they bump into each other enough (especially when you're not around), they may get to talking and realize they kinda, sorta like each other. If you're tempted to yell, "Yahoo!" and plan an overnight for the three of you, don't. If they're to be friends, it has to evolve naturally, over time. Any sign of pushing from you will send them running in opposite directions again. So stay cool!

**When things go a little too well:** Maybe your buds will start to see in each other what you see in them. They may actually enjoy time together when they don't feel they're competing for your affection. They might even hang out with each other, share private jokes, or create their own cryptic messages. Hey! Are you being excluded? You wanted them to get along, right? But you're not so sure anymore. It's easy to feel insecure when two friends who couldn't stand each other become friends outside your domain. Let them. If you accuse them of leaving you out, you're not only going to seem jealous, you'll be a hypocrite. You assured them there was room for both of them in your life. So take your own advice and enjoy the fact you have such fantastic friends.

# I Just Got Dumped!

It's something for The X-Files. For months you're totally in with a group—passing notes, making sleepover plans, and sharing lockers. The whole thing. Then one day it happens. The very girls you thought were your best friends in the entire world suddenly let you know, subtly or otherwise, that you are now out. Way out. Somehow, it doesn't matter how long you've been friends, or how much fun you've all shared in the past. There's a saying for times like this: "Into each life, a little rain must fall." And baby, it's pouring.

Welcome to the darkest, loneliest hours girls have to face. We cannot tell a lie—this is one of the most unexplainable, mean-spirited phenomena that happens to girls. And it does happen—all the time. No matter how popular you are, sooner or later the winds shift, and it's your turn to be isolated, gossiped about, and completely shunned. Thankfully, it usually only lasts a few days, often just one.

Ask older girls about it, and many will tell you about the time their so-called friends ganged up on them. They'll tell you how it started, what it felt like and how relieved they were when it finally blew over. Why do girls do this to each other? What if it happens to you? We can only hope it never will. But if it does, here is how to ride out your social storm.

First, we'll tackle the "why." The simple version goes like this: You do or say something that offends one friend. Maybe you tell Jill you think Lisa's new hairstyle is "so last year"—and it is—"but don't tell her I said so." Before you know it, Lisa is furious you're talking about her—and her hair!—behind her back. Or you admit to another bud you got a note from the guy she likes—and she goes ballistic. Or you say something as trivial as, "Ew, gross," when one friend unwraps her tuna sandwich at lunch. Whatever you did, for whatever reason, you've ticked someone off. And she's not planning to let it go.

Ideally, your friend would pull you aside and say, "Listen, you hurt my feelings. Can we talk about it?" Some girls have friends mature enough to actually handle it this way. But many girls seem to think the best tactic is to strike out and hurt you back. What better way than to get all your friends mad at you? All it takes is a little manipulating on a girl's part. She goes to each friend and informs them about the horrible thing you did, blowing it way out of proportion. Then, she tells them what a jerk you are and how anyone who would associate with you is obviously a jerk too. Next thing you know, you're under group attack.

Let's face it, no one wants to be an outcast. So even if the others feel badly for you, there's a good chance they won't risk defending you. (Note: This is not a "girl thing." Many guys also aren't willing to defend another kid if they think they might get shut out of the group.)

Some of you know the next scene well. You're sitting alone during lunch. Your friends are whispering to one another—about you, no doubt. Or they're passing notes to each other and laughing. When you try to talk to them, walk near them, or smile, they turn away like you're the villain who cursed their kingdom.

## WHAT DO I DO?

We know what you'd like to do: go up to the other girls and scream, "Knock it off!" Or cut out of school, go home, and crawl under your covers. We also know what you think you might do—break into uncontrollable tears. Don't. The best thing to do is keep your cool. Take a deep breath, and let it out. Tell yourself you are going to get through this (you will) and that it has an ending (it does).

If this sounds like Mission Impossible, here's what not to do: Go to your friends when they are in a group and remind them you're not the enemy. Fair or unfair, they've already decided you are. And as we said, it's doubtful anyone will break from the group to help you. That takes guts and maturity—qualities these girls are lacking at the moment, or you wouldn't be here.

Approach the girl you've angered when she is alone. She is not as likely to ignore you if she doesn't have the others backing her. Tell her you're sorry for what you did (assuming you are). Most likely, she will start talking. This is good. It's not fun, but it's conversation—and it keeps the focus between you two. Hopefully, you'll work things out at this point. If you do, tell her you're glad you resolved things, but it's important she comes to you next time she's mad—instead of involving third parties.

If you can't work things out—she ignores you or keeps yelling—walk away. Do not beg forgiveness, scream, or play victim. You'll feel stupid, and she will learn that ganging up on you helps her get her way. Keep your head up and get through the day—hour by hour. If there are others you can hang out with, do so. In the meantime, the gang will tire of treating you like a victim.

## I DON'T KNOW WHAT I EVEN DID!

The only thing worse than the situation above is when you have no idea why you're being outcast. You're Target Without a Cause.

Leslie, 13, says that in her grade, it's usually fake girls who get targeted: "If a girl lies just for the sake of it, and once the word is out that she is a liar, look out. The other girls will make her miserable." She says it's especially the girls who act phony in front of guys who get it. "This one girl in my class acts all giggly and dumb in front of guys," says Leslie. "We hate her for it. We were mean to her for a few days just so she would cut it out. But of course she didn't know why she was being left out. We should have told her the reason."

Adds Tara, 12, "It's strange because it even happens to popular girls. It's like girls want to show someone who's popular what it's like to not be so popular." She also says when it comes to being dumped some girls fare better than others.

"Some girls cry or beg forgiveness. That's the worst thing to do," says Tara. "Yeah," adds Leslie, "You just look desperate." So how should you handle it? They both agree: If no one will talk to you, keep your chin up. Have a little attitude, as if you couldn't care less about their stupid game and remind yourself that it'll pass.

## WHAT IF THINGS DON'T GET BETTER?

A day or two has passed, and you're still sitting by yourself at lunch. Just going to school is making you sick to your stomach, and you worry that it might never end.

Now is the time to bring in your guidance counselor, who is trained to deal with problems like this. Believe us, she's seen it before. The counselor will sit with you and hear your side of the story, and then bring in the other girls. You may feel you're tattling or making things worse. But, heck, it beats being tormented one more day. The counselor's job is to get everyone talking—and that's the first step to clearing things up.

## YOU CAN BREAK THE CYCLE!

If you think, "I have never seen anything like this at my school," or "My friends would never pull something like this"—great! We wouldn't wish it on anyone. However, if in the future you are asked to join a group in shutting another person out, you'll be on guard.

You can be the one to ask the group to stop and think about what they are doing to the poor girl they are turning on. Ask them why they are exiling her and whether it's something they'll feel good about later. (If they answer yes, rest assured they'll get around to doing it to you. Run, do not walk, to a new group of girls and start making some new friends!)

If they go ahead and strike, don't play along. Not only will you feel stronger for not taking part, but your fairness will be remembered when this ridiculous war is over. You don't even need to make a big statement. Just sitting out is often good enough. In addition to winning the undying loyalty of the girl in question, others will notice your strength and courage. This will drastically cut down your own risk of attack. It's never easy to go against the group, but it sure beats going against your belief system. Here's to hoping we all can someday live in peace.

# After the Blow Up

## Making Up & Moving On

You and your bud have made a pact to be best friends forever. You plan on buying houses next door to each other, marrying identical twins and having daughters that will be the best of friends. So why are you two no longer even speaking to each other? It happened so quickly. First, there was the out-and-out fight, when you both spewed some nasty words. Then you stopped speaking. Now you are taking the long way from homeroom to first period just to avoid passing her in the hall.

Or maybe you haven't exchanged a single hateful word—but it's obvious to you and the rest of the school that she's flat-out ignoring you. And what's really weird is that you're clueless as to why she is so ticked off.

Having a fallout with a close friend feels terrible. You may be upset, hurt, shocked or confused. If the conflict lingers, negative vibes make everyone within a five-mile radius squirm. Friction between best buds is as common as the cold and makes girls just as miserable, especially when they have no clue how to deal. Are you supposed to ignore your friend and hope the whole thing'll blow over? Should you wait for her to apologize? What if—your worst fear—she never does? As if all this weren't bad enough, you have to deal with news of The Fight spreading, causing the whole school to take sides. Could your entire social life become a casualty of friendship warfare?

In the icy aftermath of a fight, it sometimes seems that way. As painful silence stretches across hours and days, it gets harder for you and your bud to know how to stop it. But you can choose to get your relationship back on track.

## FIGURE OUT WHY YOU'RE FIGHTING

If your argument is totally stupid, it's likely to blow over by itself. For example, your friend's gum cracking gets on your nerves, or she's upset you accidentally ripped her geography book cover. These issues are hardly biggies.

More serious disagreements occur when someone's genuinely upset, disappointed or hurt over something the other person said or did. Sometimes it's clear as crystal you've messed up, like when you blab a secret or badmouth a friend. If you want to make up, it's up to you to apologize and make nice.

If you're peeved 'cause your friend ignores you when her crush is around or treats you like a homework hotline, she should agree to change her ways. But it's usually not so simple. More often, it's nobody's fault, both your faults, or unclear whose fault it is. That's why it's so tricky figuring out how to fix broken friendships.

## UNDERSTAND THIS MAY BE NO-FAULT

The fights that are hardest to resolve are the ones where you can't pinpoint who's right and who's wrong. Tina, 13, says her friend Bethany began ignoring her one day. "When I asked what was up, she said, 'Nothing—I'm not ignoring you.'" Tina later found out Bethany was acting strangely because another friend was angry at Tina, and Bethany "felt she had to hate me to keep that girl as a friend." Since the girls never talked it over, their friendship was severely damaged—even after Tina made up with the other girl. Tina says, "Bethany and I are no longer best buds."

Other times, after a dose of silence girls gradually start talking again. Erica, 14, reports her friend Karin was mad for an unknown reason and completely ignored her at a party. "But the next Monday, she acted as if nothing had happened." Since Erica was confused about why Karin "got mad for nothing," she says, "things haven't been the same."

Even if you and your friend can't agree, it's important to talk it through. It may seem easier to avoid each other, but ignoring small disappointments hurts a friendship. Unless you and your friend understand how each other feels, you're likely to keep upsetting each other. Also, bad feelings linger and damage trust. Instead of letting your friendship go down the tubes, try these steps:

## 1. Face your fears

What gets in the way of friends being straight with each other? Fear, plain and simple. Many people's worst fear is rejection. You may worry that after pouring your heart out, your best friend will continue to blow you off. Or maybe you're scared of saying what's on your mind when you're so upset. What if you don't choose the right words, or start crying and your friend laughs at you?

It's possible you won't be perfectly poised, but coach yourself to face the fear. If you break the code of silence and your pal gives you a dirty look, so what? Rejection might sting, but it is never fatal. If your friend dumps you, the friendship probably wasn't the best. So, take a deep breath and relax. The occasional spat can help you and your friend air what's been bugging you. Conflict can help you reach compromises that will strengthen your relationship, if you handle it well.

## 2. Make the first move

Once you get past the anxiety, it's a lot easier to gear up for a talk. Don't wait for your friend to come to you. Even if she should make the first move, does it really matter? If you let the fight fester, you both lose. If you make up, you both win. So instead of waiting for her to fix the problem, take charge.

As for timing, the sooner the better. It limits the chance everyone on the planet will dish the dirt, take sides, and make things worse. Also, the longer you wait, the more you waste on what should be awesome friendship time. If you feel too angry to approach her, take a day or two to collect your thoughts.

## 3. Offer the olive branch

Instead of pretending nothing happened, test the waters. Bring up the tension in a neutral way ("Hi, I miss you." "This stinks, doesn't it?" "Should we call a truce?") If you feel uncomfortable saying it to her face, slip her a message on a piece of paper with a hopeful smile.

Since everybody has different timelines for cooling off and moving past fights, remember that your style may be different from your friend's. If you get a nasty scowl in response to your kindness, don't despair. You can say, "You're still upset. When you cool off, let's talk."

Then give her space. Even though you may be eager to make up, respect your friend's need to chill. When she's ready to talk, you'll get better results.

## 4. Hear each other out

When you're both convinced you're right, listening to each other is tough. But how else can you find out what your friend is feeling? If needed, spell out the ground rules: "I'll listen to your view and then I'll tell you how I feel." Don't interrupt or argue while the other person is speaking.

And here's the hardest part—Listen! Think about what your friend is saying and imagine what it's been like for her. Maybe you can understand her position. Even if you didn't mean to be gossipy or exclude her, you can see why she felt that way. Hopefully, she'll do the same. That means you two respect each other.

## 5. Agree to disagree

Sometimes, no matter how hard you try, you won't agree with your friend. She sees it one way; you see it another. It's okay that you may never see eye-to-eye, as long as you hear each other's point of view without dissing it. Agree to disagree. Then move on. Each of you can take responsibility for your part. Saying, "I'm sorry" doesn't mean you admit guilt. Instead, it lets her know you care for her feelings. Even if you did nothing wrong, you can be sorry your friend was hurt. And you're both probably sorry the whole fight ever happened.

## 6. Do things differently

Can you do things differently to avoid similar fights? Maybe next time you can warn each other when you're in a bad mood or ask before borrowing stuff. You can even remember to be extra sensitive if your bud feels ignored next time you start soccer season or make a new friend at chess club.

## 7. Forgive each other

To rise above a fight, you must forgive. That doesn't mean forgetting what happened, but putting it in the past. As tempting as it may be to bring up the fight or rub it in, focus on the present and future. Even though it often takes a while for things to get back to normal, memories of the fight and uncomfortable feelings will fade over time.

## 8. Move on

Sometimes getting over a fight seems to take forever. One of you may be a world-class grudge holder. Or perhaps emotions run too high to talk things out. In these cases, ask for help. A neutral friend, counselor, teacher, or parent can help without taking sides. Working through fights is worth the trouble to keep valued friendships intact. Blow-ups, even with your best bud since kindergarten, don't have to be the end of the friendship. You have the power to put the healing process into action. And knowing how to move on after a fight leaves you confident to say what's on your mind in all of your relationships.

# Bad News Buds

In that cool picture from last summer of you and your buds, you're all standing in a row, arms linked, with matching smiles and tankinis. Whether that picture lives on your dresser or only in your mind, you remember the happy feeling of being part of the group.

But things've changed since then. Your friends are exploring new paths, some of which make you not-so-comfortable. Maybe you found yourself part of a spontaneous shoplifting trip to the mall that left you wanting to crawl under the fake shrubbery. Or you may have considered moving to Bora Bora when you discovered everyone else in your group (except you, that is) was planning to cheat on the mid-terms.

Maybe it's not your whole group that's gone astray, just the one BFF who really matters. You've known her for a trillion years, but suddenly she's morphed into this, well, not exactly terrific person. You want to remain friends, but you wish she'd stop acting so high-and-mighty, weird, slutty, whatever.

As much as you'd like the power to turn everyone magically into how they used to be, you're not Sabrina. So what to do? Besides worry, that is. What follows are some answers to girls' top tricky questions about moral choices.

**1. Why have things gotten so complicated?** It was so simple when your biggest debate with buds was whether to play Pictionary or Monopoly. Sometimes you got your way; sometimes you didn't. But now, with friends venturing into iffy or off-limits territory, you feel pulled in different directions.

Louisa, 12, has struggled since her group started lifting stuff from the mall. "It was so great to hang with my friends without any parents around," she says, "but then it felt really weird when I realized they didn't exactly buy all the stuff they got."

When a similar thing happened to Maura, 11, she felt "like such a baby because I got so scared a cop was going to come up and arrest me. My heart started pounding so fast I almost burst out crying."

Whether your friends are sneaking around the rules, bending them a bit, or boldly smashing them to smithereens, part of you probably still wants to keep on hanging with them. You might even think they're pretty cool because they're daring or acting kind of grown up. A little thrill is not such a bad thing, right? But you don't want to get in trouble.

You also may think what they're doing is unhealthy, like smoking, or wrong. If you're associated with something a wee bit too shady for your taste, you have to deal with that awful, anxious sensation you get in your chest, like a hand squeezing your heart.

Things are complicated now because what your buds want and what you want don't always jive. This doesn't just seem complicated; it *is* complicated. So if your situation feels tough, don't beat yourself up. Give yourself a pat on the back instead for realizing you have a dilemma. It's the first step in figuring out some real solutions.

**2. What's wrong with me?** Of course, being part of a tight group feels terrific. If you're having a yucky day, your buds can give your self-confidence a reassuring boost. But the opposite is also true. If you're not doing what your friends are doing, you worry that there's something wrong with you.

Charlotte, 13, says, "My best friend Gia started wearing the teensiest tank tops this year. It's completely gross. But maybe I'm just jealous 'cause she has boobs or I'm just shy about my body."

"Even worse," says Tina, 14, "is when your friends start acting trashy. My close friend tells me she's been messing around with guys at parties. It's disgusting, but what if I'm just mad that nobody likes me? Maybe if I weren't a complete jerk, I'd have some fun with guys."

In every grade, it seems, girls who lead the pack often seem older and more confident than they probably actually feel inside. It's easy to think of these girls as having fun 24/7—and being way more popular than you and the others who aren't in the fast lane.

Like Charlotte and Tina, maybe you've been second-guessing yourself. Are you hopelessly uncool? Terminally infantile? Do you think that if you're different, you must be not as good? Although some girls are tempted to do "bad" things to prove they're okay or to impress their buds, this strategy is usually a dud. Ever see a girl trying too hard to wear makeup? She doesn't look glamorous—she looks clownish.

Finally, remember that social and emotional changes, like physical ones, come at different times for different girls. There's never a perfect timetable. Even if all your friends are way ahead of you, relax. Growing up is not a race, and no one is watching the clock. Years from now, no one is going to think you're awesome because you smoked a cigarette or stole a bracelet during middle school. Bottom line—if you don't feel right doing something, it's probably wrong for you. Waiting until you are ready—or deciding it'll never be right for you—is always a good thing.

**3. Am I going to lose all my friends?** Some girls dread being separated from their friends for a single minute, so the thought of being worlds apart is scary. You may worry that if you don't go along with the group, your buds'll kick you out.

As Mira, 13, puts it, "I'm always the one saying, 'Maybe we shouldn't,' like I'm the mother or something. Maybe they think I'm no fun anymore?"

Henny, 11, says, "Sometimes my friends are like, 'Come on, just try it.' If I say I don't want to smoke, they might not want me around." Even if your friends aren't blatantly pressuring you, you may worry that they think less of you or feel uncomfortable around you because you don't go with the flow.

Your worst fear could be that one day all your friends will drop you, and you'll be palling around with your little brother. Although we can't give you airtight guarantees, your truest bluest buds probably won't toss you off just because you say "No thanks" to something. You wouldn't have chosen such superficial clods as friends, right?

It's possible, though, that some of your friends might choose to hang out with other girls. While this may be painful, remember that it's perfectly normal for friendships to change. Circles of friends always shift as you meet new people and find you have more in common with some than others. This doesn't mean there's anything wrong with you, just that you're taking different paths.

**4. Should I cover for my friend?** Aaargh! You need King Solomon, or someone just as wise, to figure out what to do when a friend begs you for a favor that makes you break out in hives. Says Eghrin, 10, "My best friend was out of school for a while and had to make up a big science test, so she asked to see mine." Since Eghrin's teacher had asked everyone not to do exactly that, she was in a jam.

"I felt terrible," she says, "because she's my good friend and really needed help. Friends should help." Like Eghrin, however, you may feel torn when doing right by your friend puts you in the wrong. Eghrin realized, "Giving her the test would be the same as cheating." She also worried that helping her bud was too risky: "I know my teacher would figure out that someone showed her a test, and I could get in big trouble with the honors committee."

It's important to remember that being a good friend doesn't mean you have to violate your own values or honor code. You can choose a different path from your friend without totally abandoning her. In fact, if she's a really good bud, she will care about your feelings too. She wouldn't want you to do something that makes you feel low.

You can tell your friend you want to help her but have to find a different way. Try, "Let's see if we can think of what else will help you." In Eghrin's case, offering to tutor her friend was a workable solution. That way, she helped without compromising her honesty.

**5. Should I try to change my friend?** Sometimes you're truly upset about what your friend may be doing to herself. Charla, 14, was stuck with a dilemma when she learned her best friend Lizzie was riding around in cars with older boys she met at the mall.

"She's not thinking right," Charla insists. "She doesn't know these guys, and something really bad could happen to her. I don't know what to do." Basically, she struggled with whether or not she has the right to tell her friend what to do and wondered whether she could even influence her if she tried.

One option was for Charla to do nothing. She could decide that it was none of her business. Or she could consider approaching an adult (more on that later) to deal with a problem that seemed too big or too difficult. Or, and this takes guts, she could certainly bring up the situation with her friend. If that's what you choose, don't think you have to (or can) change your friend. You may just want to draw attention to the problem so she can decide for herself if she wants to change or not.

How you say your piece is critical. Compare, for example, "You're so stupid! Are you trying to get yourself killed?" with, "You know, I worry about you when you do that. Can we talk about it?" While giving advice may be tough, it's always okay to let your friend know you care about her, that you're happy to talk things over and that, if she likes, you'll be glad to help her.

**6. Will people think I'm bad news, too?** You've probably heard a parent or grandparent say, "You're judged by the company you keep." You may have found this to be somewhat true if, say, you sit at the loudest table in the lunch room— the one that's always giving the cafeteria aide a hard time and has to be asked over and over to clean up. Even if you're the quietest girl in your group and never talk back and always bus your tray, the cafeteria aide judges you as a group. This is called "guilt by association."

Same goes for hanging with buds who get caught doing something bad. Despite your innocence, sometimes you go down too. That's a risk you take.

But it's also true that you can have a friend who flirts with calamity without being just like her. You can definitely remain your own person, even when your best bud is

**Dear Carol:** My best friend always brags and lies. She brags about her blond hair, grades, cheerleading, and being allowed to shave her legs. And she lied about going out with this boy. I told her I was going to ask him if it was true, and that's when she finally came clean with me. What should I do?
—NON-BRAGGER

**Dear Non-bragger:** Sometimes people brag to cover up insecurities. When you feel great about yourself, you don't have to work hard to convince others how amazing you are. Of course, some crowing is okay. It's ideal when friends can tell each other their triumphs and setbacks. But when friends tell lies, that's a different story. Since you call this girl your best friend, let her know that you cherish her and think she's terrific, but you wish she'd be honest and wouldn't brag so much.

way different. In fact, sometimes we're attracted to people who are our opposites. We find pals who are abundant in the traits we think are decidedly lacking in ourselves.

Debbye and Randi are seventh-graders who have been friends since nursery school. While Debbye is quiet and shy, Randi is the "wild one." When they hit middle school, these differences became more exaggerated, especially around boys. At first Debbye was horrified by Randi's exploits, but now she says, "I realized I enjoy her stories. I get to have fun without actually doing that stuff myself." Like Debbye, you can learn from your friend's experiences without taking the risks. It may not be easy, but it helps to have an agreement: Don't put each other down, and respect her right to make her own choices.

**7. Should I stop being friends with her?** When your friend does the very thing your parents have drilled into your head not to do, you may think, "That's it. She's history. If the folks find out what she's up to, they'll put an instant kabosh on the friendship." You yourself may think this drastic solution is the only one.

Not necessarily. Rather than ditching your friend, pick and choose when and how you'll see her. Maybe you'll decide hanging in school is fine, but you won't get together afterwards. Or it's okay to invite her to your house, but not go to hers. Or you may feel comfortable being with her when adults are handy, but not at the mall or other unsupervised places. Another possibility is that you'll avoid one-on-one situations, but you'll include her when others are around.

If you've decided that none of these solutions are do-able and you definitely want to cool the friendship, you can avoid an ugly mess by doing it gradually. You don't have to stage a whole scene over it.

Branch out a little by talking to girls you don't know very well. Make plans with people you've always wanted to get together with. Avoid the temptation to tell anyone what you're doing and why. The less said, the better. That way, you're also keeping the door wide open to getting together again if you feel more comfortable hanging with her in the future.

**8. What if I'm worried about my friend?** Let's say your friend is doing stuff that's totally not okay—just in bad taste or wrong, but possibly dangerous. Beyond deciding to avoid the activity yourself, what should you do?

Miranda, 13, became worried about a friend who was drinking from her parents' liquor cabinet. Miranda wasn't sure if her friend was "just experimenting" or "had a problem." If you find yourself wondering whether your friend's behavior is normal or scary, it's a good idea to ask an adult for some advice.

You can't expect to know all the answers. So talk to a parent, school guidance counselor, or trusted teacher. If you're concerned about your friend's privacy, don't give her name. The important thing is that you and an adult figure out a way to get your friend help if she needs it. She may not appreciate it at first, but that's being a good friend.

# Branching Out

## Make New Friends But Keep the Old You

Just before the clock struck midnight on New Year's Eve, Melissa made a promise to herself this would be the last year she'd spend without a ton of friends. Melissa swore that she'd be one of the few, the chosen—the popular.

And Melissa wasn't sitting idle, waiting for her fairy godmother to come along and wave her magic wand. She took back all the teddy-bear sweatshirts her grandma gave her for Christmas and bought some cool new jeans. The money she earned baby-sitting was invested in a great haircut. She even took the new diary her mom gave her and used it to record goals for her new and improved self. She vowed to make one cool new bud every month. "It won't be hard," she thought. "I can be friendly, and the cheerleading tryouts for basketball are just around the corner. Lots of cool girls are on the squad." Melissa was sure she was destined for social success.

So how did the year go for Melissa?

"Awful," groans Melissa, now 12, looking back. "I thought that by looking like the girls who are popular, making the cheerleading squad and doing what they did, the cool girls would accept me. And a few of them did. For a couple of months there, things were going according to my plans."

Melissa shouldn't have been surprised. It's not that she didn't know how to be a good friend—she did. Matter of fact, Melissa had two great friends *before* she decided to change her persona. Sara, also 12, had been her best friend since third grade. And her next door neighbor Sam was someone Melissa could always count on for a quick game of hoops, or for help with memorizing those history dates.

"When I came to school that first day after Christmas break, Sara said she didn't even recognize me. And it wasn't just my clothes and hair. I thought I had to act like a snob, too. I saw that some popular girls excluded people, so I thought my first step should be to snub my old friends in favor of new ones. I really hurt Sara."

Even Sam, her trusty guy pal, was confused. "One day, Melissa was on my driveway playing basketball with me, the next, all she wanted to do was bounce around and yell for guys on the team. I never got it. Heck, she could beat half of the guys on the basketball court."

Thinking back is harder for Sara, "I knew what Melissa was doing. Both of us used to sit around and think how great it would be to be popular. But she treated me like dirt, so I made friends with this girl who likes to write and act, like Melissa and I used to. After a while, it was fun to have new friends, and I assumed Melissa was having fun with her new friends, too."

But it wasn't long before Melissa's new "popularity" came crashing down. "As soon as basketball ended," says Melissa, "so did my new social life. The girls I had been hanging out with sort of faded away. By that time, Sara had a new friend and Sam stuck to hanging out with the guys. I was left alone. And that's when I realized that even though I looked and acted like a popular girl—and, in a way, hung out with them —I wasn't really their friend and they weren't mine. Like when they would talk to me on the bus on the way to games, they were just chatting. I took it to mean they were interested. But all of those girls already had friends. They really didn't see me as part of their group."

After spending a few lonely weeks trying to figure out what went wrong, Melissa called Sara and Sam. Many long talks, apologies, and a little time later, things went back to normal. "I still like my haircut, and I wear those new clothes to the mall, but when it comes to friends, I am happiest with Sara and Sam."

At some point or another, each of us resolves to get out there and make new friends. That's perfectly natural, and it's always great to find new people who are fun to be around. But like anything else, making lots of new friends is a skill. Just like you might be good at basketball or writing, some people are good at making friends. They have what experts call "social skills." Popular people have skills that *get* them friends, skills which are different from the skills you need to *be* a good friend.

As Melissa found out, people aren't well-liked just because they have the right clothes or hair or do a certain activity. Take a good look around your school, and you'll notice that all kinds of people have tight groups of friends. Funny girls, athletic girls, girls who act and create art—all have their own fun social scenes. Maybe in your school, "being popular" means hanging out with a certain person or glamorous clique. But again, as Melissa learned, these connections hardly guarantee you a hopping good time. A truly awesome social life means having good friends that share your interests, or support you and your beliefs, or make you laugh, or help you create. Or all of the above. Or whatever you think is important. Melissa wasn't wrong for trying to expand her social life. While some girls crave just a few tight buds to hang out with, other girls prefer being friends with lots of different people. Talking to people with various opinions and backgrounds opens your mind to all sorts of amazing ideas and activities. Who could blame anyone for wanting that?

Melissa's big mistake was the way she went about making new friends. Dropping old friends for new ones is incredibly lame, and so is picking friends based on how good it might look to be seen with them. So what's the right way to add new friends to your life? What follows are some hints to help you make all the new friends you want. We've all heard about being friendly (say "hi!") and open (get involved!). What follows are the less obvious tips for making new friends.

**Hint #1: Pick the right people.** We know—we said it's not the people that make you popular. The point is to pick people you have stuff in common with. It's not so much that the popular basketball cheerleaders snubbed Melissa. They just realized something that Melissa didn't—they had absolutely no mutual interests past the pom-poms.

You can have some people as "friends," some as "good friends," and some as "best friends." You can also have "math class friends," "youth group friends," even a "friend who will watch X Files without screaming uncontrollably and having nightmares afterward." It's great to have a mix, especially if you get a kick out of people with different interests. But the truth is that unless you have a few things in common, things get boring—fast.

When you do find girls with a shared interest (it's not that hard), it's a plus if they like to make new friends too. Some "popular" people create that illusion by excluding others. But some are just "people" people who are always looking to make new buds. They are usually the ones who are eager to organize your team's fund-raising bake sales, host scenery-painting parties for the school play, and lead the student council. Since doing their thing requires the help of others, they'll be as into meeting you as you are into meeting them. Even if you don't become new best friends with them, they might bring you into a group where you will make another connection.

**Hint #2: Pace yourself.** Another one of Melissa's mistakes was to push things too quickly. Unless you are starting over at a new school, you really should take this new friend thing slowly. Like it or not, people have a certain image of you, and if you do a 180-degree turnaround, everyone will wonder what's up. One day you're Susie Smith, next you're Miss All-That.

Better to be yourself with some frosting. Think about the last time you were in a really killer mood, right after you aced a test or scored the winning

**Dear Carol:** Some girls in my class are really preppy and rich and they have big houses and wear new clothes. They are nice to me and say hi and stuff, but sometimes I think they are laughing behind my back. —LESS LUCKY

**Dear Less Lucky:** No matter how much you have, there is always someone out there who has more. Rather than dwell on what others have, you're better off looking at what *you* have. Do you have a loving family? Are you rich in friends? What are your special talents? You say you are less lucky, but money is not the only measurement. I doubt these girls are laughing at you any more than you would laugh at a girl whose home is smaller than yours.

goal. Remember how you felt like you could do anything, talk to anybody, and it didn't matter if the cutest guy in school said hi back or not? Try to project a bit of that infectious spirit every day. Yes, some days are hard enough to get through without trying to be perky on top of it. But it's worth the effort.

Instead of thinking you are a kiss-up, new people will notice your good mood. And people like to surround themselves with people who are positive—that's how life goes. While you don't want to be totally fake (people don't expect you to crack jokes if your dog just died), you do want to put your best face forward. There will be enough time later for your new friend to help your lows as well as share your highs.

**Hint #3: Learn to read.** No, not Shakespeare—body language. This is a difficult thing to learn and takes some practice. But it's the thing experts say separates the socially skilled from the rest of us. By watching people's faces, expressions, posture, and body positions, you can tell how they are reacting to you.

You probably already have some experience picking up subtle clues. If your mom slams the door on her way in and smacks the grocery bags on the counter, chances are this isn't the right time to ask if you can have a friend over for dinner. That's body language.

But often, when we try to make a good impression we focus so much on what we are saying and doing that we forget about the person we're trying to impress in the first place! Smiles are an easy way to tell if someone is into you. But is that smile real? Nervous? Do her eyes say one thing and her face another? Every few minutes, check out the facial expression of the person you're chatting with. Is she giving you her rapt attention? Or looking down the hall?

And while you have to start a friendship somewhere (talking about the weather counts), try not to make too much out of first encounters. Every once in a while, you'll instantly hit it off with someone, but most people will be a bit reserved until they get to know you better. Respect that distance, and keep things quick and light for a while.

**Hint #4: Keep some mystery.** It's hard to resist the temptation to spend every waking moment with a new friend. You want to share everything with her. But some people feel overwhelmed by so much instant attention, so don't Krazy Glue yourself to her.

Plus, you don't want her to think you had no life before. Keep up with old friends (oh, by the way, did we mention that only the lowest of the low dump their old friends while making new ones?), practice your flute, write a play, whatever. As the comedian Groucho Marx once said "I don't want to belong to any club that would have me as a member." As odd as that sounds, remember that most people are suspicious of anything that comes too easily. If you are desperate to be friends with someone, that person will pick up those vibes. And, let's face it, no one wants to hang out with someone who comes off as being really needy. So enjoy your budding friendships, but also keep other interests kicking.

**Hint # 5: Consider doing the unexpected.** Don't have much in common with the masses? While it's great to be the golden girl, some people just aren't comfortable in groups or don't find what they are looking for in clubs or sports. So, why not start your own club? Girls who enjoy writing may find themselves solo a lot more than they like. Instead of going it alone, why not start a writers' workshop? Get together with other scribes to talk about your writing.

Computer-savvy girls also spend mucho screen time alone, but that's when on-line chat rooms come in handy. Having an e-mail buddy is tons of fun, even if you just send silly lists or poetry to each other. So, even if your passion tends to require a lot of alone time, don't give up on friend-ships. Use your hobby in a creative way to connect with like-minded souls.

Don't like organized groups? There is another option. It's called being friends with everyone. Literally. Some girls are uncomfortable with the pressure of being a best friend or find that belong-ing to a clique is super limiting. Like Switzerland, you can become a country that doesn't take any one side, yet remains a part of the big picture. By being friends with everyone, you can play Sega with the guys, hang at the mall with the mallrats, be in a play with the drama gang, and then play tennis on the team. While this may sound like the perfect solution, it's not for girls who need a lot of security. Often girls in these situations are extremely self-reliant and have no problem relating to anyone. They are social chameleons. But if that's you, this is the way to go.

**Hint #6. Don't forget the basics.** Have something to talk about, be it the latest movie or what you did over the weekend. Be supportive when someone needs it. Be a good student (no one wants to hang out with troublemakers—detention is not cool). Really listen to what other people are saying, and resist the temptation to hog the spotlight, even if you think you have a million great stories to tell. And finally—yep, we'll say it—be yourself. As Melissa found out, pretending to like being a basketball cheerleader is a lot harder than playing basketball: "The whole time I've played basketball, no one ever asked me to do splits." Aaarghh!

# How to Be a Happy Camper

About all you need to pack for summer camp are T-shirts, shorts, bug spray, and sunscreen. Wish you could pack your BFFs, too? Not so fast. "Even though I only have a few weeks with my friends from camp, those are some of the best weeks of my year—and some of the best friends I have," says Madison, 11. While it might seem easier to hide under the nearest swim dock instead of mustering up the guts to introduce yourself to complete strangers, almost every happy camper we know has this advice: "Just do it! Everyone else is there to make friends, too." Here are some tried-and-camp-tested hints to get the ball rolling.

**Just say hi.** "Walk over to the person and say, 'Hi! My name is [your name here]. What's yours?' Sounds simple but it works."—CHARITY

**Find an icebreaker.** "I was waiting for a hot dog with another girl, and the guy making them was taking his time. So I turned to her and said, 'We're not the only ones on vacation here!' She laughed, and I introduced myself." —JENNA

**Don't limit yourself.** "Don't dismiss a girl just because she isn't the type of person you would normally spend time with. Try to find common interests, and accept generosity. Be open and honest, and let other girls know they can be open and honest with you." —LUCY

**Get involved.** "Focus on having a great time. Be yourself, but don't be the one who never wants to do what the group is doing. Take part in activities and compromise." —EMILY

**Be friendly, and put the other person first.** "You can make a person feel really good by making her the subject of your sentence. Try my trick. Instead of saying something like, 'I love your sweater!' say, 'You look great in that.' That puts the focus on your new friend." —TARA

**Be courageous.** Jenna, who shared her icebreaker, reminds herself that if someone isn't friendly back, it probably has nothing to do with her: "I say in my head, 'I don't sound like a dork; I sound friendly.' After all, what would I think if someone tried to be nice to me? I'd think she was pretty cool!"

# The Girls' Life
## Guide to
# Family

I MUST HAVE BEEN SWITCHED AT BIRTH.

Mother        Daughter

# Battle of the Sibs

Some days you're sure your sib was put on this planet strictly to annoy you. Unfortunately, brothers and sisters know just which buttons to push to make each other certifiably crazy. Does any of the following sound familiar?

"I'll flip if my sister barges into my room one more time, steals any more of my stuff, or butts in at the exact moment I'm spilling a story to my friends." —NAT, 12

"My brother only needs to hear the tires of my parents' car leaving the driveway to start busting on me. Then he moves onto teasing, followed by insults, and finally onto name-calling that's so mean I burst into tears." —JENNI, 11

"My so-called sister thinks the best way to handle battles is pushing, pinching, and shoving. I'm sick of being on guard all the time and feeling absolutely powerless." —BETHANY, 15

"Fights with my brother start over the remote, which video we watch, or whose turn it is to be on-line. It's like summer reruns—we have the same scenes over and over." —MELISSA, 14

In most cases, it's not that your sib is a 24/7 nightmare. You probably have some moments when you don't think your baby sister should be stuffed inside her bedroom closet for all of eternity. You probably even enjoy your big bro's company from time to time. And you may be capable of seeing the positive side of having sisters and brothers, like having a sidekick for car rides and rainy days, and that essential extra player for two-person PlayStation games.

"My younger sister Melanie does worship me and can be downright cute...well, when she's asleep," admits Cari, 10. Older sibs can drive you to the mall and give advice on how to cope with, say, the same treacherous teacher they had in middle school. Big sisters occasionally loan you clothes and earrings (not the primo stuff, of course). Brothers bring their very fine friends right to your front door.

"The benefits sometimes make up for the bothering, bickering, and other bad scenes," says Lani, 15. But more than a few girls tell us their home turf is a battleground in need of a United Nations peace-keeping force. The worst fights seem to start when girls are forced to fend off hostile sibs alone—without adults to intervene and referee. "It's like combating bullies at school, sometimes worse," reports Mia, 13.

Since so many parents work, lots of girls have to take care of themselves—and sometimes younger sibs—after school and into the early evening. And your folks probably expect you guys to be okay on your own while they run errands. That's dandy—that is, if you don't routinely serve as your sib's number one punching bag. But if you draw battle lines the second the 'rents hit the road, being parentless for even a half-hour is torture. To exterminate the pestering, we'll help you figure out what might be causing all the conflicts and outline some tactics for turning war into peace.

There are as many reasons for sib fights as there are sibs. Sometimes, there doesn't even seem to be a reason. That's just the way you relate to each other. You speak to each other with an edge in your voice or an obnoxious tone you wouldn't dare use with anyone else. You tease or belittle each other out of sheer habit. Or, as Christina, 10, says, "We're just taking our anger out on each other."

When you're frustrated or upset about overdue book reports, backstabbing friends, or detention (again), it's easy to lash out at the nearest target—a sib. Plus, it's a pain sharing space with people whose habits may pluck your nerves. Add normal feelings, like jealousy and competition, and you have kindling for rip-roaring sibling blowouts.

And don't dismiss good old sibling rivalry. One 11-year-old reader, whose 14-year-old sister regularly picks fights, says, "I think she secretly envies me because I go to the mall a lot with my friends, get invited to parties, get good grades, and am better at sports." Whether it's school performance, appearance, social status, whatever, if your sib is sure she's a dark shadow compared to your ray of light, she'll probably attempt to even the playing field the first chance she gets.

It's doubtful you've sat around just whining, hiding, or hoping your sib will get bored harassing you. Instead, you've likely tried a tactic or two or three that just hasn't done the trick.

While the folks might tell you to just ignore taunting sibs, that strategy (as you know all too well) almost always fails. Nicki, 13, says, "When my brother starts in with me, I don't even look at him or answer him back. My mom says if I ignore him, he'll realize he doesn't get to me and will lose interest. But it just makes him hotter, and he doesn't let up until he gets a reaction out of me."

Keeping to yourself in your room or basement or attic is also usually a no-win. "If I'm home, my sister always finds me," says Henny, 11. And you've definitely told your offending sib to cut it out so many times that it falls on deaf ears. No wonder you feel helpless! What you need are time-tested strategies that will absolutely obliterate the problem. Take your pick from the arsenal that follows.

**Choose your battles wisely.** If you get caught up in petty problems—like your sister took a bracelet or your brother gets to sit in the front of the car—you and your sib will be in combat virtually all the time. Who needs that? Instead, decide what you can live with and what you can't.

Maybe you can tolerate your brother controlling the stereo when your parents are out—but you can't deal with him barging into your room. Or you can stand the teasing, but not the arm-twisting. Sit down with your sib when things are peaceful and a parent is around. Relay your message simply, clearly, and firmly: "Look, from now on, I'm not going to stand for this." Don't whine, threaten, beg or cajole. Just say it—and mean it.

**Do your part.** As tempting as it may be to blame your sibling for 100 percent of the problem, that's often unfair. Ask yourself, honestly, how you may contribute. Julia, 12, thinks her sister is perpetually peeved with her. Julia admits, however, that she constantly goes into her sister's room and "borrows" her newest clothes without permission.

If Julia changes her behavior— like by asking first—her sister may get less ticked and won't be as likely to retaliate. Sounds simple, but seeing that you're making an effort might be all your sib needs to cool the crossfire from her side.

Another example? Suppose you tattle on your brother (the one who thinks he's so cool and superior) just because it's fun to see him crash and burn. You may win the battle—but once you guys are alone you may be in for some ancient Chinese torture treatment. Is it worth it? We don't think so.

Resist being baited. Sibs are masters at knowing precisely how to make you go ballistic. Then, when you lose control and swear at them or take a swing, they use your reaction as an excuse for beating you up or getting you grounded. As Lyndsey, 11, reports, "When your sis or bro lies, accuses you of something you didn't do or says rude things, it's easy to retaliate." But losing it is precisely what they want you to do.

Instead of taking the bait, stay cool-headed. Distracting your sib ("Why don't we see if we can program the VCR?") sometimes works, too. Amy, 13, suggests going to your room, putting on headphones, reading, or thinking about something else. Do anything to resist spewing words or actions that will infuriate your sib and, therefore, backfire.

**Make a pact.** Draw up a peace treaty. Promise not to do the three things that most annoy your sib as long as he agrees not to do whatever bugs you. This can be applied to attitudes (no overprotectiveness or bossiness), aggression (no hitting or tickling), or annoying habits (no borrowing stuff or tattling).

Maybe your big bro is mad about having to be in charge when your parents step out because you always make a huge mess. Offer to organize the cleanup if he stops barking orders.

**Call in the reinforcements.** Your parents may tell you not to tattle—and you may fear things will get worse if you blow the whistle. But if you are being hurt or feel truly frightened, you must tell an adult. Even if your mom and dad have told you not to interrupt them at work, don't hesitate to pick up the phone in serious situations. But there's a huge difference between getting your mom out of a meeting to say, "Steven won't let me watch my show," and, "Steven sprained my left arm." Tell your mom it's important, and then describe exactly what's going on.

When your parents get home from work, ask for some discussion time ASAP. Tell them what's been going down and that you need help. Hopefully, they will respond seriously. If not, tell another trusted adult, such as a relative, teacher or counselor. You have a right to feel safe.

Life is peachier when you and your sibs get along peacefully. You'd love for even one day to hang out in the living room without worrying about being taunted, teased, or put into a headlock. As impossible as this may seem, it will more than likely happen down the road. Okay, so it might not happen until your big brother leaves for Dartmouth. But don't give up hope.

**Dear Carol:** My brother is in tenth grade and obsessed with girls. He's always on the phone with them, and he's never nice to me. He was never mean to me before he got obsessed with girls. I feel like I'm losing my brother. Can you help?
—SCORNED SISTER

**Dear Scorned:** Ouch! Who needs a nasty brother when you had a nice one? What to do? You could yell at your brother to stop yelling at you, but that never works. How about inviting him to do something fun, or sending him a note saying you miss him? That should turn him around. Also explain to him that girls like guys who are kind to their siblings. And be patient. Girlfriends come and go, but brothers and sisters stay in each other's lives forever.

In the meantime, take positive steps toward getting along. And when your sib eventually treats you with respect, appreciate it. It may be the start of a beautiful friendship.

# Superstar Sibs

## How to Reclaim Some of That Spotlight

You're somewhat athletic, nice enough, and you've certainly got one or two things you're pretty good at. But you're no superstar. Unlike, say, your brother or sister, whose radiance seems to shine all over the entire house—he's a star soccer player, or she's a piano prodigy. Many girls with superstar siblings wish they, too, could be ultra special, or even noticed—as in, "Hel-lo? Remember me?" It can be positively miserable living in the lonely, dark space of someone else's shadow. But that doesn't have to be your destiny. No matter what type of attention-getter your sib is, you don't have to let his or her star status shrink your own self-esteem.

### THE TALENT

Sibling stars come in dozens of varieties. Crystal's sister Leah is the state tennis champ. Crystal, 11, says, "Dinner conversations are always about Leah's last win, her next tournament, how she'll train, blah, blah, blah." Crystal is quick to point out that her parents also ask about her activities and include her in conversations, "but which is more exciting—my A on a history quiz, or Leah's win in her age division? Sure, they might say, 'Way to go,' when I get a good grade, but big deal. Our family room looks like a showroom with all of Leah's ribbons and trophies." But the worst part, according to Crystal, is "being dragged all over the place, to this tournament, that exhibition—sometimes all weekend long. It's not even for me!"

It's not that Crystal has anything against tennis. In fact, she thinks playing with her friends might be fun—but she doesn't even try because, "I'd feel like a dufus when Leah's so great at it." So how does Crystal deal with her sister's success? "I try really hard to be happy for her," she says, "I mean, she is my sister. But sometimes I just want to scream, 'You know what? I don't even care about your stupid matches or your stupid victories!'"

### YOU'RE HER SISTER?

Some sibs don't even have to have any talent to shine. They have looks that people think are perfect, and they don't have to do a darn thing. Says Janine, 15, "Having a younger sister who looks like a fairy princess is a major drag. Alessandra's so gorgeous that wherever we go, people stare and smile. I swear, I could fall down and die, and nobody'd notice! Sometimes, people say, 'You don't look anything like your sister,' and I say, 'Gee, thanks.'" It doesn't help that, unlike Janine, Alessandra loves the frilly, fussy clothes their mom picks out. While Janine's wardrobe is confined to the few items she and her mom can agree on, "Alessandra goes through major costume changes."

For a while, Janine tried to copy Alessandra's look but eventually gave up. "Alessandra is just lucky—she has the perfect hair, sparkly blue eyes, pearly teeth. How can I compete with that?"

What did Janine do? "I went the total opposite direction," she confesses, "I stopped taking care of myself." In the past year, Janine quit eating healthy foods, gave up her dance class, and gained fifteen pounds. Now Janine's sloppy appearance makes such a statement that she, too, draws stares—and not very complimentary ones.

Several factors can make sibling stars even less bearable:

## IF NOT BEST, FIRST

Many girls feel it's far worse when a younger sibling leaves them in the dust in a meteoric rise to glory. There's an unwritten law that says older sibs hit milestones first. They're supposed to master long division, learn the butterfly, and get braces off before the younger sib. So if little sis steals your thunder by getting the first bra or going on the first date, the universe may seem out of whack. "To be honest, I wanted to strangle Lisa," says Cindi, 14. "She developed way before me and pranced around in a bikini all summer. I was so humiliated I stayed away from the pool as much as I could."

## SOMETHING ABOUT SISTERS

When younger brothers beat girls on the lifeguard test or master black-diamond slopes before them, they may feel un-special, but usually less murderous. No doubt about it, most girls agree that having a star sister is significantly worse torture than having a star brother.

Why? For starts, comparing ourselves to other girls seems automatic. The thinking goes, "We're both girls, so we should be equally good at (acing tests/scoring goals/making guys drool, whatever.)" With brothers, on the other hand, girls can take the sting out of their achievements with consolations such as "He's got the genes," or "He's been allowed to do stuff first," or "He and Dad have a male bonding thing." As Becca says, "Tim is built like a football player, so it makes sense that he excels at sports that take a lot of strength."

## AND YOU DO WHAT?

When the star sibling's interests and talents mimic those of a parent, this can also make girls more inclined to hate-filled fantasies. Take Melody, 12, whose younger sister, Jill, goes golfing with their dad every Saturday. "The first time he took Jill out, he said, 'She's a natural.' I got the Fisher-Price plastic clubs, and she got real ones," says Melody. "I hate the fact that she and my dad are like best friends now. It's not my fault I'm not good at golf."

## KEEPING SCORE

So where does all this leave you? We have a news bulletin: Having a star sibling has no effect on your own potential—really. It's not luminous sibs themselves, but rather the need to compete with them that does girls in. Once you truly accept this, you'll find time to focus on your own life! What your sister or brother does—or doesn't do—has absolutely no bearing on what *you* can do.

A sib who scores home runs, for example, has no effect on your own RBI or potential to make team captain. If your sib is a concert pianist, you can still play for fun—or be a concert pianist yourself. Contrary to popular opinion, there aren't limits on "smart genes" or "sports genes" in each family. Who you are is up to you.

So why is the need to be best so strong? Deep down, the real question may be, "Do my parents love my sibling more than they love me?"

As Crystal says, "Every time Leah brings home a tennis trophy, I get a sick feeling and think, 'How can I compete with that?' Then I tell myself I don't have to." Although there are rare exceptions, most parents have enough love for all their children, regardless of how they look or what they accomplish.

## FACING REALITY

No, you may never dive as well as your dolphin-like brother or sing like your soprano sister. And you know, there will always be super-whatevers who are prettier, smarter, or more talented than you and everybody else. But just because a girl in skating class glides like Michelle Kwan, do you unlace and vacate the ice? Of course not. Even though you can't be tops, you should never stop being your best or simply enjoying an activity.

There are certain factors you can't change. Older sibs will usually drive first, date before you, and get more privileges. You have to deal. Besides, think of the advantages of your sibling position (they've paved the way, you get rides, etc.). Don't automatically assume your sib gets things because he or she is a star. You may get hand-me-downs while your sister sports brand-new trendy clothes simply because an older sister may grow faster or develop first.

## NOTHING'S PERFECT

Thinking your sibs (and their lives) are perfect is a huge mistake. No such thing, sis. It's easy to think a sister who brings home straight A's or a brother who stars on every team has an enchanted life. But being good at one thing doesn't mean everything comes easily. Many star sibs have their own struggles.

Jen, 12, whose 11-year-old sister Monica's math talent is a constant source of irritation, admits that Monica has trouble making friends: "She really relates better to numbers than people."

Being a star also means sacrifices—missed parties, mall trips, and other fun stuff. Being a ranked tennis player is cool but, says Crystal's sister Leah, "Sometimes I just want a normal life— you know, hang out, go to movies, shop. At school, I'm not sure people like me for me or because I'm in the paper." The flip side to fame is also tremendous pressure to perform. Stars may even be expected to "set an example."

When we asked Leah if she thinks about how her star status affects Crystal, she sighed and said, "I feel bad that Crystal is dragged around to tournaments. I know she hates it. But I wish she understood that tennis can be grueling, especially all the pressure I feel to win. She seems to think my life is blessed."

Seeing the universe from your sib's point of view may help you see fame as less enviable and maybe even lonely. See, stardom doesn't guarantee happiness.

## FINDING YOUR OWN SPARKLE

In a misguided belief that "If I can't be 'the best' I won't even try," many girls neglect activities, schoolwork, or appearance. But you don't have to set lofty goals or be the best. Just be you. If bowling, writing poetry, or taking guitar lessons seem fun, go ahead. So what if they seem unglamorous or aren't prize-oriented? Or you may be good at taking chances, have a way with animals, or be capable of surfing the Net. While these qualities seldom win awards, they do bring significant rewards.

## REMEMBER ME?

No matter what you do, things aren't always "fair." Sometimes, parents devote more time, money and attention to you, other times to sibs. Hopefully, your parents will treat you each as an individual who needs specific things at specific times. Just like kids, however, parents may need reminders. If you want more attention, you might have to ask for it. Try "I'd like to spend some alone time with you. When could we have an hour together?" Recognize that your special time might have to be arranged around your sib's games, performances, or schedule.

If you still feel lost in the shuffle, you might need to ask your parents to make as big a fuss over your achievements as your sib's. If parents compare you to your sib, point out that you're trying your best. And as long as you really are, you'll light up any room.

# You Say Potato, I Say...

## Are You and Mom Like Night and Day?

The woman is driving you batty. Yes, she's your mom and you love her to pieces, but sometimes you'd swear you were switched at birth with some other baby in the hospital. How could this person who's responsible for half your genetic makeup have seemingly nothing in common with you? How can your appearances, personalities and/or preferences be so totally opposite? More important, how are you supposed to get along with her when your differences seem like a canyon that can't be bridged? She can't even relate to the things that matter most to you.

   If you and your mom seem like night and day, you're hardly alone. Most girls, in fact, find that they part ways with their moms on at least one if not a ton of important issues. And while you think life would be easier if you and your mom were two peas in a pod, you should know that your differences don't necessarily spell disaster. In fact, with an open mind and a bit of effort, you two can learn to tolerate, respect and—believe it or not—even appreciate each other's uniqueness.

### HOW DIFFERENT ARE YOU TWO?

When it comes to answering this question, some girls don't even know where to start. Addie, 14, for instance, only half-jokingly asks, "You got a couple days? My mom and I are nothing alike. We look different, we act different, and we think differently." Says Mika, 14, "My friends don't believe it when they meet my mother. I like wearing jeans and sweat shirts, playing sports, and getting messy. All she cares about is shopping and makeup and looking perfect."

   For other girls, the differences between them and their moms aren't as overwhelming. Jill, 11, focuses mostly on the physical, "My mom is tall and blond and I'm short and dark," she says. But when asked about stuff that's more than skin deep, Jill adds, "I guess we both like to do outdoor stuff, like hiking and biking, and we also care about animals a lot."

   The truth is, it's probably impossible to find any two people whose looks, tastes and habits are perfectly the same. You and your mom are no exception. But maybe it's not the actual differences that you mind. Maybe what you can't stand is your mom's disapproval of these differences. Whenever you don't agree on something, she's convinced her opinion's right. This is a major problem because your mom, after all, gets the final word on what you do.

Fourteen-year-old Alexis adds, "I'm sick of my mom trying to make me a little version of herself. I just want to be me!" Although you can't make your mom enjoy the things you do, you can figure out ways to make life more bearable despite your separate tastes. Let's break them down by issue. Below are the ones that seem to spark the most frequent mother-daughter clashes.

## TWO SHIPS PASSING...

Some of us are "morning people," while others of us live and breathe for the snooze button. These aren't things we can change at will, they're just quirks and characteristics that make up our personalities.

Marta, 11, says, "Living with my step-mom is torture. I can't sleep in on weekends because she's up at dawn doing chores and making a racket. All I want to do is get some sleep." Things get pretty heated because Marta's stepmom keeps telling Marta she doesn't pitch in enough; Marta is infuriated because she doesn't see why her chores can't wait until later when she wakes up. "I would help her," Marta claims, "but by the time I get up, she says it's too late!"

Natalie, 13, reports the reverse situation. "My mom goes to bed practically right after dinner. She's always yelling, 'Light's out!' and 'Be quiet!' I can't help it if my friends call at nine and wake her up. My schedule is normal, hers isn't."

These conflicts happen because people—and that includes moms and daughters—are born with distinct biorhythms which, at times, don't mesh. Since this can happen between sisters sharing a bedroom and even roommates in boarding school, it's important to learn how to cope.

First, realize that nobody's at fault here. Rather than blaming each other, use that energy to admit that differences exist and find workable compromises. For example, Natalie and her mother agreed to accept calls until 9 P.M. and then to turn off the phone's ringer. Marta and her step-mom figured out a schedule that allowed her a few extra zzzzs in the A.M. and yet enough time to make a dent in the laundry pile. She and her step-mom both felt less resentful and more content.

## THE TWINKIE ZONE

Dinnertime can really bring out the differences in people. Danielle, 13, says she used to love her mother's cooking until she lived on a farm last summer. "Ever since then, I can't look at the stuff my mom makes, much less eat little chicks or piglets." Danielle's mom hasn't taken too kindly to her daughter giving the thumbs down to meat. "She's really judging me," Danielle complains. "She's telling me I'm just being difficult, like I'm doing it on purpose or something. But I'm not."

Snacks are yet another biggie. Some girls prefer snacking to eating, which drives their mothers wild. "My mother's always telling me I'm 'ruining my appetite' when I make myself a mini-pizza or grilled cheese in the afternoon. But who cares if I'm not hungry for dinner? Just because she likes a huge meal at the end of the day doesn't mean I have to."

It's important to make sure that battles over food are really about food. If you're upset with your mom about something else, deal with that issue directly. If it's truly a question of different tastes in food, you and your mom can deal with that. You might go through some cookbooks together and find meals that appeal to everyone. She might agree to cook your favorite meal once a week. Or you might learn to cook a few of your favorite dishes for your whole family. Chances are, your food likes and dislikes will change a zillion times in the next few years. Just make sure you're not making a fuss about dinner to make a point about something else, and your mom's not taking your pickiness personally.

## CLASHES OVER CLOTHES

Another topic that often sends girls and moms spinning into different directions is clothes. Let's face it, the days of Laura Ashley matching mother/daughter outfits are way way behind you. You're enjoying experimenting with clothes and finding your own unique style. So what's the problem with having your own look?

The problems begin, girls say, when mothers balk at their daughters' choice of clothing. Margaret, 13, reports "I guess my style is just too much for my mom. She's so stuffy that she freaks out when I wear anything she considers too tight. She keeps saying my outfits are 'inappropriate' and making me change my clothes. What does she want me to wear? Turtlenecks in July?"

Okay, let's make a distinction here: having different taste from your mom is one thing, having poor taste is another. It's crucial that you and your mom discuss and define the difference for yourselves. When your choice of clothes isn't too skimpy, suggestive or offensive—but merely a matter of preference—perhaps you and your mom can agree to disagree.

This strategy worked well for Tamara, also 13. "My mom wears these flowy long dresses that make her look like a hippie from the 60s, and I dress pretty preppie. People think we look weird together, but it really doesn't bother us."

Accepting differences in style goes both ways. Next time your mom shows up in an atrocious straw hat, you may just have to clamp your lips. In fact, to avoid ugly scenes and hurt feelings, why not make a pact with your mother? You'll both accept the fact that from time to time (or every day, in some cases), your outfits will make each other cringe. But no matter what, you won't insult, tease, or critique the other. In fact, maybe you won't even hint about the merits of each other's accessories—unless specifically asked.

## MUSIC TO WHOSE EARS?

It's hard even to imagine a daughter and mom agreeing on music. In fact, moms sometimes insist their daughters' musical tastes are designed to give them migraines. Debby, 13, says "I'm really into Fiona Apple, but whenever I listen to it, my mom asks me, 'Can't you find a CD that's not so dark and intense?' She thinks the words are too angry, but that doesn't mean I should." Sam, 12, has a similar complaint. "My mom likes music like Simon and Garfunkel—oldies and stuff, which she plays real low. So when my music's at normal volume, she freaks and tells me to turn it down." These situations call for immediate negotiation and compromise that both of you can live with— before hard feelings accumulate. And a good set of earphones might be a lifesaver for everyone.

Moms and daughters disagree not just on what kind of music and how loudly it's played, but also on when and how much girls listen. Lauren, 11, likes background music when she does homework and falls asleep. "My mom doesn't understand how I can do two things at once. But listening to music actually helps me." You may need to demonstrate how music affects you. For example, Lauren's mother backed off when she showed her mother her solid homework record and proved she could wake up on time on school mornings.

Why not take the approach "Different strokes for different folks?" Maybe you  can describe to your mom what you think your music says and why you like it. You probably won't convert her, but it might help her to be more tolerant. And the next time some sappy love song your mom loves comes on the car radio, don't pretend to hurl or change the station. Fair is fair.

## PARTY ANIMAL VS. COUCH POTATO

Yet another potential danger zone is personality. Katelyn, 12, describes herself as pretty soft-spoken and shy. "My mother is anything but. She practically screams and shrieks in public," Katelyn says, "and I get so humiliated I want to hide. Plus, she's always telling me to stop mumbling and speak up."

For Hillary, 14, the differences between her and her mother have even worse consequences. "My mother is a homebody. She's happy just blabbing on the phone to her friends once in a while. She doesn't understand why I want to be at my friend's house all the time." What makes Hillary feel bad, she says, is that "It seems like my mom thinks there's something wrong with me because I like to go out with my friends. When she was my age, she hung out with her mom." Once Hillary realized her desires were pretty normal, she spoke to a sympathetic aunt and then got the courage to broach the subject with her mom. "My mom actually thought I couldn't stand her," Hillary says, "but once she realized that I was just trying to have a social life, she seemed to relax."

This, too, is an important distinction. Be clear that your desire to do things differently from your mom is not an indirect way of showing you're angry or pushing her buttons. Then make sure your mom knows it, too. It's a whole lot easier for each of you to deal with the others' differences

**Dear Carol:** My older sister is 15 and won't stop spying on me. When I'm out, she goes through everything in my room—e-mails, cards, everything. I tried talking to her about it, but she said, "I have a life of my own. Why would I want to spy on yours?" It gets worse. She went through my underwear drawer and found some bras. Then she called her friends to tell them I was wearing a bra. Can't a girl have any privacy at all?—ENOUGH IS ENOUGH

**Dear Enough:** Sounds like she's threatened by the fact that her kid sister isn't as much of a kid anymore. Don't scream at her (though it may be tempting). Instead, tell her two things you like about her and that you feel hurt and betrayed when she goes through your stuff. Remind her that if there's something she wants to know, she can just ask you. Also if you can, confide in her at times. She may imagine that the only way into your life is to invade it. Point out that you respect her privacy (do you?). If all else fails, enlist the help of a parent.

if you know they're genuine—and not intentional or personal.

We realize you could probably add about a dozen more issues to this list. We also realize there will surely be times when there'll be no terrific compromise in sight. No matter how much you discuss, negotiate, or agree to disagree, the differences between you and your mom will threaten to drive you both up a wall. What do you do then? Here are strategies that can alleviate painful differences between you and your mom:

**1. See each other's point of view.**

Actually stop and think how you would feel if you saw things as your mom does. Let's say she's always getting upset about stuff lying around the house, but for you, the more clutter the better. Because you see the world so differently, not a day goes by without sparks (and clothes) flying. Try to think of something you yourself like neat and organized (like, say, your favorite accessories) and imagine how you'd react if someone scattered them around the house. It's perfectly okay to ask your mom to do the same when she's having trouble seeing your viewpoint. If you and your mom put yourselves in each other's places, you won't necessarily agree, but empathizing will put you in a better frame of mind to smooth your differences.

**2. Let little things go.** Getting riled up about every teensy-weensy difference of opinion, like who likes which style of napkin folding, will wear everybody out. Actually, most girls report feeling most panicky about the differences that show up in their mothers' fashion choices. Even the thought of being seen with a mother who perms her bangs, wears moccasins and purple jumpers—well, you can imagine. But who cares if her hot pink lipstick is vile? Try to remember that your mom's tacky vest or ugly hair clip does not reflect on your choices. Ignore the little stuff and make a stink only when it truly counts.

**3. Appreciate your differences.** Hard to imagine, huh? But it can work. Rather than each of you trying to "convert" the other, why not learn to make the most of differences? Well, let's start with just accepting differences. Suppose your mom is high-strung, always flying off the handle, while you're more laid back. Since it's unlikely that even your best, cleverest or sneakiest efforts will do a thing to change her, maybe you could learn to accept her instead. Just say to yourself, "It's okay, it's just mom's way." Anyway, there'll be plenty of personality differences between you and various friends, teachers and future roommates. By working things out with your mom, you'll learn to get along with all kinds of people.

**4. Relish your differences.** Consider this: What if it were a friend, rather than your mother, who suggested doing something pretty offbeat? You might still think it was weird, but you'd probably be a whole lot more open to the possibility. So just because it's your mom try not to immediately trash new experiences she offers. Sure, if your mom is gung-ho on your joining the church choir or a ham radio club and you're aghast, you can nix the idea. But if she's into bicycle races and you're into shopping sprees, what do you lose if you give her passion a try? And don't hesitate to ask her if she'll be open to your game plans, too. Instead of treating your differences as bones of contention, think of them as the spice of life.

**Dear Carol:** My dad ran away when I was a baby and I haven't seen him since. I keep wishing he would come back. I do have a stepfather but I wish I had a real father.—DAD LEFT

**Dear Dad Left:** I'm sorry your biological father has not been there for you. That is a big loss for him and you. While it's tempting to idolize your dad and dream about a reunion, he has a new life and hasn't been responsible for you for years. It's time to accept this and focus on the adults who care about you now. You say you wish you had a real father—but is your stepfather there for you? If so, *he* is a real father. Parenthood is about taking care of children, not just having children. Your feelings are natural, but being realistic about your past will help you heal and have a brighter future.

**5. Find your commonalities.** When all else fails, it may be comforting to know that aside from looks, personality, biorhythms, and hobbies, you and your mom do have something in common. Just what is it, though? It could be something small—like your love of singing silly songs in the car or watching lightning storms. Maybe you share things as basic—and important—as values. You both, for example, think women's rights, world peace, a clean environment, or protecting animals are key issues. Most likely, you also have in common something pretty helpful—an interest in getting along better with each other.

# Mom Envy

## When Your Mom's Too Cool or Not Cool Enough

Mom's red-and-blue plaid pants never embarrassed you before. You didn't used to cringe when she called you "precious" in front of friends or danced around shaking her thing to Richard Simmons' *Sweatin' to the Oldies* video. That was just Mom.

But suddenly, Mom's endearing little traits are grating on your every nerve. Your friends' moms are so much cooler. Well, listen closely because we're going to help ease your nerves, while keeping your relationship with Mom intact.

Take Jenny, 12, who used to be totally proud that her mom was so fashionable. She once loved clothes shopping with her mother, who had a flair for matching clothes with tons of funky accessories. But lately, seeing her mother so dressed up really bugs Jenny. The situation came to a head one day as she was standing in the school courtyard talking to her friends. When her mom came to pick her up and got out of the car, Jenny hated what her mother was wearing—pants that matched her blouse that went with her sweater, shoes, scarf and earrings. It was too much. "I was humiliated," Jenny says. "It wouldn't have been so bad, but I heard two guys from gym class laughing at her."

Similarly, Alice, 13, used to be proud that her mom was younger and prettier than her friends' moms. But now that Alice's mom dresses in the same clothes Alice and her friends wear, she feels ashamed of her. One day her mother came downstairs in a funky pair of jeans and beaded bracelets, in front of Alice's best friend. She wished she could tell her friend that her mom didn't usually dress like that but, in truth, she does. "At first, I didn't realize it," says Alice, "but whenever I thought she was trying to be cool, I found myself saying some pretty nasty and insulting things." Her mom became hurt and angry, and before they knew it, the two were arguing about all sorts of unrelated stuff.

It's pretty easy for hurt feelings to start arguments that get out of hand quickly. You don't want to tell Mom that she's embarrassing you, so you take it out on her in other ways. You say things that are really cruel or refuse to do the dishes. Of course, this makes things worse. The best way to handle the situation is to gather your courage and talk to her honestly about your embarrassment. If you express your true feelings and listen to her side, you should be able to work out ways to solve the problem.

You may want to talk to a friend before sitting down with your mom. For one thing, you'll get all the pent-up anger out of your system so you don't blow up at your mom later. You'll probably get sympathy from your pal, but you may even get a whole different viewpoint. For example, when Jenny complained to her friend Wendy about her mother's slick outfits, she was shocked by Wendy's reaction. "At least you have a mother who's with it," said Wendy. "My mother's still living in the '70s. She sews me these awful dresses and expects me to wear them to school. I don't want to be mean, but people would think I'm totally weird if I wore them." Jenny realized that maybe her situation wasn't so horrible after all.

When you do sit down to talk with your mom, try to say something positive first. That'll take the sting out of telling her that she embarrasses you. Say something like "Thanks for trying to fit in with me, but it bothers me when . . ." Tell her specifically what it is that embarrasses you. Saying "You always play stupid music" is insulting and will probably just make her angry. Instead try "It's embarrassing to me when you play your Sonny and Cher albums while my friends are over. Could you please wait until they're gone?"

Always keep the discussion on track. Do not go off on the way she nags when you don't clean the dishes or finish your broccoli. That will only cause you guys to get sidetracked, making you both even more upset.

**Dear Carol:** My parents are divorced, and I live with my dad. I see my mom every other weekend. I am happy the way I am living now, but my mom wants me to live at her house. She just finished school and has a job. I told her I don't want to live there, but she insists. My teacher even said I should live with my mom. I love my mom and like seeing her, but I am happy the way I am now. —TUG OF WAR

**Dear Tug:** Laws differ from state to state, but it seems to me that if your dad has custody and you're happy, things are settled. What caused your teacher to get involved? Does she distrust your dad? Ask if you're curious, but the point is: If you and your dad are content where you are, you don't have to move. Do, however, reassure your mom that you love her and like your living arrangement.

For Wendy, it was hard talking to her mother about the handmade clothes without hurting her feelings. Feeling trapped, she finally decided to speak to her guidance counselor, who gave her great advice: "I didn't tell my mother how awful or out-of-date the clothes are. I just said I appreciate her making them for me, but my tastes have changed and I want to experiment with different stuff. She didn't get mad at all. We even talked about ordering from some catalogs."

Once you tell her the problem, ask her if she'd like a cooling-off period to think about what you said, before trying to come up with solutions. Show your mom that you still like her—you just don't like something specific she's doing. Once you tell her what embarrasses you, don't go off and sulk or ignore her. Hug her. Now's the time to do something thoughtful. Also, cut her a break. You may need to remind her a few times to change her behavior—old habits die hard.

What if you gather your courage, wait until your mom seems relaxed and say all the "right" things, but she still goes ballistic? When Jenny told her mom she was embarrassed by her overly funky fashions and wished she'd dress a little more "normal," her mother exploded and told her to mind her own business. Jenny, hurt and surprised, yelled back, making things much worse.

"At first, I wished I'd never said anything," says Jenny. "But I'm glad I did. I now know that she might get angry, but she will eventually calm down. And then we can deal with the problem. I also learned to say 'Time out!' if she is yelling, which means 'I'm not going to stand here and listen to you scream at me.'" Just because you make your mom angry doesn't mean you're a bad person or that you necessarily did something wrong. Says Jenny, "I feel horrible when Mom and I get into a fight, but it's always worth it once we figure out what to do about it."

There's something else you should be prepared for. There are times when it isn't possible—or even appropriate—for your mom to do something differently just because it's embarrassing to you. It's okay to ask Mom to stop calling you "pumpkin" or telling you to clean up while friends are over. But there are some things you'll just have to deal with.

Let's go back to Alice. No matter how much Alice dreaded her mom's jeans and jewelry, she couldn't really expect her mother to stop wearing them. Just as girls want to choose their own outfits and be their own person, so do mothers. When Alice told her mom she didn't like her outfits, her mom basically said "too bad" because she really did like her clothes. Says Alice, "I knew we would never agree about it, but it's not going to change. So I guess I'll just have to live with it."

If talking face-to-face just seems too awkward or scary, try writing a note to your mom. Many girls find it easier to describe their feelings on a piece of paper, taking all the time they need. You can think through what you want to say. It might also be easier for your mom to understand your message if she can read it quietly in her own time. That way, she has a chance to think about her response without being put on the spot. Often, these notes between mothers and daughters can become a great way of communicating with each other.

Girls are most comfortable when their mothers aren't extreme—too cool or too uncool. They want friends to like their moms, but not too much. They want their moms to chat with pals, but not spend the afternoon hanging out with them.

Thirteen-year-old Hillary was tired of her mom spending so much time with her and her friends. Her excitement about an upcoming school ski trip was dampened by the thought of her mother sitting on the same bus as chaperone: "My mother is the type who wants to be one of the gang. It used to be great. But now when I have my friends over to the house, my mom is always around. I just want to have time with my friends—alone. I used to love it when she came along on field trips, but now I want someone else's mother to be the chaperone."

Fortunately, Hillary was able to explain how she felt so her mother didn't take her request as a personal rejection. "I told her the truth—that it was important to me to have some privacy with my friends," Hillary says.

Katie, 11, had the opposite problem. Katie's mom was at work or on the road a lot, and she wished her mother would hang out more with her and her friends. She felt bad going to her friends' houses all the time, but she wasn't allowed to invite her friends over when nobody was home. Says Katie, "Actually, my mom felt good when I told her I really wanted my friends to meet her. So we planned a sleepover one weekend when she wasn't traveling." They also decided Katie should invite friends over whenever her mother had the day off from work.

It's wonderful to enjoy and admire other people's moms. They all have their good and bad points. The truth is no mother is perfect—no birth mother, no stepmother, no adoptive mother and nobody else's either. Mothers can and do make mistakes, just like daughters. As one mother put it, "My daughter didn't come with an instruction manual."

One of the best things mothers and daughters can do is respect each other. That includes accepting each other's mistakes. Surefire ingredients for a great relationship include apologizing and quickly moving on afterwards.

Also, spend plenty of time doing fun stuff together. Spend the day window shopping, planting a flower garden, or going to a movie or for an afternoon hike. Set aside a regular, special time just for the two of you. You may want to go for breakfast on Saturday mornings or for dinner on Wednesday nights. During your time together, arrange to be alone, away from interruptions of siblings and the telephone. Not only will this time make your friendship stronger, it will also make it easier to start discussions if and when things bother you in the future.

# Daddy's Little Girl?

## Not!

> ...SO I CAN'T DECIDE WHETHER I SHOULD PIERCE MY NOSE OR MY NAVEL. WHAT DO YOU THINK, DAD?

> UH-HUH.

Every Father's Day you buy Dad something nice—a book or tie, give him a card signed with loads of love, then spend the day doing something fun with him.

But what about the rest of the year? Is your dad someone you can hang out with? Does he have any clue what's happening in your life? Let's face it—for many girls, it has become much easier to go to friends for advice. And if you can't talk to them, chances are you head to Mom (being a survivor of weird girl stuff herself). So where does that leave Dad?

For some, Dad is Mr. Disciplinarian—the one who lays down the law. Maybe he's the wallet holder, the one who rules the cash flow. Or maybe he's just the guy who says, "That's great, honey," before he buries his nose back into the paper. He has his job, his hobbies, and his pals.

A lot of girls have dads just like that. And they all want to know "How can I get closer with him?" It's not that most girls and their dads don't get along; it's just that after age ten or so, things sometimes take a turn for the distant. And if he wants a closer relationship with you, he'd have said something, right?

Not necessarily. Just as you may feel uncertain about your relationship, so does he. Don't forget, he has watched you choose to become closer to your friends. And he understands that you have more in common with Mom. But there's a good chance he feels left out.

What should you do about it? You can ignore it—but you'll be missing out on plenty. For one thing, Dad can introduce you to a whole new way of thinking. Men and women think and respond differently. (As one author puts it, men are from Mars, women are from Venus.) Whereas women tend to listen to others' problems and offer understanding and support, men tend to seek practical solutions to fix problems.

Dads can also explain the often confusing "male point of view." Who better to explain why the guys in your class do and say what they do than another male?

Last is this important fact: You are the product of him and your mom. Understanding your dad will help you better understand yourself.

So how do you start building a friendship? Here's a radical thought—tell him you want to. We're not saying it's a piece of cake. It takes courage to tell your dad you want to spend more time with him. It can be equally difficult to go to him with a problem for the first time. There's the risk that he might not act like you'd hoped. Sometimes he won't. But think how great it will be once you are able to gain each other's trust.

Here's what three girls did to get closer to their dads. All three started by admitting they wanted more from their dads than they were getting. Although none of them would say it was easy, they all feel the effort was worth their while.

## WORK COMES FIRST

Eleven-year-old Molly looks a lot like her dad and has always been told she "has his eyes." The two used to spend a lot of time together. But something started bugging Molly this year. She played basketball in an intramural league, but her dad never came to any of her games, despite the fact that they were scheduled on late afternoons, evenings, and weekends. All the other kids' parents seemed to find time to watch. What made it worse was knowing how much her dad loved watching basketball on TV. When Molly admitted to a teammate how much his absence disappointed her, the teammate suggested she talk to her dad. But how—and what if he didn't care?

After his no-shows at a few more games, Molly realized she would have to say something or end up really angry at him. So the day before a big game, Molly sat and watched basketball on TV with her dad. They did lots of cheering and pigging out on chips. And at the end of the game, Molly took a deep breath and decided to chance it.

"I asked him why he never came to my basketball games, since he obviously likes the sport so much," Molly says. "He told me it was because he has to work. So I told him the next game wasn't until 7:30 P.M., and he just said, 'We'll see.'" Although Molly could have left it at that, she decided to go the final step: "I told him it would really mean a lot to me if he showed up." He said he'd try, and Molly tried not to be too hopeful.

Happily, Molly's father did show up at the game to cheer her on. It wasn't picture perfect. "I made a few clumsy moves on the court," she says, "and I wanted to tell him I usually play better. But on the way home, he said I did well and gave me suggestions on playing my position. He doesn't go to every game now, but he goes to a lot more than he used to." Best of all, Molly is more comfortable telling her dad about personal stuff now that she knows he takes her feelings seriously.

## STEPPING IN FOR MOM

Last year, Melinda, 14, was having a major friend problem. Jen, the friend, told a boy that Melinda was sometimes "so stuck up." When the boy went back and told Melinda, she was devastated. Worse, Melinda had no idea what to do.

Normally, she would have just talked to her mom. The two had always been close, and Melinda could tell her mother about almost anything. But there was one problem. Melinda's mother was away on business for a few days and Melinda didn't feel comfortable talking to her dad, who was always involved in his own activities. When she was younger, her dad was constantly taking her to restaurants, concerts, and other neat places. It seemed, however, he had less and less time for her these days. So why would he have time for her now? How could he even begin to understand or help her deal with her feelings?

Melinda sat and moped in her room, hoping her mom would call. But the longer she waited, the worse she felt. So she decided to brave it. It was scary, she says. She kept wondering what she'd do if her dad ignored her or said she should just wait until Mom gets home.

When her dad got home from work, Melinda asked if she could talk to him. It started off badly. "When I asked if he had a minute, he said, 'Let me unload my briefcase.' I couldn't believe it," Melinda says. "Once again, work was more important than me." But instead of walking away hurt, Melinda told him she really needed to speak with him right away. He looked surprised, but asked what was up.

"I told him everything that happened," Melinda says, "and I kept waiting for him to nod his head like Mom. She always handles problems right away." Her father, on the other hand, listened and then said she should give him an hour to think it over to come up with an idea. She went up to her room, disappointed.

"I really thought he was trying to blow me off," says Melinda. "I just about gave up. But he called me downstairs forty-five minutes later. He suggested I tell Jen how angry I was that she gossiped about me. He said I should, however, measure this one incident against all the good ones I'd had with Jen. We could definitely get through it. But the best thing he said was that guys aren't going to base friendships with me on what Jen says. I think that's what I needed to hear."

Melinda now goes to both parents when something is really bugging her. They always have different approaches, but both are usually helpful.

## CHOOSING FAVORITES

Twelve-year-old Ellen likes her older sister Amy but couldn't stand that Amy got all her dad's attention. When Amy talked about school, Dad asked questions and joked around. He even went to all Amy's dance recitals. But when Ellen complained to her dad about always having to sit in the back seat of the car, he was annoyed with her for whining. Ellen explains, "I can't believe it now, but I actually counted the number of times in a week Amy got to sit in front with Dad and how many times I got to. It came out that she got to sit up front twice as much. I know it was dumb, but I was trying to prove that he was nicer to Amy."

Since scorekeeping didn't work, Ellen tried a new strategy. She tried to be as much like Amy as she could. She dressed like her, took dance class and talked about the same stuff Amy talked about. But soon Ellen realized she hated dance class, and wearing dresses. Amy constantly screamed at Ellen for being a "copy cat," and Ellen got no more positive attention from her dad than she started with.

"Finally, I got so mad that I went and talked with Dad," says Ellen. "I told him I felt like I was being ignored, and I could not be Amy. He looked surprised and said he didn't want me to be Amy. He told me to try activities I enjoy."

So Ellen followed his advice. She took up chess after school and got hooked on figuring out math problems. When Ellen discussed her hobbies during dinner, her dad asked questions about the problem-solving she was doing. He even asked if she would teach him to play chess. "He's pretty bad," Ellen confides, "but at least he's taking the time to learn. That's cool."

According to Ellen, she's also been spending a lot less time worrying about how much attention her dad gives Amy.

As Ellen found out, it's a pretty bad idea to take on activities because you think it will please your dad (or anyone else, for that matter). You're much better off joining clubs that make you happy. Ellen's advice: "Trust me, you can't win your dad over through whining or trying to be someone you're not. If you want to spend more time with him, there's only one thing to do: Tell him."

One last point. After letting Dad know that you want him to take more of an interest in your life, return the favor. Ask him what activities he enjoys, and take part once in a while. Find out his likes, dislikes, talents and dreams. Asking him questions from the quiz on this page will get you headed in the right direction.

## HOW WELL DO YOU KNOW DAD?

1. Where did your father grow up?
2. Did he go to college? Where?
3. Who were his best friends growing up?
4. Who are his best friends now?
5. What are his hobbies?
6. What's his favorite sport?
7. Does he like to read?
8. What does he do at his job all day?
9. What did he want to be when he was growing up?
10. How did he meet your mother?

To score, go sit with Dad and ask him for the answers. Whether or not your answers match, you're bound to find some interesting conversation starters.

# 'Fess Up to the Folks

## Tips for Coming Clean to Your Parents

"Shoplifters will be prosecuted." The sign was glaring at Jessy from above her friend Tam's head in a dressing room. The same dressing room where Tam was stuffing a shirt into her backpack. "Come on," Tam said, shoving a pair of socks at her, "Take 'em." Jessy heard herself say okay, as she stuffed them in her pants. "Meet me outside!" Tam whispered. Her heart pounding, Jessy followed Tam through racks of clothes toward the door. The guard at the entrance looked right at them. Did he know? They kept walking. This was it. Act casual. Walking, walking….

"Excuse me," the guard said, blocking their path. "You have to come with me."

Busted! With the socks wedged between Jessy and her jeans, the security guard searched her backpack and found nothing. When they searched Tam's backpack, they found the stolen shirt. So who got in trouble? Just Tam. While she got to meet the mall police, Jessy was escorted out of the store. On her way to the bus stop, Jessy wondered what would happen to her friend. Will Tam tell her mom what really happened? More important, will Tam's mom call Jess's mom? Should she have confessed about the socks? Should she tell her mom everything when she gets home? Talk about a long bus ride!

And talk about a dilemma. If you've ever been in a situation where you've blatantly screwed up, you know how hard it is to make everything right again. Jessy made a major mistake and had to decide how to deal. Not easy. The obvious solution is to just confess and get the inevitable over with. Moms, dads and even psychologists will tell you that's the decision you ought to make.

Still, it's not hard to understand the back-and-forth panic you go through when there's a fifty-fifty chance you might not get ratted out. That little devil on your shoulder sometimes tells you to play the odds by taking the easy way out (crossing your piggies and hoping you don't get caught). Of course, there's the other fifty percent chance Mom's going to get the dreaded call, and you'll be in double trouble for not spilling the beans yourself.

Our advice: Turn yourself in. Yeah, we know you want to hear about a magic potion to make the whole thing just go away, but we just don't have that recipe.

We can, however, tell you how to make the task of telling your folks a bit easier. If you're in a dilemma where you need to tell Mom or Dad about a bummer situation—or even if you just want to buff up on your parent strategies for the future—here are five basic tips to remember.

**1. Expect to be nervous.** Knowing you need to confess when a bad scene has gone down is just the beginning. We admit the actual act of choking up a confession is harder than French-braiding your hair with two broken arms. The best plan of action? Don't pretend it's not a bad situation. It is.

Your mom and dad usually know when you're hiding something or when something is bugging you. The chances that they won't read your bad vibes are pretty slim. But your parents probably aren't going to be as concerned with *how* you tell them, just as long as you *do* tell them and own up to your mistakes. So when you're thinking about how to announce the messy details of your latest (gulp!) screw-up, expect a band of butterflies to flutter around. Throw in sweaty palms, pounding heart, throbbing head, and stuttering voice, and you have yourself a ticket to Confession City.

**2. Don't predict the reaction.** You're sure fessing up is going to cause a reaction. With that confession just minutes away, you have important things on your mind: Exactly what will that reaction be? Will they be high-voltage ballistic, mildly angry, or low-level peeved? The answer: flubbaglup! Meaning: Don't bother trying to figure this one out! Your parents' behavior is not predictable.

No matter if you're exiled to your room until your eighteenth birthday or simply forbidden to watch Simpsons reruns (which you've seen a million times anyway), the punishment does not always match the deed. Rumor has it moms and dads own a parenting manual to consult when you commit a kid crime. But parents only wish they had it so easy.

**3. Get straight to the point.** Ever have a friend rush up after class to tell you how crushed she is over getting a C in history? But before she actually gets to the C part, she has to explain how the teacher hates her, how the test wasn't fair, how her head was throbbing, blah, blah, blah. The point is she got a bad grade. Period. When too many details tie up the story, the truth gets confused in all the drivel.

That's why this is the most crucial part of the strategy. When it comes to stuff that's going to raise eyebrows of disapproval, there's only one plan: Spit it out! Otherwise, parents will get lost (and probably ticked) in the build-up. Start with these words: "Mom and Dad, I have something important to tell you." Then tell them the climax of the story first! No speeches about events (and no philosophies on grounding).

**4. Don't blame others.** You dropped the bomb. Now what? There you are, sitting across the kitchen table from the let-down faces of the folks. It's 7 P.M., and you have no idea what's coming next.

Did someone say "lecture?" Lec-ture. Say it to yourself because that's what you're likely to get once you've admitted your mistake. Though you've fessed up, you still have to deal with the consequences of your mess up. (Remember? That's why you're here.) Sorry, but if you expect your parents to pat you on the head like the family retriever and tell you thanks for owning up, you're living a fantasy.

Now that you've gotten straight to the point and confessed, it's time for the parents' verdict (commonly called "The Talk"). But don't fret. The key to getting through The Talk is to actually listen to what your parents have to say and answer third-degree questions directly. Now is when they'll want those details (the parts we told you to tuck away until you got the real goods out in the open).

Jessy's mom wanted to know what happened in the dressing room. "I told her Tam made me take the socks," remembers Jessy, "but for some reason, that made her more upset." Jessy's mom was angry because Jessy wasn't owning up to what she did. How does a girl own up? Say you're sorry. When you fess and then apologize for what you've done, you show you take responsibility for your actions.

Even though that may sound like a cliché to roll your eyes at, the truth is, accepting responsibility is what will keep the steam from shooting out of an angry parent's ears. Don't blame the other kids who were involved. If you own up to your actions by saying you're sorry, you trumpet to mom and dad that you didn't mean to do wrong. It's a gesture that may also, by the way, lessen restriction time and change chore lists from heavy-duty overhauling to light dusting. Think about it.

**5. Promise it won't happen again.** When we make mistakes, we're supposed to learn something. That's why certain promises have to be made. A promise that you won't make the same mistake twice puts a big Band-Aid on the situation and helps rebuild that trust. You can repair the trust-injury by promising a ten-foot pole between you and all future dabbles in whatever trouble (future or right now) you may attract. Then you have to keep that promise. And trust us, you can do it.

# The Big "D"

## How to Cope When Your Folks Split

Sure, you know people get divorced. Until recently, however, it was only other kids' parents. Now maybe you've joined the ranks of 1.5 million kids whose parents divorce every year. Maybe you felt numb when you first heard; then came sadness, confusion, anger, fear. Face it, there are loads of changes to get used to—having two homes, juggling a different schedule, and remembering in whose house you left your math homework. As if that weren't bad enough….

Perhaps the biggest challenge of all is when parents are waging battle against each other. In this giant tug-of-war, you're smack in the center, feeling pulled apart. But the most important thing to remember is that your parents are splitting from each other, not from you.

So no matter what happens between them, your goal is to have the best relationship you can with your mother, as well as the best relationship you can with your father. Separate relationships. How? Stay out of whatever conflicts arise between your parents. It's almost never advisable to take sides. We can't say this strongly enough. No good will come out of getting involved. None, zip, nada. Thankfully, there are ways to stay neutral…and stay sane.

## OPEN WARFARE

In a perfect world, adults would never argue. In a semi-perfect world, they would argue in private. Kids would be spared the raised voices, icy tones, and harsh words that spill in the heat of anger. Although many parents try to protect kids from conflicts, sometimes their emotions get the best of them, particularly during the stress of separation or divorce. As a result, kids witness fights they wish they'd never seen. Katie, 12, went through this for two years before her parents finally divorced. "As soon as I heard them yelling," she says, "I'd go in my room, get under my covers and put my Walkman on real loud."

It's even tougher when parents openly express hostility about each other to their kids. "All my mom and dad did was badmouth each other," says Minnie, 12. "As soon as they got me alone, they'd each say hateful things about each other. I didn't know what to do." It's hard to hear a parent you love speak badly about the other. Although your first instinct may be to defend the parent who's not there, that tactic backfired on 14-year-old Martha. "I ended up getting into fights with each parent about the other one." Ellen, 13, perhaps has the best suggestion: "I listen, but don't say a word."

If a parent doesn't pick up the silent message that you're uncomfortable hearing your other parent get bashed, you might have to speak up. Rather than scolding, say what you feel: "It's awful to hear bad things about Dad," or "I know you're angry, but it hurts when you say you hate Mom," or "I love you both, so please leave me out of it." Ideally, your parents will keep their problems with each other separate from you.

## IF LOOKS COULD KILL

Sometimes disapproval is expressed subtly—not with mean words or flying objects, but with a certain sigh, an eye-roll, or raised eyebrow whenever the other parent's name comes up. Says Katherine, 14, "My parents would never come out and say anything, but every time I talk about my father, my mother gets a weird look on her face. It makes me wonder what I've done wrong."

Ignoring the signals of hidden anger won't make them go away, so you might want to mention that they make you uncomfortable. Many parents don't realize their body language screams hostility. And for a while, you may want to put a lid on gushing to your mom about the awesome time you had with your dad. Or skip mentioning your mom's cool new friend to your dad.

## THE BLAME GAME

When it's clear one parent wanted the divorce and the other didn't, it's harder to avoid taking sides. You and one parent want to be a family again; the other parent is to blame for all the misery!

Becky, 14, confides, "My mom found someone else and didn't want to be married to my dad anymore. He was devastated. I felt sorry for him—and myself—and blamed her. It was years before I realized it wasn't that simple." Even when you think you know what's going on, you may not. Taking sides may help you express your anger, but placing blame won't accomplish much. In fact, you could wreck a close, healthy relationship with each parent.

## WHAT'S IN IT FOR ME?

Girls think they're being neutral, but sometimes—maybe without realizing it—they manipulate situations to their advantage. Say you and your dad are fighting about privileges. You think he's setting unreasonable rules. Mom has her own beef with him. So when she complains, you don't zip your lip about your own issues with Dad. You fuel the fires of her anger. Now she's in complete sympathy with you about Dad's stubbornness and pressures him to lighten up. Good work? It may seem so. You've gone to more parties and finagled extra phone time, but you've gotten nowhere in the process of working out stuff with your dad. Having a relationship with him where you can negotiate rules is far more important in the long run than a short term victory.

## TELL ME ABOUT IT

Parents often ask girls for info about the other parent. It can be as innocent as "Did your father get the photo albums I sent him?" or as probing as "Is your mom getting serious with that man?". When parents are in conflict, communication between them might be at a standstill. So they may use these questions as easy ways to find out stuff they're curious about.

But when girls feel parents are pumping them for information, they're understandably uneasy. "When my dad asked me what time my mom gets home at night, and if we were ever left alone," says Sara, 12, "I was worried that whatever I say might be used against her." Andrea, 11, agrees. "I never know what to say. If I answer, I wonder if I'm telling on the other parent."

This can be tricky for parents too. One divorced father confessed, "I'm so tempted to ask my children things about their mother. I actually have to stop myself because I know it's not right."

If your parent doesn't realize this is a problem for you, you may have to say, "Why don't you ask Mom?" or "I'd feel better if you could ask Dad that question." That way, you're wiggling out of the middle without being cagey or rude.

But if you're being placed in a dangerous situation—or truly being neglected or mistreated—do not keep quiet, even if telling someone might make your parents' conflict worse. Your safety comes first. If you'd rather not tell the other parent, speak to a trusted relative, teacher, guidance counselor, friend of the family, doctor, or religious leader.

## HE SAID, SHE SAID

"At first I thought, 'What's the big deal?'" says Anna, 12. "My mom asked me to tell my dad about my teacher conference, but he flipped out. He started yelling about how come he wasn't told before, why was it scheduled in the middle of the workday, blah, blah, blah. He just went off on my mom."

Emily, 12, confides, "My father asked me to tell my mom that he needed to switch weekends with her. I didn't want to, but what could I say? So when I got home and told her, she got all quiet and went to her room. It wasn't my fault!"

It may seem like a perfectly harmless request: "Tell your mother I'll take you to school in the morning," or "Ask your father about that child support check." But carrying messages back and forth is a surefire way to get yourself smack in the middle—even if you thought there was no conflict. To keep out of the crossfire, suggest that parents leave messages on each other's office answering machines or send e-mail. That way, they can avoid face-to-face or phone confrontations, and you can avoid being the messenger.

## OH, THERE'S MORE?

When parents split up, they lose a lot too. So it's only natural they might try to hold on to what they value most—you. Sometimes parents try to show how much they love their kids by giving them lots of toys, clothes, jewelry, whatever. To make up for the hurt of a divorce, other parents try to have fun every minute they spend with their children. Constant outings, movies or zoo trips, anything to entertain. "I can't believe I'm saying this," says Sally, 11, "but it gets to be a bit much. He never did this when they were married."

For Fran, 12, it came down to a competition. "It's like they're trying to outdo each other." It's bad enough when parents have equal resources. But often, one parent doesn't have as comfortable a lifestyle after a divorce. Evi, 13, found the gap painful. "My dad bought this great house and got me the horse I always wanted. He gives me anything I ask for. Meanwhile, Mom and I live in a tiny condo, and she can barely afford everyday stuff."

It's important to keep material things in perspective. It's fun to visit great places and get gifts, but if it feels like parents are competing for your love, it's time to say, "Time out!" Nobody likes to be fought over. When you're in the middle, you don't come out a winner. Yes, you might have your own horse, a box full of movie stubs, or enough nail polish to get you through 2010—but your relationships with both parents should be based on genuine caring, honesty, and affection.

Sometimes, you might have to point out to a parent that you don't expect—or even want—him or her to keep pouring money out for you. Molly, 14, says, "I was torn between enjoying all these great clothes my dad bought me and feeling bad because that was all we talked about. Finally, one night I blurted out, 'Dad, instead of going shopping this weekend, could we just go have lunch?' He seemed uncomfortable at first, and it seemed strange, but it was a start."

Toby, 10, spoke to her dad after realizing she was exhausted after weekends with him. "We were always running around—fun stuff—but it was too much. I told him I really wanted to just hang out with him sometimes, maybe play a game. I think he may have even been a little relieved."

Divorce or no divorce, if a parent unselfishly gives love and time, offers patience and a sympathetic ear, he or she is giving the ultimate gifts.

## CUSTODY BATTLES

It's one thing for parents to disagree about where you'll spend a weekend or holiday, but quite another when they wage war over whose house you live in. Nearly everyone agrees when it comes to divorce that custody battles are the worst nightmare. Girls vary, however, on how much input they want in the decision that will transform their lives. "I don't want to have to choose who to live with," Ariel, 10, says directly. "But what if they make me?"

Susannah, 14, feels differently. "I love both my parents," she says, "but I get along better with my mom. I'm more like her than my dad, so living with him would be uncomfortable."

What should girls do if they have a preference? Can they say their piece without offending either parent? What are their rights? Although rules vary according to what state you live in, most laws say children are entitled to be appointed an adult representative (a guardian or attorney) by the court, who represents their best interests in the custody process. So, if you wish, you should have a chance to make your preferences known.

**Dear Carol:** My parents are divorced. My dad moved away to a different state. My mom won't let me spend the summer with my dad, but I want to. —MISSING MY FATHER

**Dear Missing:** I'm sorry you're going through a rough time. Can you ask your mom why she doesn't want to let you go all summer? Is it because she'll miss you or because she's mad at your dad or maybe doesn't trust him to take good care of you? Who has custody during the summer? If you can find out these answers, it will help you decide what to do. Explain to your mother that you miss your dad. Reassure her that you love her tons and will call and write her letters and send email and that you'll be back before she knows it. If there's a grandmother or aunt whom you trust, perhaps you can ask for advice or help from her, too. It's important to be sensitive to your mom's feelings, but it's also important to stay close to both of your parents, if possible.

Your feelings, we admit, will be harder to deal with. There's no getting around it. Girls feel worried, angry, frustrated—even devastated—when parents fight over them. These feelings are perfectly normal and, hopefully, temporary. But it's an awful position to be in. Whatever you do, don't keep your feelings to yourself. This is the time to confide in trustworthy, neutral adults like school counselors, teachers and religious leaders. They may not be able to sway the process, but their caring and support can definitely help ease the pain and anxiety of this stressful situation.

The best thing you can do is take care of yourself. Where there's parent conflict and separation, there's hurt. Even though it was not your decision for parents to split, you have to accept what you can't change and find happiness in new ways. Though painful, a divorce doesn't have to destroy anyone's life. And, believe it or not, you can influence much of what happens after a divorce. How well you come through this process and get on with your life depends on your parents, of course, but also on your outlook, how much you deal with your feelings and how you handle situations that pop up. You can start by doing a lot of thinking about what's best for you. Here are some tips on how you can continue to take care of yourself by not getting caught in the middle:

**1. Accept divorce as a permanent reality.** In hoping that their parents will get back together, many girls are desperate to "help." The thinking goes "If only Mom realized what a great guy he is, she'd give Dad another chance," or "If Dad understood Mom's feelings, he'd come back." Sadly, nothing good ever happens when girls dive into the conflict. When their efforts fail, they often feel guilty and blame themselves. As hard as it is to accept, girls must realize they aren't responsible for fixing parents' problems. It's up to parents to work it out—or not.

**2. Avoid conflict as much as possible.** The fewer arguments you see or hear, the less you'll be drawn into the clash between your parents. If you find certain routines usually cause major scenes, such as when your dad brings you home after a weekend or when your mom drops you off, think about how to get around them. Consider staying outside until parents finish "talking." Call a friend, play loud music, go for a walk, cuddle a pet, or take a bike ride.

**3. Make your life easier.** When there's tension so thick you can practically touch it, special occasions can turn ugly. Think of how you can work things out to minimize weird vibes. You may have to celebrate your birthday and religious holidays twice. (This could have advantages.) There may be a way for one parent to visit camp one day, the other parent the next. Or split a school visiting day in half. Teachers usually are willing to have separate conferences if parents can't or won't go together. By speaking of your own discomfort and wish to keep peace, you avoid blaming either parent and let them know they're valued.

**4. Monitor your own life.** As you remove yourself from your parents' conflict, you'll be better able to pursue normal routines, activities, and friendships. But make sure you're not taking your feelings about the divorce out on others. For example, if you're suddenly mouthing off to teachers, getting in trouble or going ballistic on friends, this may be a sign your anger isn't resolved or being channeled well. It may take a while to feel like your old self, so give yourself a break. Be sure you're taking every chance to care about others and have them care about you. Enjoying healthy relationships is an important way of moving on after a divorce.

**5. Feel the feelings.** Divorce is hurtful—no doubt about it. It's tempting to avoid facing feelings. Some girls pretend they don't exist: "Oh, I could care less about the divorce." Others use alcohol or drugs to dull the pain, and some get so busy they don't have time to think. But if you don't deal with the feelings—that is, allow yourself to feel them, no matter how painful—you can't move on. You've experienced a huge loss, which can cause sadness, anger, worry, and confusion.

Don't let yourself suffer needlessly. Talking about what you're going through, confiding in special friends and caring, trusted adults, is a must. Sharing your feelings isn't betraying family business. Counselors, religious leaders, relatives, and friends' parents can keep discussions private. Support groups especially for kids whose parents are divorced are another resource.

In thinking about your future, post-divorce, here's our wish list:

★ You will continue to have separate, healthy relationships with both your parents.

★ They will put aside their differences enough to parent you together wisely.

★ Parents will be supportive of your feelings.

★ You'll still get to be a kid.

★ You will stop blaming yourself for causing or not preventing the divorce. It had nothing to do with you.

★ You will have loving relationships in years to come.

★ You will forgive your parents.

**Dear Carol:**
Lately, I've been feeling left out of my dad's life. Since he got a new girlfriend, I feel like she and I have to compete for his attention. —NEEDS ATTENTION TOO

**Dear Needs:** I wish I could write to your dad and not just to you. Since your father can't read your mind, you'll have to tell him how you feel. Don't say "You pay more attention to her than me." Instead try "Dad, I miss you. I don't see you often enough, so when we do get together it means a lot to me if we can do something, just us. What do you think?" I hope he realizes he's lucky to have a daughter who loves him. If all else fails, leave this book open on the desk with a Post-it that says, "I confess—I sometimes feel that way."

# Wedding Bell Blues

## What to Do When Parents Tie the Knot... Again!

"If anyone is against this union, speak now or forever hold your peace." When Cindy, 13, heard the minister make this announcement she thought, "That's it!" Why hadn't she con- sidered it before? All she would have to do was yell, "Stop! Hold everything. I am against this union!"

For an agonizing moment, Cindy tried to summon the nerve to do it. But she was living that nightmare where you're trying to scream and no sound comes out. "I realized at that moment that my dad was going to marry Monica no matter how I felt, and there wasn't a darn thing I could do about it."

Wait—weddings are supposed to be happy occasions, right? Well, Cindy was definitely experiencing a lot of emotions, but happy wasn't one of them. Anger, resentment, betrayal, and jealousy were just a few. Not to mention she felt a tinge of guilt for even having those feelings. But experiencing such emotions is perfectly normal because watching a parent remarry—even if you adore the soon-to-be-stepparent—can be an excruciating event in a girl's life.

There are ways, however, to make the new situation tolerable. Bear in mind, though, that things may not get better overnight—or even in a few weeks or months. It takes time to adjust.

### ACCEPTING CHANGE

Getting used to the idea of a parent remarrying can be frustrating, but it does no good to sit around and mope about it. Cindy had an especially hard time shaking her negative attitude because she was just getting over the sting of her mom and dad being divorced. She wanted her parents to live out the happy fairy tale—married and in love forever. When they announced they were splitting up, it rocked Cindy's world. And now that her dad had a new wife, that ruined any chance of her parents reuniting.

Brianna, 12, had no hopes of her parents getting back together because her dad died when she was six. But when her mom got married to Rick, Brianna couldn't help feeling uneasy—even though "he's a great guy." It had been just Brianna and her mom for so long that she couldn't imagine it any other way. "You and I are a team," her mom always said. Now, a whole new player had been recruited. And even though he passed "tryouts," Brianna couldn't help feeling like she was being benched: "I liked Rick, but I couldn't help thinking he was trying to split us up."

It's normal to feel overwhelmed. But, unfortunately, there are some things in life you have no control over—like when a parent decides to tie the knot. Cindy couldn't stop her parents' divorce, and Brianna can never bring her real dad back. Changes happen all the time in life, and the best thing you can do is try to change with it. "Once I accepted that I couldn't end the marriage," says Cindy, "it really did take the edge off of my bad feelings."

## SHARING

Many kids say the hardest part about being in a step-family is having to share a parent. Because Cindy's stepmom has two daughters, she has to share her dad with Monica, his new wife, and two stepsisters. "I was enjoying the special time my dad and I spent together on weekend visits," says Cindy. "And now, while I get only weekends with him, they get to live with him all week long. Like that's really fair!" And who could blame her for feeling that way? If you miss spending time with a parent, you should say so. After about two months of gritting her teeth over it, Cindy decided to sit down with her dad and chat.

She explained that she really missed the alone time she used to have with him. Her dad was cool about it, and they worked out an arrangement where every other weekend he and Cindy would do something together for at least an hour—just the two of them. They'd go for walks, get ice cream, whatever. Just so they had special time together.

But for some kids, like Jesse, 10, a parent might not be willing to spend one-on-one time. When Jesse, who has two stepbrothers, tried to talk to her dad, he said, "I have four children now, and I won't give special treatment to just one." Jesse was bummed, but she accepted it as one of those things that she just can't change. She takes solace knowing her dad really does love her. She also knows he's just trying to be fair to the other kids.

## HOUSE RULES

A new stepparent sometimes comes with a roster of new rules and regulations—from seating arrangements at the dinner table to having the towels folded a specific way. For Brianna, the new rules were about curfews. Her mom used to let her go to Skateland every Friday night until midnight. That was her favorite part of the week, and half the kids from her grade went. "Well, Rick freaked out," she explains. "He changed my curfew to 11 P.M.—and Mom let him!"

The new rules were an equal surprise to Cindy. When her dad first moved out and got his own place, it was pretty cool because things were so laid back: "I could put my feet on the table and eat Snickers bars for breakfast. I swear, I think I could have stuck wads of gum under the furniture and my dad wouldn't have cared." Not anymore! Cindy's stepmom is like Martha Stewart and expects everyone to help keep the house spotless. "Even Mom isn't this tidy," says Cindy.

It's hard adjusting to new rules, especially when things have been a certain way for so long. However—unless you think a specific rule is terribly unreasonable—you just have to deal. Rules can be particularly confusing when you live in two homes with two different sets of laws. If this is the case, write down the rules of each house and post them in plain sight.

## ALL IN THE FAMILY

Dividing bathroom time with virtual strangers can be pretty unpleasant. Suddenly, your shampoo bottle is half empty or replaced by a stepsister's shaving gel. Even worse is being forced to share a bedroom.

On weekends with her dad, Cindy has to share a room with her oldest stepsister Samantha because they're about the same age. (Five-year-old Stephanie gets her own room. Go figure!) "I was an only child before Dad married Monica," she says, "so I always had my own room. It was weird to be sleeping in the same room and sharing drawer space with a girl I hardly knew. Not to mention that I thought she was a complete dork."

But Cindy decided to at least try to get along with Samantha. "Once I gave her a chance, I realized she's not so geeky. Honestly, I would probably never choose her as a friend, but we were thrown together so we make the best of it."

As for five-year-old Stephanie, Cindy thought, "What's wrong with me? Here's this cute little kid who's supposed to be my sister, so how come I don't feel like I love her?" Cindy soon figured out she doesn't have to love her stepfamily. Love is something that grows—it doesn't just happen because of some marriage certificate. You might never love (or even like) your stepkin like you do other relatives. Then again, maybe one day you will. Either way, it's okay. The important thing is to do your best to get along.

## SOMETHING TO TALK ABOUT

If you're trying really hard to get along with members of your stepfamily but still having trouble, find someone to talk to. While it feels good to vent to a bud, you need someone who can offer trusted, helpful advice.

Lucky for Brianna, she was able to approach Rick when she was feeling angry or scared. But remember Jesse? She had a super hard time getting along with her stepmom. "She was mean," says Jesse. "She just waltzed in and took over. It seemed like Dad was totally brainwashed by her. He even stopped paying as much child support, and Mom was so stressed." Her mom being upset was rubbing off on Jesse, and her stomach was in knots.

"Things were spinning out of whack, so I knew I had to talk to someone," she explains. That's when Jesse went to see her school counselor. The counselor helped Jesse a lot and referred her to a support group with other kids from stepfamilies. They got together once a week, talked about things that bothered them, and helped each other deal: "That's where I learned all about accepting change and how to share and stuff."

Jesse found out that child support shouldn't concern her: "My counselor explained that it's an adult issue and it wasn't fair for Mom to burden me with it—though she didn't mean to hurt me."

She also learned an important lesson in communicating. If you plan to talk to a parent about something that's bothering you, use "I feel" sentences, such as "I feel hurt," or "I feel left out." Sentences that start with the phrases "You always..." or "You never..." make people feel they have to defend themselves instead of solving the problem. "I feel" sentences keep things in perspective and help others put themselves in your position.

For example, instead of "You always treat the other kids better," try "I feel that I'm not being treated fairly." When Jesse talked without blaming, her stepmom was able to better understand what was bugging her.

## OH, THE GUILT

A lot of girls build an instant wall between themselves and a new stepparent. Jesse admits she was afraid to be nice to her stepmom because she felt guilty. Why guilty for trying to be nice of all things? Because she felt like she was betraying her mother if she started to care about her step-mom—especially since her mom didn't like her dad's new wife.

As much as Brianna liked Rick from the very start, she too went through tremendous guilt: "I felt like I was trashing the memory of my real dad. I didn't want to feel like I'd replaced him."

It's all right, even healthy, to have a good relationship with your stepparent. It takes nothing away from your feelings for your other parent. But what if you sense your parent, like Jesse's mom, feels threatened by this closeness? Jesse finds it works best to avoid blabbing on and on to her mom about her stepmom.

## TIME OUT

If you're having a bad day, fighting with the stepbrother over the Game Boy or something, distance yourself for a while. Go for a walk, read a book, call a friend. Everybody needs and deserves private time. Because Cindy has to share her room, she had a hard time finding her own space at first: "If I went in the kitchen, there was my stepmom. If I went in the family room, there was little Steph. I felt smothered." So Cindy found herself a little spot in the basement where she goes just to chill and write in her diary.

She reminds herself of her role in keeping the peace. "Sometimes I think it's unfair that I have to make an effort for a situation I didn't choose, but it's okay."

# The Evil Stepmother

## Fact or Fiction?

Your parents divorce, and suddenly your picture-perfect family isn't so perfect anymore. It takes time, but most girls do get used to their parents leading new and separate lives. What might take more getting used to is their new and separate loves. While getting a new "mom" or "dad" can be equally daunting, it seems stepmothers present unique challenges. We can credit some of that dread to fairy tales. We all know what happened to Cinderella and Snow White. While we don't know any girls who spend their post-stepmom days scrubbing floors, wearing rags or eating poisoned apples, many say having a new "mom" brings on complicated questions and feelings.

Though Callie, 12, liked her stepmom-to-be well enough, the big announcement left her cold. "I knew I should feel happy for them—it's not that I didn't like her—but all I felt was hurt. My school counselor helped me realize how hard my parents' breakup was on me. She also pointed out that while I rationally knew my parents would never get back together, it took hearing Dad's big news to know in my heart that our family was really over."

Callie's feelings aren't that unusual. No matter how much you wish or pray or watch *The Parent Trap*, hearing that one parent is getting remarried forces you to accept that your family will never be the same again. But you can survive this final chapter of your parents' breakup…and survive the first chapter of having a new family member.

## FIRST REACTIONS

Sometimes, dealing with your feelings—good or bad—isn't the hard part. What's difficult is being told those feelings are wrong. It doesn't help when everyone tries to paint a cheerful picture. Just ask Susan, 12, who admits: "My aunts kept telling me how great having a stepmom is, but it didn't feel great to me."

Christina, 16, had the opposite experience when her father remarried. In the same way Susan felt pressured to be psyched about gaining a new stepmother, Christina was made to feel bad about being open to the idea. "My sister acted like I had stabbed her in the back, but I couldn't help liking my stepmom," she says.

Whatever your feelings about hearing your family portrait will be repainted, they are yours and yours alone. People can feed you opinions to chew on, but it's your decision to swallow them or spit them out. Remember, nobody can (or should) ever try to force you to feel a certain way. As time passes, you may change your views, but in the meantime it's perfectly okay to say to others, "Give me some time to get used to all this" or "I see what you mean, but that's not how I feel right now." Likewise, you should give other people, like sisters and brothers, room to have their own feelings. No fair asking, "How could you possibly like her?" or "Why don't you try harder?"

## "IT'S ALL HER FAULT."

When telling the kids about a divorce, most parents present a united front and stay away from issues of blame. It goes without saying that you should not feel responsible for the breakup. But when a girlfriend appears soon after a divorce, it's hard for girls not to point a finger her way.

Right after Heidi's parents called it quits, her father married his co-worker Stacey. "I hated her," Heidi, 14, confesses. "I thought if she had just stayed away from my dad at work, my parents would still be married and we'd all be happy." Heidi is the first to admit her fury made life pretty uncomfortable for everyone. When she finally struck up a conversation with her mother about the situation, Heidi says, "She told me I shouldn't blame Stacey, since both she and my dad had a lot of problems in the marriage."

If one of your parents immediately takes up with someone new, don't jump to conclusions (as hard as that might be). The changes in your family may seem sudden, but your parents have probably been adjusting for a while. It would be great if they had been happy together, but the best thing you can do is understand their wanting happiness and accept that a new person brings that into their life.

## TWO'S NO LONGER COMPANY

Diana, 13, believes her stepmother has driven a wedge between her and her dad: "She makes my dad do so much stuff after work that he has no time for me." It's understandable if you're frustrated and upset about not getting as much alone time with your dad. But instead of taking it out on the family, your best bet is to pull your dad aside and talk to him. ("I miss our early breakfasts, just the two of us.") Then ask directly for what you'd like. ("Can we spend a little time alone together?")

Although it's unlikely things will go back to the way they were BSM (before stepmom), your dad might be happy to arrange some special time for the two of you. If your dad has trouble carving out time, don't lose hope and definitely don't blame yourself. The family changes affect him too, and he's probably having difficulties balancing it all. If he seems pulled in 200 new directions, give him a little time to adjust. Then try again. If he just can't seem to fit in some special time, accept that visits with him now include your stepmom and make the best of it.

## SHE DRIVES ME CRAZY!

Nobody's perfect, and that includes your stepmother. You'll undoubtedly find things about her that drive you batty. Maybe she'll talk too loud, expect too much from you, give too much input on your fashion choices, feed your dog the wrong way. But the two most frequent complaints girls give about stepmothers are "She tries too hard" or "She doesn't try hard enough."

Some girls resent overzealous stepmothers who try too quickly to get close or act like a parent. Amy, 10, believes that as soon as her stepmother met her, she "lost no time in stepping right in and telling me what to do and not do. I hate that. She's not my mother." That's true, she's not your mom. But she is an adult and she has probably been entrusted to take care of you, just like a teacher or an aunt.

Try to separate your anger over her presence from your anger at her barking orders. No one likes being told what to do, but we all make an effort at school and with family. If she is a 24/7 drill sergeant, you may need to bring in a trusted adult to help you and your stepmother communicate more effectively. But if she's just trying to keep things running smoothly, try cutting her a little slack.

Debbie, 13, complains that her stepmother acts too familiar, "like she's known me my whole life. She drops my friends' names as if she's known them forever!" Amanda, 14, whose father just got engaged, says of her future stepmother, "The lady acts like she's my best friend. If she plops down on my bed one more time, I am going to scream!" You may have to point out to your stepmother (gently, of course) that you need more time to feel close to her. It's better than flinching every time she puts an arm around you or plants a fat smooch on your cheek.

At the other extreme are girls who feel their stepmothers don't put enough effort into having a relationship with them, ignoring them or behaving as if they wish the girls weren't around.

Mindy, 13, says, "My stepmother acts all weird around me, like I'm an alien." Patty, 10, believes her stepmother can't stand her, since "she hardly ever talks to me, and whenever I say something to her, she acts like it was just stupid."

If you're feeling awkward around your stepmom, remember that she may be feeling just as anxious as you. She may want to get to know you but is afraid to push things or seem too eager. Perhaps she's never had a daughter or children of her own. Maybe she's not used to being around a girl your age.

And if you know that you might be doing something to make your stepmother feel bad—like the daggers you keep shooting her way, the sighs and snippy remarks, the eye-rolling—think about how it's impacting you and your family. It's hard for everyone to get along when one person is actively pushing others away. It may take time and even some counseling, but you need to try to find a way to at least have some family peace.

### CHANGING FOR THE BETTER

You don't have to look for four-leaf clovers, throw pennies in a well, or snap turkey bones in half to improve your stepmother situation. Nor do you have to wait for Dad to clue in that you and she are not exactly tossing rose petals at each other. Instead, take matters into your own hands.

Start by being friendly and trying to get to know her, just as you would a new girl in school. Ask her to do something, just the two of you, like go for ice cream, play a video game, or take an afternoon hike. If you're not sure what to talk about, bring up things you have in common (other than your dad, that is), such as movies, books or sports. Ask about her job, her family or where she used to live. If none of this works and you still feel she is shunning you, bolster your courage and ask, "Could we try to get to know each other better?" or, if necessary, "Is there a reason you ignore me?"

Some problems with stepmothers, however, are too hard for girls to figure out—much less solve. Brenda, 13, found herself feeling bad because "nothing I try with my stepmother works. She took over our whole life along with our whole house. She even turned my old playroom into her personal home office. It's almost like she can't stand the sight of me."

Unfortunately, there are times when, no matter how assertive or creative you are, you won't be able to make a dent in your stepmother's armor. It's not your fault. Remember, it takes two to have a relationship. Talking it out with someone else might help. Sometimes, however, girls report that when they speak with their dads, they aren't sympathetic, or believe that their daughters are putting them in the middle. Then girls end up feeling even more upset, disappointed, or hurt. If this happens, it doesn't mean you've done anything wrong. It may be a good time to turn to a trusted relative, guidance counselor, religious leader, or family counselor.

### COMPETITION WITH MOM

As if dealing with a stepmom isn't tricky enough, some girls have to grapple with Celebrity Deathmatch featuring "Mom vs. Stepmom." Competition can be subtle, such as one or both of them asking questions like "What did your stepmother make for dinner?" or "What did your mother get for your birthday?". For Donna, 10, the competition was obvious and fierce. "I can't stand it," she says. "My stepmother took me to get a haircut and it practically caused World War III. Mom got furious and said that was her department."

The fight factor between mom and stepmom can usually be boiled down to one thing—insecurity. Both of them are unsure of their positions in your life now, and each of them is probably just a tad jealous of the other.

The best policy: keep mom and stepmom apart. Don't talk about one to the other, and don't give either of them the bitty details of time spent with the other. If your stepmom makes the most delicious holiday cookies you've ever tasted, do not (we repeat, do not) get the recipe for your mom and suggest she give it a whirl.

Same goes for the other direction. If your mom asks you about your stepmom, you might think you should tell all—after all, she's your mom. But this isn't about loyalty. You never know when a teensy bit of info can cause a heap of trouble. So if either of them pries for specifics, tell them you're uncomfortable and suggest she ask your father.

## WHEN YOU LIKE HER TOO MUCH

Despite all the pitfalls, many girls find themselves, to their amazement, growing fond of their step-mothers. So what's bad about that? Well, sometimes it can make girls feel disloyal to their moms. Bethany, 14, describes getting closer to her stepmother when she and her mom went through a rough bout together. She says, "My mom and I were fighting so I spent more time with my dad and stepmom, and I found I could really talk to her."

It's not so surprising, really. Relationships with stepmoms are sometimes less intense than those with moms. Over time, the relationship you have with your stepmom might evolve—less disciplinarian, more like an older sister or friend.

You may also come to appreciate your stepmother's finer points. She solves computer problems like a pro, makes the best tacos this side of Mexico, or proves a fantastic running partner. It's okay to like these things about your stepmother. You don't have to feel guilty or disloyal—it doesn't mean you love her more than Mom. There's always enough love to go around for everybody.

By being open-minded and positive, you and your stepmom can have a decent relationship. It might take time, but eventually you and she should find a balance that's comfortable for both of you. Stepmothers can be valuable people we both learn from and enjoy. And you just might find yourself writing your own stepmother fairy tale... one with a happy ending.

# The Girls' Life

*Guide to*

# Crushes

# You're Not Sick, You're Not Crazy... You're Crushed!

A new school year—you were just getting used to new teachers, mastering your ultra-stubborn locker and getting into the social swing of things. Then—wham!—you started coming down with some mighty strange symptoms. Your heart's been beating fiercely, you've actually started planning outfits and you're always on the lookout for someone—well, this one guy in particular. And when you finally see him, you find yourself blushing, stammering, and tripping over air pockets. Yep, you've got yourself a serious case of The Crush.

## SAY WHAT?

Having your first crush can be as nerve-wracking as it is exciting. You're suddenly facing sweaty palms, obsessive thoughts and confusing decisions. Many girls wish their feelings would just up and vamoose so they could go back to their normal lives. Unfortunately, having a crush isn't something you can zap away.

Dana, 11, says having her first crush was like getting hit by a lightning bolt: "I could have used a little warning. I always swore I wouldn't be all gushy for a guy. Now here I am hoping I run into this one guy all the time." Many girls admit the plotting and planning can be exhausting. Every time you pass the phone, you will him to call. You find yourself lingering near his classes and trying to figure out his schedule. For Jenna, 12, scribbles were the big clue. "I looked down at my notebook," she confesses, "and had written David's name about a dozen times."

Sometimes having a crush is even, well, kind of embarrassing. As Jenna describes, "I promised my friends I would never put a guy first. But I want to be with David all the time. There's no way I can tell them that." Maybe you're having thoughts you vowed you'd never have: "The way he rakes his hair with his fingers is amazing," or "I can't believe how blue his eyes lo[ ] wears that sweater." Now you're "one of those girls"—and wishing you could hib[ ]

It used to be easy. If you thought about guys at all, it was that you'd like a cool[ ] and he'd like you back. If only having a crush was that simple. Now in addition to [ ] your own thoughts, you're trying to figure out all of his. "What did he mean when he said 'hi' to me?" "Is he looking at me because he's interested or because he saw me looking at him?" "Would he think it was weird if I saved a seat for him?" It's confusing! So don't beat yourself up for having these feelings. Instead, give yourself time to sort through them.

## BUT I FEEL LIKE AN IDIOT!

Your symptoms may not be fatal, but turning beet red every time you picture him is hardly comfortable. Annie, 13, reports, "Every time I try answering a question when he's around, nothing comes out. It's humiliating." Gabrielle, 14, confesses, "If he's in view, I can't seem to get from one place to another without tripping or dropping something."

If you've been feeling klutzy when you get within yards of your new crush, you're in good company. You're probably so preoccupied (being on the lookout for him and figuring out what to say) that you're forgetting other stuff—like holding onto your books or pushing the door open before walking through. Not to worry. This is all temporary, and you will function normally again.

## OH NO, NOT HIM!

Just as you can't plan *when* you'll have a crush, you can't plan *who* it will be on. This guy may even be someone you'd normally put on your list of least desirable guys. It could be your best friend, the class clown, the super-brain who cries when he doesn't get an A+, or the guy who desperately needs a wardrobe consultant. Or maybe it's someone completely inaccessible, like your oldest brother's friend, your friend's older brother, or a Hollywood celeb with exceptional hair.

For Deb, 11, it was her piano teacher, who'd been giving her lessons for years. "It was weird. All of a sudden, I started playing like I had ten thumbs. I felt so awful, I wanted to quit." For Amanda, 14, it was the cashier at the local pizza hangout. "I constantly wanted to go there, but I didn't want my friends to know I had a crush on him so I'd always tell them to go without me." No one gets to pick a crush like a grocery item, so try not to feel disappointed about your choice. Life—and lunch—would be totally boring if everyone had a crush on the same guy!

## CAN'T STOP THINKING ABOUT HIM

One of the most shocking things is how much your brain becomes consumed by "him." As Amy describes, "It's taking over my life! I've even figured out his schedule so I can pass by his locker at the exact moments he does. I can't take it!"

When you like someone, it's natural to want to see him. Problem is, you can't focus on anything else. Even when you have tons of homework, letters to write and chores to complete, you can't stop envisioning his milky-white teeth or the splash of freckles on his nose. You're constantly spacing out in class, reliving what he was doing when you saw him last. You're up all night thinking of him, even asking the Magic 8 Ball a million times if he likes you back. When it says, "My sources say no," you shake it furiously and ask again.

Mary, 14, claims the reason girls develop a one-track mind is the not-knowing part. "You like him but don't know how he feels about you," she says. "Does he like you back or hate you? You'll die if you don't know." It's maddening. So do you tell him? Not tell him? Flip a coin? Tell a friend of his friend's friend?

Let us make this perfectly clear: You don't have to do a thing. You do not *have* to declare your feelings. This crush is yours to tuck away in your mind and take out to savor. By keeping it secret, you never have to face potential ridicule, third-degrees questioning or humiliation. If, down the road, you change your mind, fine. Otherwise, mum's the word for as long as you want.

## BUT I'VE GOT TO TELL SOMEONE!

Maybe you're dying to share the news. You're ready to blab every teensy detail to the first person who'll listen—the way he elbowed you, shared his world view, or asked if he could borrow a dollar (it was the way he asked).

This is a normal—but potentially hazardous—reaction. Once the info's out there circulating, you can never take it back. So tell your best and most trusted pal—exclude anyone who can't keep their lips zipped. If you're not sure you can rely on anyone, tell your diary, pen pal or secret-keeping cat. They'll never tease you, grill you or spill the beans.

If you're considering telling him—the dude of your dreams, that is—question your motives. What are you expecting to happen? At best, he'll tell you he has a crush on you too. Only what if he doesn't? Will you regret your confession? Also, consider whether telling him will make things too uncomfortable. If it's your best bud or math tutor, for example, things might get pretty hairy—and you do have to face this guy. If you know in your heart of hearts it can't work out, you're probably best off saying nothing. If there's as good a shot as any, it's your call.

"I'm doing it," some of you are thinking. "You only live once! Seize the day!" Okay, brave girls, if you're going to tell him, do it right. Avoid the bombshell. If you walk up to him and announce, "I have a crush on you," you'll put him on the spot. Even if he likes you back, he may feel too embarrassed to admit it.

## STEER CLEAR OF MESSENGERS

It's tempting to hint to his best friend that you think so-and-so is cute. That way, you don't have to tell your crush to his face and put him on the spot. There's only one problem. You have no idea what the best friend is going to tell your crush. He might be jealous and say something mean, or choose not to tell your crush at all—and you'll never know.

If you have one of your people (a bud) talk to his people (his bud) you're really asking for trouble. Crystal, 14, can tell you all about it. "I asked my best friend to let his best friend know I liked him," she says. "Well, she told him during lunch, and the guy I liked started cracking up. I thought I was going to hurl."

So how should you let him know? Treat him like a friend you'd like to get to know better. Say "hi," save him a seat on the bus, share your notes when he's absent. Radiate a genuine smile. Basic skills apply: Start conversations, be a good listener, ask questions about stuff you're both interested in. Ask about a mountain biking trip he took, his old neighborhood. You get the idea.

## DO NOT LOSE SIGHT OF THE WORLD AROUND YOU

It's easy to get so wrapped up in him that you abandon your old life. Some girls start skipping after-school activities so they can watch their crush play sports, perform in band practice, whatever. Lots of girls ditch friends to spend even more time around him.

Says 14-year-old Kirsten, "My friend Brittney keeps bailing on plans so she can drool over this guy KJ. It's so annoying!" Don't be one of those girls. Enjoy your crush, but don't take your buds for granted. If your grades or social life outside of him are starting to suffer, it's time to chill out.

## YOU'VE HEARD IT BEFORE, BUT WE'LL SAY IT AGAIN: BE YOURSELF.

Maria, 13, knew the deal but still dyed her hair blond after discovering her crush's love for Cameron Diaz. "My hair looked terrible," she says, "and when he saw me, he started laughing with his friends." Others play dumb to get attention. Imagine hiding your smarts to impress someone! This makes no sense! If he needs you to be less so he can be more, forget him. The guys you want to hang out with should appreciate, not dislike, your know-how. If he hints he could use help surfing the net—and you know your stuff—show him the ropes. If you're a good athlete, invite him over for a game of hoops or whatever pick-up game you both like.

## "HE LOVES ME, HE LOVES ME NOT..."

You can yank all the daisy petals in the world, but how can you tell if he *really* likes you back?

**He's always cracking up when you're around.** Guys get nervous too and are often more comfortable making jokes. If your crush always teases you (with a big smile), he may be hooked.

**He's trying to be your bud.** Is your guy being helpful, confiding in you, asking for help on an assignment? Is he showing up at your games? If you notice he's trying extra hard to be social, it's a good bet he's interested. Take note: Few guys are mature enough yet for this method.

**Dear Carol:** I have a problem. I really like this boy who everyone else thinks is a dork. I think he likes me too, but he acts like he's afraid to say something. We're nearly best friends and he has the same interests as I do. What should I do? —BOY TROUBLE

**Dear Boy Trouble:** Who'll be going out with him? You or your friends? If you like him and he likes you, maybe you don't have a problem after all. And maybe your friends will soon see what you've seen in him all along.

**He wants to know everything about you.** When a guy gets incredibly curious about whether you'll be on the debate team, who you think is funniest on *Friends* and what your favorite flavor popsicle is, it's a good tip off he has feelings for you.

**Is he pulling strings behind the scenes?** Some guys have a hard time being direct, so you just have to read between the lines. Does he pick you first to be on his sports team? Get you invited to a party? Push someone out of the way so he can stand behind you in the water fountain line? Definite signs.

## THE VERDICT IS IN

You just found out he likes you. Now you're flipping out. Do you have to go on an actual date? Do you have to go public? No—again, you do not have to do anything. You can continue to be his friend, or not. You can call him on the phone, or not. If you're not ready to date, get together with him and other buds. Pace your relationship according to what you feel comfortable with.

Don't let friends or anyone else push you into anything. You can just enjoy the fact that he has feelings for you too. If, on the other hand, you learn he's not interested, it's his big loss. We know it feels horrible—that's why they call it a crush—but we promise you're going to be okay. It's intense, but it will pass. In fact, for good or bad, there's probably another crush waiting for you in the wings.

Remember to take things slowly and enjoy the good parts—like when you're so excited, you could skip through the school halls. The anticipation, the suspense, the bliss…it's the best a crush has to offer. Live it up! Just remember not to let him become your whole world. And do beware of glass doors—you actually have to push them open before walking through.

# Is He Crushworthy?

1. You and your crush are walking home from school together when you spot an injured bird. What does he most likely do?
   a) Wrap the bird up in his jacket, take it home, and nurse it back to health.
   b) Say, "Hmm, looks like a rare species from the Laguna tribe."
   c) Poke it with a stick and pluck a feather for his collection.

2. You ask your crush if he wants to go to the carnival with you, but he says he can't make it. When you spot him there with his friends he says:
   a) "I'm really sorry. I was planning on staying home to study for the history exam, but the guys talked me into going out instead."
   b) Nothing. As soon as he sees you, he bolts behind the cotton candy counter.
   c) "Well, see, my aunt died and I was supposed to go to the funeral, but the thing got postponed 'til next Friday."

3. You tell your guy a funny story that happened at summer camp. How does he respond?
   a) Laughs and tells you how hilarious you are.
   b) Says, "Yeah, so? Guess what happened to Hunter at camp..."
   c) Yawns and says, "Huh? I don't get it."

4. You're at the mall with your boy, and you walk into Wacky Willy's Silly Sweets. What does your crush do?
   a) Buys you a bouquet of lollipops.
   b) Gets himself a jawbreaker and asks if you want a taste.
   c) Slips a handful of gummy worms into his pocket and leaves the store without paying.

5. You run into your crush at Skateland. His appearance is as follows:
   a) Khaki pants, a nice shirt and a new haircut. And, mmm, is that CK One you smell?
   b) A pair of jeans and a T-shirt that looks like it was yanked from the dirty laundry pile.
   c) A pair of cut-offs and a shirt that says, "Who Cut the Cheese?"

6. Your guy agrees to help you study after school for tomorrow's language arts test. How does he follow up?
   a) Shows up on time, equipped with *Webster's*, *Roget's* and the newest edition of the *Prentice-Hall Handbook for Writers*.
   b) Knocks on the door twenty minutes late with three of his friends by his side and says, "Can we make this quick? I have a basketball game in half an hour."
   c) Stands you up entirely, doesn't call, and avoids you the next day.

7. You're walking with your guy when you trip and fall flat on your face. How does he react?
   a) Helps you up, wipes gravel off your knees, and seems genuinely concerned.
   b) Asks, "You all right?"
   c) Keeps walking, shakes his head and mutters, "Klutz."

8. You're at the park and your crush is hangin' out with some of his friends. Suddenly, his mom yells for him, "Ed-waaaard!" How does he respond?
   a) "Must be time for dinner. Gotta go, guys."
   b) No response. He pretends he doesn't hear her, hangs out for about ten minutes longer and then moseys on home.
   c) "I have no idea why she insists on calling me Edward. Everyone knows I'm Big E."

9. You invite your favorite boy to your house for dinner so your parents can meet him. What is his conduct at the dinner table?
   a) He puts his napkin in his lap, holds his fork correctly, and says, "These are the best brussels sprouts I've ever tasted. How did you make them?"
   b) He cleans his plate but skips the dinner conversation.
   c) He dips his half-chewed roll in the gravy boat, licks his butter knife, and recaps last night's *South Park*—word for word.

10. An older kid in the school parking lot offers your guy a cigarette. He says:
   a) "No thanks, man. I don't smoke."
   b) "Well, maybe. I'll try anything once."
   c) "Gotta light?"

11. Your school is devising a gender equity program so girls are sure to get fair treatment in education and sports. What does your guy do to participate?
   a) Helps you write a letter of support to submit to the board of education.
   b) Asks, "Gender what?"
   c) Paints posters that read, "Hey, girls! Forget what's fair. Go do your hair!"

12. A big science project is due on Monday. What does your boy do to prepare?
   a) Spends all weekend collecting data to support his hypothesis on water conservation.
   b) Sticks the stem of a pinwheel inside a soda bottle and calls it a windmill.
   c) Knocks over the smartest kid in class, steals his ant colony, and turns it in as his own.

## SCORING
*Mark 3 points for each A answer, 2 points for Bs, 1 for Cs. Add up the total.*

**28-36 points:** Good for you. You know you deserve the best and won't settle for anything less. You have no interest in wasting your time on a guy who isn't caring and respectful of girls. Congrats on having a good eye, and have a blast with this sweetheart of a guy.

**20-27 points:** While your crush has potential, he's probably not quite ready for a girlfriend just yet. Spend time hanging out with him in group situations, which will give you a chance to check out whether he's worth your energy. Hey, he might come around and grow up some. But if he doesn't, you can still keep him around as a bud.

**12-19 points:** Turn around right now, and run (don't jog)—as fast as you can! This guy is trouble and certainly not worth your time. He's sooooooo cute, you say? He's also rude, inconsiderate, and dishonest. Trust us—cute only goes so far when he lies to you for the ninth time in a row. Say good-bye to this crush, and work on setting your sights a little higher.

# Controlling The "Crush Crazies"

It doesn't take a brain surgeon to figure out what a new crush can do to a girl. Suddenly, you smile a little bigger. Your step has an extra bounce. You think nothing of rolling out of bed at 5:45 A.M. to blow your hair dry. Yes, now that your crush has come along, each new day brims with possibility. Even though it's November, you're sure you hear birds singing as you pass his locker. The rain outside isn't cold and dreary anymore; now it's cozy and romantic.

The buzz you get from having a new crush couldn't be matched by ten gallons of Frappuccino. But as good as having a crush can feel, it is our duty to inform you of one tiny detail—love can turn you loony.

Don't believe it? That's the funny thing about the crush crazies. They strike otherwise perfectly normal girls. Take Jen. At the peak of her crush, she would take her chocolate lab Java for his nightly walk around the block. Then she'd hike it an extra twenty—that's 20!—blocks north, on the off chance she might "bump into" her crush near his house.

Then there's Claire. Her crush gave her the number to his private line so they could discuss sets they were building for the school production of *South Pacific*. Two months later, Claire was still calling the number—just to hear his voice on his answering machine. Even though she worried that he might have had caller ID, "but since he never had me arrested," she just kept on calling.

Don't get us wrong. We're not talking about those little things you do to give fate the extra nudge it needs to bring you together with your crush. There's no harm in consulting your Magic 8-ball or passing by his locker on occasion. We're talking about the things we do for love that later cause us to do a V-8 headslap.

Each of us have probably had a few "What was I thinking?!?" moments that make us cringe in retrospect. But don't be so hard on yourself—after all, you weren't thinking. The crush crazies were thinking for you. The bad news is even the most sane, level-headed girl can find herself caving in to the crush crazies. The trick is to take a chance on romance—without turning into a fool for love. Below are some smart crush moves to make sure you're staying sane.

## SMART CRUSH MOVE NO. 1: BE SURE HE IS WORTHY

One of the weird things about the crush crazies is they tend to strike hardest when your crush is someone you only know from afar. Let's say you're a freshman and you fall like a rock for the captain of the football team, a senior. He's all you think about. It matters not that you have no classes with this guy and no mutual friends. Heck, you and he are barely on "hello" terms. But

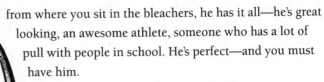

from where you sit in the bleachers, he has it all—he's great looking, an awesome athlete, someone who has a lot of pull with people in school. He's perfect—and you must have him.

Hate to be the one to burst your love bubble, but guess what? He's not perfect. You just haven't had the chance to find that out yet. Still, you are willing to stake your happiness on whether or not this is the week he figures out your name is Bridget, not Brittany.

It's disappointing when a crush doesn't reciprocate the same amount of attention and affection you dish out for him. But when you stop to think about it, how could he? While Joe Pigskin is off pumping iron three hours each night (you don't get those biceps by staying home with a good book), you've been daydreaming about how awesome it would be to have him as a boyfriend. But what do you really know about him? Do you have common interests? Would he support your efforts to write your first novel by eighteen? Who knows? You don't.

It's not that you shouldn't be flexible in your expectations or that you shouldn't consider someone who is your social or personal opposite. Some great romances happen between people who outwardly might not have much in common. But there has to be respect, caring, and understanding. Unless you have a sense of who your crush truly is, it's foolish to put all your happiness eggs in his basket. No matter how cute his basket is.

No doubt, it's fun to like someone from afar—and safe. You never have to risk rejection or find yourself in dating situations you may not feel ready for if your relationship is limited to writing his name on the bottom of your shoe. And it's perfectly okay to have a "schoolgirl" crush on people like celebrities and athletes as long as you recognize your admiration for what it is—a starry-eyed crush. (And if you are going to crush on a football player, may we recommend Brett Favre?)

But if you're ready to consider dating, look around your own group for guys you know and respect. Save your feelings for someone who will appreciate, and, hopefully, return them.

## SMART CRUSH MOVE NO. 2: DON'T GO CHANGING

Once you learn more about your crush (He plays tuba! He drinks Peach Snapple!), the crush crazies tempt you to show your crush how much you two have in common. That's how Michelle ended up spending a freezing cold Sunday chasing her amour through a frigid forest—on skis.

When Michelle heard her crush was looking for company on one of his ten-mile cross-country ski-a-thons, she professed her love for slip-sliding the day away. Of course, the closest thing to cross-country skiing Michelle had ever done was on her mom's Nordic Track. Out in the woods, it quickly became apparent Michelle wasn't cross-country savvy when she fell flat on her face the second she tried to push down the path. "It was painfully obvious I had lied," she remembers. "He was bummed, and I was totally embarrassed." Her crush left her in a hut with some hot chocolate and a magazine. "That was our first date—and our last," she says.

Rationally, we all know pretending to be someone we aren't is a bad idea. But when you are desperate to find a connection to the object of your affection, it's hard not to chirp up with "Me, too!" when he waxes poetic over ski wax. But before you find yourself hugging a pine instead of pining away, search for the truth in what is about to fly out of your mouth. There is nothing wrong with saying, "Wow, you can ski ten miles? I can't go ten feet, but I'd love to learn."

Why would that have been a smarter move? Because for most guys, the only thing better than mastering an activity is sharing that knowledge with someone else. Whether your crush writes cool song lyrics, plays piano, or is an awesome cook, one of the nicest things you can do for him is show a real interest in what he loves most. Who knows? He might get a clue and offer you a lesson. But if, after your best efforts, you can't stand the cold, then get out of the, um, forest.

## SMART CRUSH MOVE NO. 3:
## DON'T SHOW AND DON'T TELL

If you really want a "Thank heavens that wasn't me" moment, try Shari's story on for size. She had a huge crush on the star of the freshman lacrosse team. When the team reached the finals, she thought it would be fun to show her support by making a T-shirt with his picture and a big #1.

"I scanned in a photo I snapped at a game and transferred it to a T-shirt. I thought it would be a cool way to show him I care. Of course, his teammates saw me wearing it and started laughing and teasing him. He was nice about it, but it was obvious I had blown it."

When you're crush crazy, it's easy to think a stunt like Shari's will be a welcome ice-breaker. But more often than not, big gestures fall flat. Why? First, most guys hate being put on the spot. When you go over the top to get

**Dear Carol:** One of my BFFs is starting to like boys and my other friends and I are not ready for that. She's always fixing her hair, while my friends and I don't care if our hair looks like it's been in a twister. When I have her over, all she talks about is boys, and if I had my way, I would ship boys off to Planet X! I have known her for six years so I don't really want to dump her. —CUPID IS STUPID

**Dear Cupid Is Stupid:** Then don't dump her. Your long-term friendship doesn't have to screech to a halt just because you're going through different phases or have different interests. Boy-crazy girls can be best friends with book-crazy girls or horse-crazy girls or artistic girls or athletic girls. Don't criticize your friend, but next time she's going on and on about the hottie in homeroom, say, "I know you like him, but now I want to talk about..." and come up with a common interest such as books or movies. Here's another idea—spend time together doing something besides yakking. Bake cupcakes, ride bicycles, visit a pet store, rent a movie, or study for the science test.

# CRUSH HORROR STORIES

If you're feeling heartbroken over your new crush, here are some girls who can truly sympathize. Despite their experiences, they all lived to tell the tale!

"Jimmy was an outdoor nut, so I told him I loved to hike—the biggest lie. When he asked me if I wanted to climb a mountain in Vermont, I said okay, thinking it would be romantic. What a joke! I hated every step and got so exhausted I never made it near the top. I was humiliated." —MAYA, 16

"I had a crush on the lead singer of a band, and I went to see him in concert. He was amazing. During one song, he smiled at me and I thought I'd pass out. Then, at the end of the concert, he said he wanted to dedicate a song to someone in the audience. I was praying! He dedicated it to 'Julie, his brightest moon.' It was devastating." —ANGELA, 18

"I was ten, and it was my stepsister Anne's wedding. This hot college guy sat next to me and I almost died! All these pretty older girls were around, and he sat next to me. I acted chill at first, but lost my mind around dessert. He went to mingle with guests, and I followed him around like a puppy. When he went to the bathroom, I even waited for him to come out. To top it all off, I thought I should commit my smooth moves to paper. I wrote my helpful stalking hints on the back of the wedding program, which my stepsister found the next day. In case they hadn't gotten a good enough laugh before, they did now. Ugh." —ISABELLE, 15

"When I was fourteen, the couple next door hired me to baby-sit. I thought the husband was gorgeous (he looked like Harrison Ford), and I got shy every time he spoke to me. But he was super nice, always asking me about school and stuff. One night, when they thought I'd left, I heard his wife say to him, 'Beth has the biggest crush on you! It's so adorable!' I cried all the way home." —BETH, 17

"In junior high, I went crazy over this boy in study hall. He was a jock, member of the debate team, and in drama club. He was also three years older than me, so I thought he was really mature. Every day, I would rush to study hall so I could see him for as long as possible. Well, one day he was sitting with some friends at the table beside mine, and I felt something fly into my hair. I turned around, and he and all his friends were shooting spitballs at me and cracking up. He turned out to be totally rude." —ALICIA, 19

noticed, you are, in a way, forcing your crush to make a decision he might not be ready for. You may have been working on this crush for months, but on his radar screen, you are barely a blip. Asking him to like you before he knows you is totally unfair.

Second, most guys would rather get to know you without the whole school being in on it. When you publicize your feelings in a bold way, you are forcing your crush to come clean about his feelings—something many guys have a tough time doing, no matter how into you they may be.

Third, some guys get scared off by girls who are willing to go to great lengths to get them to like them. When I talked to guys who had been subjected to outrageous attention-getters, their reactions were mostly negative. Some guys wondered how their admirees could like them so much when they barely knew them. Others felt strong displays of affection meant the girls wanted a relationship more serious than they felt ready for. The most callous guys questioned the sanity of any girl who would like them enough to embarrass herself in public.

We have one word for you: moderation. There is no reason not to offer to help with his French if you're a francophile and his French sounds like Pepe Le Pew. Giving him a supportive smile across the cafeteria when he drops his lunch tray in front of the sophomore class is just plain kind. And if he's the one organizing the soccer team bake sale, why not offer to whip up a batch of your famous choco-mint chip cookies?

The key to success? Wait until you're on friendly terms. When you do something to show you care instead of trying to make someone care about you, you are more likely to get the result you want. So give it time—then give it your all.

## SMART CRUSH MOVE NO. 4: STOP WITH THE HAIR SPRAY, ALREADY

Before, it took you ten minutes to shower and two seconds in the closet to face the day. Now that the crush crazies have struck, you spend ten minutes just deciding what shampoo to use. And forget the closet—nothing is cute enough for him!

A word from the wise—relax. While TV ads show girls with shimmering, golden hair getting the guy, in real life, guys barely notice if you brush your teeth. Ditto the new duds. One guy we asked actually liked the girl crushing on him, but lost interest when she pulled an image switcheroo. "She looked great in jeans and turtlenecks," recalls our Romeo, "but then it was all mini-skirts and platforms. It's like she turned into the Britney Spears of homeroom."

The best advice? Be the same girl he already says hi to every morning. While doing your own Cinderella transformation may seem like a sure way to get his attention, it'll still be you on the inside. And if that's not good enough for him, then he isn't good enough for you.

## SMART CRUSH MOVE NO. 5: NEXT!

A smart girl knows when to cut her losses. While the crush crazies may convince you to hope against hope, there are good real-life reasons to move on.

First of all, there is only so much obsessing you—and your friends—can take. If, after your best efforts, your intended shows no intentions toward you, you must realize you might be better off as friends. As much as you might want a relationship, it takes two to make a couple.

Here's a good test: Would you accept from a friend the same treatment your crush gives you? If your friend never called and dissed you when other people were around, would you still like her? The crush crazies blind us to behavior that would otherwise send us running.

While it takes time to get over your crush, the girls I know were happy they moved on (okay, maybe after a few tears). Most couldn't remember what they were thinking when they liked a guy who ended up being a jerk. And, as many girls found out, not being known around school as "the girl who likes so-and-so" opened up a world of possibilities.

# To Date Or Not To Date?

## That Is the Question

Whether you're allowed to date or not, the idea has probably crossed—and triple crossed—your mind. (Otherwise, this book wouldn't be pressed so close to your face.) Perhaps you've watched your older sister get ready for a big night out and imagined what it's like. Or you've been rehearsing what to say in case your older brother's cute friend asks you to the movies. Or maybe you feel light years from dating but still have questions you'd like cleared up for the future.

One of girls' biggest worries is how to be sure they're ready to date—even if they have their parents' permission. To figure out this dilemma, think about why you want to date in the first place. If it's for any of the reasons listed below, you may wanna hold off till you're good and ready.

### MY FRIEND IS DATING...

One of the most horrifying experiences on the planet (barring alien abduction) is believing your best friend is about to abandon you for someone new. So girls sometimes freak when they discover their best friend is planning to date. Your first thoughts might be, "What am I going to do on weekends without her?" "Will she still make time for me?" or "We made a pact to start dating at the same exact time!" Even when girls are genuinely happy for their friends, many also feel resentful.

Jill, 14, can vouch for that. She and Tami, devoted friends since third grade, swore to each other they would begin dating at the same age. That way, they could double date. They agreed to wait until they were sixteen and even pinkie-swore. Only, Tami's feelings changed one day. More specifically, they changed when Tami decided Jake, the new guy at school, was simply too incredible to pass up.

When Jake finally asked Tami out and Tami accepted, Jill had conflicting feelings. She was psyched for Tami, but also confused. Tami broke her promise to wait. While Jill wanted to be supportive and encouraging—she knew that's what best friends did for each other—she felt completely phony every time she confirmed to Tami how great it was about Jake.

Well, the date went great, and Tami became obsessed with Jake—telling Jill every little move, gesture and facial expression that was just the "cutest" or "sweetest" thing. More and more, Jill's resentment grew, and she decided the only way to save the friendship would be to start dating too.

That way, she wouldn't feel so abandoned. The two could talk about their guys and share the experience.

So Jill asked out Scott, a boy from class she knew liked her—thanks to grapevine gossip. He eagerly said yes, and the two planned to go out on Saturday night. The situation would have been perfect if it weren't for one simple thing: Jill wasn't emotionally ready to date. For three entire days, Jill felt sick to her stomach. As she put it, "All of a sudden, I was worrying how I was supposed to act, what I was supposed to say or not say, what to wear, what if he tried to kiss me. But I didn't want to leave him hanging since I was the one who asked him out. The whole idea of it was making me sicker and sicker."

Which is how Jill ended up getting out of the date. Saturday afternoon she called Scott at home, and told him she was throwing up and couldn't go. She put off explaining until Monday, which she said, "was awful and humiliating, and I wished I'd never asked him out."

Unfortunately, this type of situation happens a lot. One girl decides she wants to date, and her best friend suddenly feels she should start too. Sometimes, it's a result of feeling competitive ("Hey, she's not the only one who can date…"), but more often, it's because, like Jill, girls are willing to do almost anything to keep their friendships intact. But the truth is, you can't force yourself to be ready for dating just because your friend is. What you can do is come up with alternative plans to keep you from feeling abandoned—hang out with other friends, find a new hobby, sign up for a sport. Do not let your happiness hinge on how your friend's dating life is going.

## I'D LOOK COOL…

Maybe no one in your grade is dating yet, and you think it'd be awesome to be first. You'd look sophisticated and everyone would ask questions because you were "in the know." Or, maybe you want to show up your older sis, who's always bragging about this date and that. Or, maybe you think guys at school would like you more if you started to date—they'd stop seeing you as a tomboy and treat you like the girl you are. Whatever the reason, you're dating to impress.

Debbi, 14, admits she started dating Chad last year because she craved attention. "I was new to the school, and the girls pretty much ignored me—they already had their friends. I wanted to shake things up so they would talk to me, or even talk about me. So I asked out Chad, this cute guy who was a year ahead of us. Well, suddenly, girls were coming up to me and asking all these

# DATING Q & A

What's the real definition of a date? According to Webster's dictionary, a "date" is: "A social appointment with a member of the other gender." Ugh, sounds like a visit to the dentist. Forget Webster's—we'll define it ourselves. A date is when a girl and a guy hang out together so they can get to know each other better. No more, no less.

**Does there have to be a kiss or something for it to be an actual date?**
Nope. It's the time spent together that makes it a date, not whether or not there's a kiss during that time.

**What is a normal age to start dating?**
No such thing—every girl is different.

**What if my parents won't let me date yet?**
Then respect their wishes. They're trying to do what's best for you. The good news is that all the daughters who've been told they can't date until high school have lived to tell about it.

**What's a good date to start out with?**
Going out with a small group of guys and girls lets you get to know him without extra pressure. Conversation will flow easily, and you can see whether he's really the cat's meow.

**When I start dating, is it okay to ask a guy out?**
Sure. Girls no longer have to sit by the phone waiting for a call. (We can't believe they ever did.) Again, group dates make this a breeze: "Hey, a bunch of us are going to the movies this Saturday. Want to go?" Or, if he mentions after class that he likes mountain biking and you do too, ask him if he wants to go to the park.

**What if he says, "No," or worse yet, "You mean with YOU?"**
Then he's a moron, so don't waste one more second of your time thinking about him. It takes guts to ask someone out, and a cool guy will respect you for asking—whether he wants to go out or not.

**What other advice would you offer when it comes to dating?**
Don't try to be the type of girl you think he'd be attracted to. If you two are going on a date, that means he already likes you—for who you are. Inevitably, girls who pretend to be someone else will have to admit that they lied (which looks pretty silly) or be bored to death when he pops in his *Star Trek: The Next Generation* videotape for the umpteenth time. It's not worth it. Besides, you're awesome—as is.

questions: 'What's he like?' 'Did you really ask him out?' I went from being a zero to Miss Popular."

And then? "I realized I had to actually go out with Chad. I couldn't just ask him out and not do it, or I'd look like a liar. So we went to this party. I was so nervous. I kept thinking he was going to try to kiss me, and I didn't want him to. I just wanted everyone to think we were a couple." Debbi says she was so uptight that she practically ignored Chad all night. "Finally, he asked me what was up," she says. "I had to tell him that I just wanted to be friends, which confused him, and he got really mad. So he went off with his friends, and I looked and felt like a jerk."

Cara, 15, went out with Eric in hopes of changing her image as well. "I've always been a jock," she says, "and I grew up playing football with the guys on the block, so it's hard for them to see me as anything but a pal. I started flirting with Eric to show everyone I'm not a guy. When he asked me out, I said yes, but I really didn't like him in that way. I felt bad about pretending that I had different feelings for Eric, so I called him before the date and told him the whole truth. I can't say we're good friends now, but at least he forgave me and all the pressure's off."

It's not impressive to date a guy in hopes of looking like a hot-shot. Like Debbi and Cara, if you're not ready, you'll end up getting caught in your own lie. What's really impressive is trusting yourself enough to wait to date until you are ready, and knowing you don't need some guy to make you a cool person.

## IT'D TICK OFF MY FOLKS...

"I wanted to start dating," says Betsy, 14, "because I knew it would flip out my parents." Along the same lines as skipping chores and blasting music, dating before you get the okay is a sure way to cause friction with the 'rents—exactly what some girls want.

"I was so tired of my parents telling me what to do," Betsy explains. "They're always in my face about picking up my room, doing my homework, baby-sitting my little sister. I have to be, like, this perfect little girl. So when John, a guy on my softball team, asked me out, I automatically said yes. It wasn't because I liked him that way. I mean, he was nice and all, but I really just wanted to bug my parents like they bug me. I wanted to do something they had no control over."

Big mistake. "They freaked out when I told them," she says. "They said there was no way they were letting me go out with a guy, and we got into this huge fight. I told them I'd date whomever and whenever I wanted to and they couldn't do anything about it." Except they could. Betsy's parents grounded her and told her she'd better respect their rules.

All girls get mad at their parents at some point. And you will definitely stir things up if you choose to date against their wishes. But nothing positive can come from this. You'll end up losing your parent's trust, hurting a guy who doesn't deserve to be used, and sticking yourself in a tricky situation. If you're angry at your folks, sit down and talk to them—don't use dating as a weapon.

## HE ASKED ME...

Girls often find it painfully difficult to say no to guys who ask them out. They feel flustered and lost for words, and it seems there's no time to even think about what to say. The guy is nervous and waiting anxiously for an answer. What are you supposed to do? It's awkward. Sometimes it seems the easiest thing to do is say yes.

This happened to Jennifer, 13: "Adam was this guy in drama club who I knew liked me. He complimented me and stuff. Still, when he called to ask me out, I was shocked. I sat there, not saying a word, wanting to hang up." Instead, she told him she would go out with him. "I didn't want to hurt his feelings," she confesses. "I knew how hard it was for him to ask me, and it seemed rude to say no."

That night, Jennifer couldn't sleep. She knew she should have said she just wanted to be friends. Now, she'd have to explain why she said yes and tell him she didn't want to go out with him. Uck.

So what could Jennifer have done? First, you never have to give immediate answers. You have every right to say you aren't sure. Here's a way to do it: "I'm flattered that you asked, but I'll get back to you." If he's cool, he'll accept that without pushing. If not, you don't want to be with him anyway.

If you know right away the answer is no, that's okay too. You might worry about hurting him, but you have to respect your own feelings. In other words, you take care of you; let him take care of him. Is there a way to decline and not hurt his feelings? Not really. It hurts to be rejected. The kindest way to say it is plain and simple: "I really appreciate your asking me, but I'd rather stay friends." You're done. If he tries to convince you or make you feel bad, just repeat yourself.

### SO WHAT *IS* A GOOD REASON TO DATE?

There is one, and only one, good reason to date. You like a certain guy, and you want to get to know him better by spending more time with him. When you're ready and you've gotten the nod from your parents, dating can be lots of fun. Yes, nervousness is part of the package, but a good date also brings excitement and happiness. So stay cool about the whole deal, take your time, and prepare to enjoy dating for all that it has to offer.

# Waiting For Dating

## Really... It's Okay Not to Be Ready!

Nervous stomach, sweaty palms, swelling zits, and brain spasms. Well, future doctors of America, what's your diagnosis? Hint #1: It's neither flu nor the common cold. Hint #2: It's temporary. For those who guess first-date-o-phobia, we see a long white coat in your future wardrobe. Dating is fantastic fun when you're ready—and a big fat headache when you're not. Since you have years of dating in your future, why deal with the hassles now? Pre-teens and teens all over the country are saying No! to dating, and opting for co-ed group outings. It's called non-dating, and it allows girls to paint the town red, pressure-free.

### THE JOYS OF NON-DATING

"What pressures?" you may wonder. Well, let's start with pressure #1: avoiding awkward silences. He says, "What do you think of the new history teacher?" You say, "She's pretty cool," and he nods in agreement. You struggle for something to add, as does he, and then comes a deafening silence. You cough, hiccup, yawn... anything to keep your mouth moving, while silently praying for an inspiring joke to come to you. As the silence stretches out, you consider running straight into a lamp post. At least you'd have something to discuss en route to the hospital.

In the real world, gaps in conversation happen all the time—with friends, parents, your gerbils. You don't think twice about it. When it comes to dating, however, males and females alike have decided that a lull in conversation is dating death. You have no business going out if you can't sustain a conversation for four hours. As goofy as this may sound, first-daters stand behind this line of reasoning.

Non-dating means never having to spew nonsense just to keep a conversation alive. ("So, Rick, what's your very favorite kitchen utensil?") In a group of four to ten, someone's always yapping about something. In fact, try asking a group this size to be silent for thirty seconds... not a chance. It works out perfectly.

If you're feeling bashful or have run out of things to say on a non-date, let others pick up the slack. You'll join in when you feel good and ready, and it's easy to play off other people's jokes and stories when you're ready to go verbal again.

## NO MORE LOSER DATES

Non-dating also offers an escape from those who are really getting on your nerves. Say you think Josh from math class is adorable. For weeks, you've been glancing back and forth at each other, but haven't had the courage to actually converse. You're psyched when you hear he's going for pizza with the gang tomorrow.

When you see him at the restaurant, he gives you a huge smile and motions for you to sit next to him—a flying start! You strike up a conversation, and all is great—until Josh asks, "Hey, why don't magnets stick to sweaters and stuff?" Later, he asks how to spell your name. (It's Sue.) Josh has the IQ of a paper clip, and your attraction to him has plummeted from ten to zip in under five minutes.

If this were a date, you'd have to ride through some seriously lame chat. Sure, you could survive, but only after hours of explaining that you don't have to be a boxer to wear boxer shorts, and that the "g" in bologna is silent (always).

With non-dating, you have the easy out of bringing others into the conversation. It's the social equivalent of Monopoly's "Get Out of Jail Free" card. Give your buddy Jason a nudge and ask, "What do you think about Josh's theory?" If Jason is a real friend, he'll pick up your cue and enter the picture.

TOO MUCH ON MY MIND.

Carrie, 14, has used this survival tactic many a time: "I went golfing with eight of my friends, and this guy I had a huge crush on ended up being such a conceited jerk. So, when we split into groups of four, I made sure I wasn't in his group. Thank heaven it wasn't just the two of us."

Adds Lana, 13, "I went on this date with a guy from school, and we had absolutely nothing to say to each other outside of the classroom. I kept wishing my best friend were with us. That girl is never at a loss for words." If they went out on a non-date, her best friend would have been there.

If you do like a particular guy in your bunch, non-dating makes the situation a breeze. In addition to easing any social pressures, non-dating gives you a chance to see what he's like with his friends—as well as yours.

"I like this guy at school a lot," says Liz, "even more

so after we went out with a group of kids. He wasn't just nice to me—he was sweet with all my friends too. And he didn't try to show off in front of his friends. It was cool."

"In a group, you can take your time getting to know the guy you like," adds Allison, 13. It's not like when you go out on a date, and the next day at school everyone decides you're a couple— even if you don't want to be. It's more relaxed."

Or, you might learn the guy you like isn't as amazing as you thought. Says Julie, 14, "Michael, the boy I liked, treated my friends so badly the night we all went out. He kept making fun of them. I was so disappointed, but let me tell you—that was the end of Michael."

## I'M NOT READY!

Lots of girls are simply not into dating yet. Ask Lisa, 14: "Many girls in my class have started dating, but I'm not ready. I'm too nervous when I'm alone with a guy."

Christa, 13, says, "I have enough to deal with without getting mixed up in dating. But I like hanging out with some of the boys in my class, so it's fun when a bunch of us goes out."

Jody, 14, is considering giving up dating for now: "I went on a date last month, and it just wasn't any fun. I kept blabbing like an idiot, and I ended up exhausted. I'm just not ready for the dating world yet."

Other girls who'd like nothing better than to start dating have gotten the red light from Mom and Pop. Many a dad has firmly stated, "No way, no how, not until you're eighteen." Instead of getting stuck home, non-dating gives everyone a chance to go out and have a good time.

## IT'S NOT FOR EVERYONE

While the group scene works for many, there can be drawbacks. Dalia, 13, is shy in a group. "I feel like I just disappear when I'm with a crowd," she admits, "but when I'm with only one other person, I feel more free to talk about things, my opinions. I guess I'm scared about what a whole group of kids might think about me."

Angela, 14, talks about the biggest problem she has with going out as a group: "You can't spend too much time with any one person. If it's a girl you're hanging out with, the other girls tend to get jealous or think you're being snotty. If it's a guy, your friends or his might start to tease you. You kind of have to make sure everyone's being included all the time."

Yonhi, 15, also says non-dating can be sort of annoying: "You spend half the night trying to find someone who wandered away. Or you have to wait while John goes to the bathroom or Lisa calls her mom. Sometimes, I feel like there's this big leash holding us all together."

Whether you prefer hanging out with a fleet of friends or one bud, it's good to know your social options. We have nothing against dating. It can be fun and exciting—when you're good and ready. Until then, nothing in the world beats hanging out with a bunch of friends, kickin' back and letting the good times roll.

# Where The Boys Are

## You Don't Have to Go the Extra Mile to Find 'Em

At some point in your life, you probably will go on a date. You know that because you've consulted the psychic hotline, every horoscope you could get your hands on and your friend's Magic 8 Ball. But "someday" and "future" are just not cutting it anymore. Maybe you've been endlessly scribbling someone special's name in your notebooks, he who has yet to acknowledge your presence. Or maybe all you really want is the chance to befriend a cool guy—joke around, hang out, learn a little about how guys think.

The problem is, as you very well know, all the wishing in the world won't get a guy knocking on your door. Even when you actually see the "him" you want to get to know, it's not as if you have any clue how to introduce yourself. Maybe you're not even lucky enough to see a "him" that catches your eye to begin with. It's all so frustrating! Boy-girl relationships must be governed by some secret code you have no means of cracking. Listen up. Getting to meet and know guys isn't a big mystery. All you need is the ability to get out of the house, smile, and say hi with a little enthusiasm. A healthy dose of common sense won't hurt either, and that's something you absolutely have.

While we can't predict the exact day you'll meet your dream guy or best male bud—it may not occur within the next ten days—we can assure you it absolutely will happen. And until it does, taking the steps below will leave you feeling awesome about your new take-charge, adventurous and confident self.

### GO THE EXTRA INCH (NOT THE MILE)

Girls have been wishing to meet guys since the beginning of time. It's only their tactics that have varied. If you were a Victorian, for example, you'd probably swoon (i.e., faint) or daintily drop your handkerchief to get a guy's attention. Today, as you know, some girls go to other extremes: wearing revealing outfits (e.g., sweaters that look as if they were spray-painted on, skirts that barely cover their bikinis); applying layers of make-up; or developing fake mannerisms (high-pitched giggles) that seem to say, "Hey, look at me!" Other girls try to entice guys by doing foolish possibly harmful things such as getting more physical with a guy than they should.

We all know these acts will grab a guy's attention in a flash, but the wrong kind of attention. Instead of enjoying the fact that he has chosen to spend time with you because he genuinely likes and respects you, you will know he picked you because you seemed to offer the path of least resistance.

So without these easy options, what can you do? Are you supposed to just sit there, hoping, wishing or praying that you'll be lucky and meet a great guy? No way! You don't have to sit back and wait for some guy to show up.

If you haven't been like Joey from *Dawson Creek*, growing up best friends with the fabulous guy next door, you may need to give your good fortune a little nudge. What we're saying is: it's okay to be active and resourceful, to go the extra inch to make something happen. This is definitely different than going the extra mile, which interferes and wreaks havoc with your respect and dignity. As you read the suggestions that follow, note the difference between the extra inch and the extra mile.

## BROADEN YOUR SOCIAL CIRCLE

Being creatures of habit, most girls hang out with the same group of kids all the time. You stick together because you like each other, you're used to being with each other and—well, because that's what you do. Samantha, 12, believes her group of four girls is pretty typical, "My friends and I sleep at one of our houses every Friday, if we can. It's fun and stuff, but we hardly ever get together with anyone else." If you're with the same group all the time, how can you possibly meet anyone new?

Expand your social group. You can do this in two ways. First, think of joining non-school buds you've met through friends, Scouts, sports or youth groups, but haven't gotten to know that well. Liz, 12, offers what worked for her: "I made plans with my friend Claudia from gymnastics one weekend, and we ended up going to the coolest party. I met a bunch of Claudia's friends from her school, and we really hit it off."

The second approach is to include "new blood" in your usual group. If you're getting to know someone from class who you think would be a great addition to the next movie or trek to the pizza place, ask your usual pals if they'd mind if he or she came along. Shelly, 14, reports, "I really liked this girl from my Spanish class, but I was afraid of what my friends would say if I asked her to my birthday party. I'm glad I did it, though, because she's invited me back and she has some really cool friends." The idea is, each new friend you make can introduce you to other people, some of whom may turn out to have good guy friend potential.

# supersafe.com
## Tips for On-line Safety

The Internet can be a great place to make new friends, guy friends included. Being anonymous can make it easier to open up and get to know people. But when friendships are anonymous, you need to be even more careful.

A person you never met approaches you and asks you where you live and where you go to school. No chance you'd ever reveal that information, right? Well, millions of girls do it every day. Almost all the people you chat with on-line are just fellow information superhighway travelers like yourself, but there is the possibility of someone pretending to be someone they're not.

Even kids with computer know-how can still be naïve when it comes to safety. As a result, they become targets for criminals. Through computer networking, criminals develop friendships with kids by playing games or having conversations with them. The criminal usually then tries to set up a face-to-face meeting, where he can lure a child into a dangerous place. No matter how safe or friendly the on-line world seems, there is always the potential for danger. Always take these precautions:

• Never give out personal information—your real name, address, phone number, where you go to school. That's why people have code names.

• If anyone leaves obnoxious or menacing messages, do not answer. Instead, report it to the police and notify the system operator for the network you use.

• Do not ever, for any reason whatsoever, agree to meet with someone you have met through the system. If anyone you talk to on-line wants to meet you, tell your mom, dad or another adult—immediately.

Part of expanding new possibilities may also mean rethinking some of your old conclusions. Perhaps you mentally eliminated some potential male friends with verdicts like: "too immature," "makes stupid jokes," "geek," etc. But some of these labels may have worn off. Before you realize it, some guys grow up and lose annoying habits. Going the extra inch means taking a fresh look at the kid who prided himself on belching the alphabet in second grade before you permanently cross him off your list. But it's going the extra mile to ask him over if you're just using him to get closer to his hot best friend.

### EXPLORE DIFFERENT INTERESTS

A good way to get to meet new people (and that includes guys) is through activities. If you and he are both doing something fun, you already know you have that activity in common. An added bonus is that you have an instant topic to talk about, so there's less chance of awkward silence. Don't think you have to take up exotic sports like hang-gliding, skiing or scuba diving, either. Any activity or school club you join will do the trick. Believe it or not, Brie, 11, met David, who is now her close friend, simply by walking her dog in the neighborhood. "My parents made me walk my new Lab puppy to the park and back, and while I was there, David came by with his dog. We started talking, and soon we were meeting there every day."

You have nothing to lose by trying a new hobby, sport, or organization. Even in the worst case scenario, if you don't meet lots of new guys, you're at least having fun. Volunteering your time to an environmental or service project, for example, is not only satisfying, but it exposes you to people who have the same interests and values. These activities are all going the extra inch. But pretending to be interested in something just to get near a certain guy or to impress someone is going the extra mile—and tends to backfire. Geri, 13, can only now laugh at what happened to her. "I joined this science club at school because of a guy I thought was cute. But they were doing an experiment with rats and I almost barfed. I was so embarrassed I never went back."

## TAKE RISKS

Going the extra inch might encourage you to take risks that you would ordinarily shy away from. By this we mean the risk of a guy ignoring you, blowing you off, or giving you a weird look. We don't mean risking life or limb. When it comes to taking a chance on friendship, follow the old saying, "Nothing ventured, nothing gained."

For example, many girls are reluctant to start conversations with guys. "I always wonder what he'll think of me," admits Arielle, 13. "If I say anything, will he think I'm dorky or pushy?" So what does she do? "Nothing, usually. I pretend I don't see him or wait to see what he does." What happens, typically, is nothing, because guys can be just as hesitant to take the first step. They don't want to feel dumb or rejected either. You don't have to wait for a Sadie Hawkins dance to take that first step in making a friend.

If you find yourself, say, on line at the video store with a guy who looks interesting, be brave. Smile and say hi, just as you would if it were a girl in line that you wanted to meet. If he says hi back, you're on your way to a real conversation.

And if he doesn't, so what? Don't assume you did anything wrong. He might've been straining to remember if he'd already seen the movie and didn't hear you. Or, if he did hear you, he might have been too shy to respond. If he truly felt too superior to answer politely, then you wouldn't want him for a friend, anyway. In that case, his loss.

It's going the extra inch when you take risks, such as saving a seat in band for a guy you like, offering to explain a math lesson when he was absent, or loaning him a book for his term paper. *Doing* his term paper for him is going the extra mile. So is doing anything that puts you at risk for getting in trouble or harming yourself in any way.

## USE AVAILABLE INFO

Many girls wonder if it's okay to use info to their advantage. Belinda, 14, knew that a bunch of guys from her school's swim team were working as lifeguards at a county beach. So when her friends invited her to go to the lake, she suggested they go to the county beach instead. Why not? If you're trying to meet more people, it makes sense to put yourself in situations that you know can help you.

This isn't the same, of course, as going places where you're not supposed to be. Erica, 12, recalls getting in trouble when she and friends pushed that limit. "We stayed after school for soccer practice, and afterward our coach told us to wait in the gym for our parents. But my friends and I sneaked over to the football field to watch these really cute guys practicing. Our parents couldn't find us and everybody freaked out."

It's going the extra inch if you happen to walk by a cute guy's locker after lunch, when you know he always gets his coat; that helps a conversation get going. But it's going the whole mile when following him around becomes your only hobby, causes you to drop your friends, or puts you in places that are unwise or off limits.

## SHOW OFF YOUR TALENTS

Unfortunately, many girls take the exact opposite approach: they think they must hide their talents—instead of using them—to impress guys. "I read somewhere that guys don't like girls who show them up," reports Monica, 13. "So I figured I wouldn't dive off the pier this summer when guys were around. I'll just jump in or not go in the water at all."

Whether it's a guy or a girl, however, a true friend helps you to be the best you can be. A truly great guy will be impressed by your brain power when you ace a final, admire your streamlined back dive, and beg you to teach him your method of whistling.

Trish, 12, won the respect of one neighborhood guy the hard way. "They always made fun of me for being a tomboy," she says. "which hurt because I sort of like this kid, Greg. Last week when I was the goalie in a street hockey game, I made a great save and he said 'Good one!' Afterward he came over and asked me where I learned to play."

What better way to catch someone's eye than being the best you can be? Any guy who'd need you to be less so he can feel like more isn't worth the effort. Instead, use your strengths. If you've got a way with words, pass a clever note or send a witty e-mail message. If you're a good artist, draw him a cartoon of your pokey bus driver. It's going the extra inch to belt out a few bars of his favorite song to make a bus ride more pleasant, but going the whole mile if the driver has to tell you to pipe down so he doesn't hit a tree. Similarly, it's going the extra inch to roller blade past the basketball court where he's playing hoops, but you're going the whole mile if you do so while shrieking, giggling, or wearing a bikini top.

## BE YOURSELF

If you have to turn yourself into a pretzel to attract a guy, why bother? Remember, you want him to like *you*. Many girls try to conform to what they think guys want in a girl.

Zena, 14, says, "I overheard some awesome boys talking about one of my friends. When they said Gwen was way too serious, I figured I'd be just the opposite. Whenever I saw them, I tried to act like everything was a big joke. I'd be laughing and stuff. But then I felt so stupid and fake. What was the point?"

Zena's right. The only way you and a boy can be true friends is if you're both honest. This applies not only to how you act, but also to how you look. Copying flashy mannerisms or make-up may attract temporary male attention, but won't help you make a good friendship. Sure, it's always a good idea to try to look and act your best so that you feel confident. That's going the extra inch. But going the entire mile is attempting to act or look like someone else—simply because you're trying to please a guy.

## PRACTICE PATIENCE

Yeah, *right*, you're thinking. We know, it's not easy. If someone whispered to you that in five days or three weeks or four months you would meet a fabulous guy, you might take a deep breath and relax. But when you want something badly enough, the thought that you might NEVER get it, no matter how unrealistic, makes you totally anxious.

In the past, when you really wanted something, like to play a certain song on the guitar, you tried your hardest, perhaps practicing long hours, until you finally got it right. The problem is, when it comes to meeting a great guy, sometimes your cleverest schemes and greatest efforts don't pay off right away. Sometimes it takes time—more time than you'd like.

Realize there's only so much you can do. In fact, unlike mastering fractions or free throws, this might be one area where trying hard (and, especially, trying too hard) may be inadvisable. Girls can do foolish things if they feel frantic or desperate to get a guy.

But there's never any reason to feel pressured. Contrary to what many girls think, there's no race to see who can have the first boyfriend, no prizes awarded for the most male friends. There is surely no definitive timeline for any of these milestones. The most important thing you can do is be true to yourself, be the best friend you can be, and have faith that you'll meet a special guy when it's meant to happen.

In the meantime, you can apply these skills to situations other than guy-searching. Meeting different people, taking healthy risks, being informed and, using your assets are always awesome ideas. You may find yourself having new experiences, taking an active role in making opportunities happen, and developing your talents in ways you hadn't imagined. You will surely become a more well-rounded and interesting person, someone a guy would be lucky to befriend.

# Boy Friend or Boyfriend?

At the end of school last year, Jamie, 13, found herself in a situation that seemed straight out of a TV season finale. All of her friends had sworn they were blowing off freshman prom to go to the beach—that is, until one of them got asked to go. Before long, everyone was grabbing dates and shopping for dresses. Boyfriendless, Jamie was bummed that she was being left behind.

Also bumming was Jamie's best bud Sam. Now all his friends were going but, as Jamie reports, Sam didn't really have anybody he liked. The solution for both of them? Do what they had done a thousand times before when there was a party or concert—go together as friends.

"I heard that a lot of the couples were really friends going together," says Jamie, "so I thought it was a great idea." So did all of Jamie's friends. Soon she was joining them in dress shopping marathons and master planning sessions.

On the big day, Jamie went to her friend Colleen's house for a pre-prom party: "Collen's mom hired a stylist to do everyone's hair and makeup. It was really fun. Everybody wanted to look awesome for their crushes but they were a little freaked out, since none of us had ever been to anything like a prom. Everybody kept saying how lucky I was to be going with Sam—someone I know so well and have a lot of fun with. I thought it was cool, too."

Jamie got home just in time to slip into her new dress and greet Sam at the door. "My mom made Sam and me have our pictures taken. I was totally embarrassed, but Sam put his arm around me and joked around. We finally got out of my house and walked a couple blocks to where the limo was waiting in front of my friend's house. I'm not used to heels, and Sam kind of held me up for the first block. He's always been thoughtful, but he was being really sweet. I figured maybe he was just trying to play the part of a date."

"Dinner was a blast. When we finally got to prom, we just hung out and talked and danced to a couple fast songs. Then everyone decided to go look for their 'hearts.' This girl on the decorations committee had made hearts with each couple's name in glitter and made a rule that when you find your heart, you kiss your date. Everybody knew it was her desperate ploy to get her crush to kiss her, but all my friends went along with it."

"Sam and I were the last to find ours, and I grabbed it off the wall and threw it in my bag, hoping Sam hadn't seen. Then my best friend told Sam he had to kiss me! Although I wanted to kill her, I laughed and dragged Sam to the dance floor."

"At the end of the night, I was really tired and my feet were killing me after spending hours in heels. Sam asked the limo driver if he'd drop us off early and go back to the dance to get everyone else. I was so exhausted, I fell asleep during the ride. When we got to my house, Sam woke me up and I kind of was stumbling and half asleep. Sam laughed and threw his arm around my shoulder.

I know this sounds ridiculous but there I was, lolling along with him supporting me, my head against his shoulder. And something clicked. Right then, we got to the door and he started to say what a great time he had. What did I do? I started babbling. It was something along the lines of, "Me, too, yeah, it was fun, okay, bye!" And I slammed the door. What I felt like saying was, "This has been the best night of my life, I never realized how completely great you are. You're the nicest person I know, and I am totally falling for you."

Not too long after that, Sam went away to camp, leaving Jamie to spend her summer, well... confused. How could it be, she wondered, that with one simple arm-around-the-shoulder, her feelings for Sam could change so suddenly? Did she really like him, or was her imagination running wild? Could it be that he liked her? Did she dare tell her friends her childhood buddy Sam was now her crush?

Telling Sam seemed out of the question, but if she didn't say something how would she ever really know if he liked her? What would happen if they did go out? Would it be like friends, only better? Would they still be able to talk on the phone, complain about teachers, work on the school paper, shoot hoops, and catch movies as always? Jamie didn't even want to think about what would happen if they tried dating and it didn't work. Losing Sam as a friend seemed worse than never finding out if Sam liked her back. With only a few weeks left until Sam's return, Jamie was still sorting it out: "Two months and you'd think I'd have reached some conclusion. But I'm still just as confused about Sam as I was standing at my door after prom that night."

Jamie isn't alone. While many girls say the idea of dating their best guy bud is just too gross to contemplate, just as many are surprised at how their feelings can change. Friendships between guys and girls are hardly uncommon, but what might be new to you is the possibility that the two of you could be more than friends.

## ARE THE TWO OF YOU REALLY "JUST FRIENDS"?

Ben, 14, is sure his girlfriend Gabby, also 14, believes they are two friends who decided to date. But if you got Ben alone, he'd admit to a slightly different version of their story: "When we got to high school last year, I noticed Gabby right away. She's into theater like I am, loves cool music, and has a great group of friends. I wanted to get to know her, but I liked her a little, too. I had never had a girlfriend before, so I basically decided to just hang out with her and maybe something would happen someday. I'm not exactly someone who would just walk up to a girl and expect her to fall head over heels—that's not me."

It took a year and half, but one day Gabby found herself thinking how much she liked Ben. She asked him to practice a scene for an audition. Not one to shy away from making the first move, Gabby picked a scene between two characters in love, then, "I just kind of improvised my own scene. In the play, the characters decide they are better off being apart. But I started saying how I could never be without him, and how much I like him. Ben got the hint!"

We certainly don't want to make it seem like guys only become friends with you as a stealth dating technique. But, in some cases, you may be the only person who thinks you were just pals to begin with.

Says Gabby's friend Rachel, "All of us teased Gabby about how much Ben liked her. She always denied it. But, c'mon, the guy spent hours with her learning lines, calling her house, and watching *Buffy* on the phone with her. He thought nothing of getting up at dawn to wait in line for Lilith Fair tickets. You just don't really expect all that from a guy you're just friends with."

What are some clues that indicate things are more than they seem? For one, if everyone but you thinks that your guy friend has other thoughts, don't be so quick to dismiss. They are on the outside of your friendship looking in and may able to see thing more clearly.

Second, think about your guy bud's actions. If he skips baseball with the guys so he can tutor you for a math quiz, always tapes *The Simpsons* when you're at soccer games, and buys you your favorite cookies at lunch, this is someone who is trying to make himself indispensable. Still, it could all be for the sake of friendship. You have to evaluate the relationship and decide if he is just being his same great self—or if he is trying to hint at how great life could be if you'd only wake up and give him a chance.

## TAKING THE RISK

Are you willing to give up your friendship to have a boyfriend? Say you're not the clueless one here. Sure, any relationship needs to be based on the same qualities that make people great friends: common interests, mutual caring, fun times. But do you really need to complicate it with a crush? Have you thought through all the possible outcomes?

Carrie, 15, and Steve, 16, were friends for a year when she decided to push the issue of turning their friendship into romance. At first, Steve went along with it. Then, he decided he wanted to be just friends again. It took a lot of work on both their parts to repair the friendship and get things back to normal. Says Carrie, "I had this whole romantic vision of me and Steve, how we would be the perfect couple. But the second we started going out, I saw less of him than when we were friends! I called him like always, but the guy who before would always suggest fun post-study plans suddenly didn't know what he wanted to do or how to dial a phone. I was completely crushed and felt like everything had gotten screwed up."

Carrie's advice? "If you're thinking about dating your friend, think twice," she warns. "I wish I had. If you want to go for it, pay attention to how he treats his girlfriend now. The one time Steve had a girlfriend before, he never saw her or called her. They broke up after just a few weeks. Once I thought about it, I realized Steve had never really been comfortable with the girlfriend concept. I guess I thought that would magically change with me. It didn't."

Even worse is what happened to Lisa, 15: "When we hung out together with a group, Jack was Mr. Easy-going. Then, we started dating. Suddenly, every time I talked to another guy, I was 'flirting.' Jack suddenly became Mr. Possessive. I had to break up with him, and I felt awful because he was a great friend before he became a lousy boyfriend." The bottom line is: He may be comfortable with you as a friend, but having a girlfriend could turn him into a nervous wreck or worse.

It would be awesome if your guy suddenly realized the girl of his dreams is right in front of him, but you are taking a chance when you put your feelings out there. We all know the worst case scenario: You pour your heart out, and he bursts into laughter. Friend or not, only the biggest creep on the planet would do that. Still, the unfortunate reality is that not every guy you ever like will like you back. Not because you aren't cool enough, pretty enough or witty enough—just because, well, it could be one of a million reasons, most of which have zilch to do with you. And once the cat is out of the bag, it's awfully hard to put it back. (We've tried; cats don't like bags.)

## MAKING THE SHIFT

So how do you go out on a limb without sawing it off? Slowly. Very slowly. While it may be tempting to confess all to your friends, be careful who you tell. For some reason, this kind of news seems to bring out the matchmaker in everyone—getting two friends together seems romantic. So even if you make someone double-swear not to tell, word will almost certainly get back. This might not be the worst thing. If word gets back that he likes you, too, then yippee, mission accomplished. If not, you can laugh the whole thing off as dumb chatter and die a small death.

Stakes too high? Then your only choice is to keep being the friend he already loves to hang with. Try doing what Ben did with Gabrielle. Make yourself just a little more indispensable, a little more his biggest fan. Leave enough space for him to breathe, and just wonder a little. Sooner or later, not knowing whether you like him just might bug him enough to make the move. If it doesn't, if he continues to end every marathon viewing of cheesy monster movies with a "see ya!" then you have your fairly painful answer. The good news is that either way, you still have the best part of him—the part that thinks you're a really awesome friend.

# WHEN *NOT* TO THINK ABOUT DATING A FRIEND

**One of you has just broken up with someone.** Everyone needs a shoulder to cry on when things don't work out. But nothing is worse than leaping from one boyfriend to another before you have a chance to get over the break-up and sort out your true feelings. Dating a friend is not something you want to rush into.

**He just got a girlfriend.** You never liked him—until he liked her. Uh-oh. It absolutely stinks when your best guy friend suddenly forgets you exist the second Miss Thing comes into his life. Don't mistake feeling jealous for other feelings. And take heart—when she's yesterday's news, you'll still be the one he loves to hang with. If his dating her is an honest wake-up call, wait until they are way, way over before you even consider the two of you getting together.

**You want a boyfriend—any boyfriend.** It stinks to be the only person without someone. But dating someone you don't have real feelings for is being dishonest to them—and to you.

**He's dating your friend.** We'll spare you the lecture about loyalty and valuing a long friendship over a very temporary crush. Again, the reason you two got to know each other so well is what you two have in common—your friend. Even if they break up, we say pass. There are many fish in the pond. Time to throw in your own line.

**He's the class Casanova.** He's dated every girl in your grade whose name starts with the letters A through U. And your name is Vicki.

# Cracking the Crush Code

What the heck is he thinking? Does he like me or are we just friends? Here are some questions to ask yourself to decode the mystery.

1. He waits for you after school so you can walk home together.
   a) That half mile walk gives him fifteen full minutes every day to get to know you better.
   b) He has no sense of direction and is still trying to learn the way home.
   c) He's mighty fearful of stray dogs and wants your protection.

2. He always tries to be your partner in science lab.
   a) He wants other kids to know there's a bit of chemistry between you.
   b) He just happens to like that section of the room.
   c) He wants to steal your hypothesis on algae growth.

3. He asks one of your friends what you're like—or who you like.
   a) He's really interested and is trying to send you a roundabout message.
   b) He really likes your friend and just needs an excuse to talk to her.
   c) He's planning to blackmail you.

4. He's nice to you when you're alone, but distant and cold when he's with friends.
   a) He really likes you, but his friends tease him mercilessly about the crush.
   b) He has multiple personality disorder.
   c) He's two-faced and can't be trusted.

5. He calls you up for no particular reason.
   a) He's been thinking about you and wants to chat.
   b) He's just bored.
   c) Wrong number.

6. He tells you about his passion for bug-collecting.
   a) He's trying to open up to you.
   b) He thinks your backyard harbors a rare cicada species.
   c) He loves the sound of his own voice.

7. He tells you he's having trouble with the math teacher and asks for your advice.
   a) He respects your opinion.
   b) He's been asking everybody for advice, including the mailman.
   c) He thinks you're the teacher's pet and can get him on her good side.

8. He tells your friends something you told him in confidence.
   a) He's testing the limits of your interest in him.
   b) He's showing off to your friends that he's close enough to you to know your secrets.
   c) Secrets burn a hole in his pocket.

9. He promises to call you at 9 P.M.—but he never does.
   a) He cut his hand and had to go to the emergency room. Bummer.
   b) He forgot.
   c) It's his bedtime.

10. You write him a great letter from camp, baring your soul—and he doesn't write back.
    a) He's been spending time at his grandmom's and hasn't gotten your letter.
    b) Your letter was a little overwhelming, and he needs some time to think about it.
    c) He gave you a fake address.

11. He teases you in front of your friends about your freckles.
    a) He thinks your freckles are adorable.
    b) He'll probably want to tickle you when you least expect it, too.
    c) He's an insensitive creep.

12. You leave your coat in the schoolyard and he shows up at your house to give it back.
    a) He is the kind of friend who will look out for you.
    b) He's hoping you'll invite him in for a snack.
    c) His mother made him do it.

13. He bought you a big, expensive present that you feel uncomfortable accepting.
    a) He's sincere.
    b) He's confused about how much you really like him.
    c) His birthday is next week and he wants you to buy him the skateboard he has been eyeing.

14. He tells his friends you kissed him last week after the lacrosse game. But you didn't!
    a) Wishful thinking.
    b) He's offering you a chance to test your powers of spin control.
    c) He's trying to ruin your reputation.

15. You have one little spat and he refuses to speak to you for days.
    a) You've been underestimating how much he really likes you.
    b) He can't stand to lose an argument to a superior being.
    c) He actually thinks he won the argument.

16. You met at summer camp. He swore he'd never forget you. Now he's forgotten to respond to your phone message.
    a) He was so amazed you called that he's trying to figure out how to respond.
    b) He has decided he's not big on long-distance relationships.
    c) He has amnesia.

17. He splashes you while he's in the swimming pool. You're wearing your killer new outfit.
    a) He'll do anything to get your attention.
    b) He'll do anything to get everybody else's attention.
    c) He'll do anything, period.

18. He kindly offers to break the nose of the guy you're talking to at lunch.
    a) He wants to be the guy you're talking to at lunch.
    b) He thinks the guy could benefit from a little rhinoplasty.
    c) He forgot his lunch and wants to steal the guy's sandwich.

19. He wants to make plans with you that extend far into the future—like after eighth grade.
    a) He thinks he's going to like you for a long, long time.
    b) He knows you're smart and hopes to keep you around so you can tutor him for the SAT.
    c) He knows his family's moving next year.

20. He tells you he really likes you.
    a. He really means it!
    b. He's been reading the book *How to Win Friends and Influence People*.
    c. He told your best friend the same thing yesterday.

## SCORING
*Give yourself 3 points for each "a," 2 points for each "b" and 1 point for each "c". Add it up.*

**45 - 60 points:** You're reading this guy like a book. You can probably get a part-time job as an emotional interpreter. You have a gift for getting to the real truth about what people are trying to express to you, no matter how clumsy or awkward they do it. This gift will serve you well throughout life. Learn to trust it, and keep developing it!

**30 - 44 points:** You're on the right track to getting at the real meaning of what he's saying and doing, but sometimes you get sidelined by the sheer idiocy of his actions. Try to ignore the methods he uses to get across what he wants to tell you, and remember the hidden message behind it all.

**20 - 29 points:** Girlfriend, he may as well be talking to his fishbowl for all the understanding he's getting from you right now. But, don't worry—you can still learn how to interpret his strange signs. For those braver girls, simply find a quiet time to talk to him, and ask him straight out why he's done the thing that puzzles you. You'll have better luck if you're both alone, so no one can overhear and make him feel embarrassed. If confronting him isn't your style, reading novels about relationships is also a great way to figure out what's going on inside his head. Also, talk to your friends, and compare notes.

# Dance Fever

## Problems & Solutions for Your Next Dance

Knocking knees, sweaty palms, butterflies bumping around your stomach... final exams? Nope. First airplane ride? Worse. It's your first school dance. Fear not. It's not as nerve-wracking as you think. Here are some of girls' most common problems for first-dance jitters and some smoothly choreographed solutions.

**The problem:** You arrive early, and there's hardly anyone there yet. You and your friends are feeling stupid and bored.

**The solution:** Remind each other that you have fun together whenever you hang out at other times. You never needed crowds before when it was just your group, and you've all danced together around your room a thousand times. Stop waiting for others to make the fun—get out there on the dance floor and make your own.

**The problem:** A slow song comes on, and everyone in your group has been asked to dance—everyone, that is, except for you. You are standing there, by yourself, feeling like an utter loser.

**The solution:** There's no reason to stand and watch the couples until the song is over. Go to the bathroom. Get some punch. Talk to someone else who's not dancing. Go outside for some air.

Make a phone call. The song won't last an eternity—two minutes maybe—and you'll have plenty of slow dances in your future. Hey, here's a thought: Why not scope out a guy who isn't dancing, and ask him to dance the next slow song. He may be eternally grateful!

**The problem:** You ask your crush to dance, and he says "No way." He walks away, leaving you utterly humiliated. All you want to do is crawl into a bathroom stall and never come out.

**The solution:** The guy's a jerk! Anyone who is so insensitive and rude doesn't deserve to dance with you. Feel good about yourself for having the guts to ask him. The humiliation you are suffering is entirely temporary. He, on the other hand, has to live with his obnoxious personality for the rest of his life.

**The problem:** A geeky guy asks you to dance. He's the last person on Earth you want to dance with, but you don't know how to get out of it.

**The solution:** You can always say, "I'm sitting this one out, but thank you." But we'd suggest bringing him into your group to dance for a song or two. It took a lot of guts for him to ask you to dance, and it's not going to kill you to accept. If after a song or two, he's sticking to you like flypaper, tell him, "That was fun. I'm going to go the restroom." Chances are your Trekkie isn't going to beam himself into the bathroom after you.

**The problem:** You're having a blast, but your BFF tells you she's ready to go home now. But the night is still young, and you want to stay.

Fix It

**The solution:** This is a tricky one and definitely depends on the circumstances. Did something bad happen to her, like she just got dumped or tore her skirt? If so, pull her aside and talk to her. The friendship comes first, and she needs you. If she's just bored or cranky, that's another story. You can tell her you understand she needs to bolt, but you'd like to stay and catch a ride home with someone else. If that's not possible, try to compromise on a fair time she would be willing to stick it out, like a half-hour or so.

# BILL & DAVE CLUE YOU IN ON:

## *What the Guys Are Really Thinking*

**Why do guys hate to talk on the phone?**

*Dave:* Because we have e-mail to answer, silly. Actually, it is not the phone that scares us, it's this whole crazy system that you females have somehow finagled. We have to call you, we have to ask you out, we have to plan... and then we have to pay! How did this come about? Did I miss a vote? Regardless of our cool act, most of us guys are shy and shaking in our Skechers around girls. Think about it—we sit there with the cordless in one hand and our scribbled crib notes in the other. After dialing all but the last digit of a girl's phone number exactly twenty-two times, the phone rings. The girl can take the call or not. She knows she's in control because, well, we did call her. And therefore, she can shoot down every one of our well-thought-out topics like an Imperial Navy TIE fighter. The only thing with greater pressure involves a No. 2 pencil.

*Bill:* As usual, Dave speaks for all men. I would like to add, though, the dreaded end-of-phone-call-sign-of-affection problem (i.e., "I like/love you, too") which is fully expected by the girl at the other end of the line but results in intense social pressure, scowls and various sound effects if a fellow guy hears it. The typical guy just says, "Me, too," and turns red.

**Why do guys dump nice girls?**

*Dave:* To go out with cheerleaders. Just kidding.

*Bill:* Sheesh, Dave, no way. I only dump nice girls to go out with supermodels. (Kidding, too.) Guys date girls for a million reasons, not all of them, um, nice. The guys who only go out with the "hot" girls (I call those guys losers, Dave prefers "lucky") are most likely insecure and not cool enough to look beyond the superficial stuff. Instead of dating girls who are kind, have made a lot of achievements and are fun to be with, many guys look for the flashiest girl, even if the odds of a successful relationship are pretty slim. But not all guys. There are definitely plenty of nice guys who would love to spend time with a great girl. Unfortunately, you'd probably dump them.

**My boyfriend and I go out for a couple weeks, and then he breaks up. Two weeks later, I'm almost over him when he calls, says he misses me, and we get back together for another couple weeks. Then it starts all over again. How can I get him to make up his mind?**

*Bill:* Actually, it sounds like maybe he *has* made up his mind. He wants to date you for two-week stretches and test the waters with someone else, then go back to you. Good deal for him, not so great for you. You have choices: Play the long-suffering woman standing by her man; test the waters with someone new while he's doing the same thing, and then get back together when you're both ready; or dump him and move on with your life. The last option may seem the obvious way to go, but it's not always easy to do. Just ask Hilary Clinton.

*Dave:* I'd never argue that men are not pigs. What I would argue is that we only take our swine-like behavior as far as women let us. As soon as someone who matters gets mad, we stop acting like the low-life species we are. If not, then perhaps we don't care as much about our mate as she'd like to think, and the superior sex should figure it out. Pronto.

**Is Valentine's Day a good time to let your crush know you like him?**

*Dave:* Two schools of thought here. If you're a girl who needs an excuse to ask a guy out, then trumped-up occasions like Valentine's and Sadie Hawkins dances serve a wonderfully convenient purpose. On the other hand, I'd rather have a girl confess her undying devotion to me on some random Thursday in March than on Valentine's Day. Just write me a mash note in the colors of my favorite NFL team, and I'm all yours.

*Bill:* Valentine's Day is a hugely high-pressure day for guys in relationships, but it's a total freebie when a guy's unattached. What girls don't realize is that Valentine's Day for a guy is like Christmas for a Jewish person. You know it exists, and you see a lot of hoopla going on, but it's not your holiday. Expectations for Valentine's Day come from girls, not guys.

**This guy always majorly flirted with me. Then when I asked him out, he said no. What's up with that?**

*Bill:* Maybe he had temporary hearing loss. Or he's an identical twin, and you asked out the wrong one. But more likely, he has a touch of fear of success. After all, it's one thing to fantasize about having a romantic dinner with someone. It's another to see that big green splotch of pizza oregano on his teeth. You can ease his fear by creating a low-pressure event (like going to a school basketball game with a bunch of other friends) so he can see that the reality is even more fun than the fantasy.

*Dave:* I agree. It is a breeze to be the guy a girl wants to go out with in theory. It can be downright flattering. However, it is a much more difficult task to actually be a guy a girl wants to go out with in practice. That's partly the reason a smart guy always seeks to be in the company of girls, even if they are not dating. It makes him all the more attractive if it appears he's a person girls like to spend time with on a regular basis. Beware the dude sans friends who are girls.

**Do guys like girls who will kiss them right away?**

*Bill:* If you listen to guys talk to each other, you'd think they really, really like "fast" girls. But guys are like boxing promoters—they tend to inflate everything by a factor of ten. So they'll say they're looking for some quick physical affection, but most guys really want what everyone wants—to be cared for.

*Dave:* There's a lot to be said for spontaneity, rather than plotting out a grand smooching scheme. If you really like a guy and want to kiss him (and you think the feeling is mutual), there's nothing wrong with letting him know. Don't make the guy play a torturous game of "Should I or Shouldn't I?" If you've decided you want to kiss him, go ahead and do it. I've never heard any post-practice locker room conversations along the lines of, "I had to dump her. She kissed me."

**How can I tell if he likes me or LIKES me?**

*Dave:* Ask him. Try to be funny: "Do you have a girlfriend who could beat me up in a fair fight?" The bottom line is that it is best to find out. There's nothing worse than not knowing whether or not someone you like likes you.

*Bill:* Eventually, you'll probably learn to pick up the signs when a guy likes you. For example, if he shows up for a date with his little brother ("Do you mind if we go to his Scout meeting?"), he may not like you as much as you'd hoped. Brings flowers? He likes you. Brings a book to read? Likes you less. Gives you gifts? He likes you. Gives you his cell phone bill? He likes you less. You'll pick up on these things after a while.

# Are You Star Struck?

Have you ever been star struck? I mean, have you ever had a crush on a movie star or famous celebrity? Do you go absolutely ga-ga over 'N SYNC, or drool over pictures of Nick Carter? There are different types of celebrity crushes, ranging from the "almost nonexistent" type, all the way to the "almost over the edge" type. To find out just how major or minor your crush is, clear your starry eyes long enough to take this quiz!

1. You're talking to your best friend on the telephone when you see your famous guy on a talk show. What do you do?
   a) Politely wrap up your conversation so that you can go to the tube and hear what words of wisdom your crush has to say.
   b) Continue your conversation, sneaking a peek at the screen every now and then.
   c) Hang up on your best friend, sprint to the TV and plant your lips to the screen.

2. When you daydream about your crush, what type of dream is it?
   a) That you actually get the chance to meet him in person and get his autograph.
   b) You dream about how cute he is, but that thought leads you to that gorgeous guy in your algebra class.
   c) You fantasize about the day he'll propose to you. You'll be married right away, live in his two million dollar mansion, and live happily ever after.

3. While reading the *TV Guide* you come across an address where you can write to your star crush. How do you use that information?
   a) Write a letter to him, stating that you are a fan and would like to request an autographed photo.
   b) You're too busy to sit down and write fan mail to someone you'll probably never get an answer from anyway.
   c) You write to your crush every week, pledging your undying love and you make sure to include your phone number, asking him to call on a weekday, after ten, so you'll be home to answer the phone.

4. Your celebrity crush will be attending a Planet Hollywood grand opening two hours from where you live. What do you do?
   a) You get there an hour early, hoping to snap a photo of him and maybe get an autograph. You're there to have fun!

b) Get real! Standing in a crowd of 10,000 screaming fans, just to catch a glimpse of someone isn't your idea of a good time.

c) You arrive five hours early, wearing your best outfit, and wait for your true love to pick you out of the crowd as his escort.

5. You get the news that your star crush is dating a famous model, Zoe. How do you feel?
   a) You're a little disappointed, but you want your celebrity hunk to be a happy hunk, so you wish him the best.
   b) You've seen Zoe in the magazines. She's really beautiful and they look like a great couple.
   c) You are devastated! How could he do this to you? You find a picture of the famous model so that you can draw a mustache on her face. Then you go to the salon and get your hair done exactly like hers and ask your friends to call you Zoe.

## SCORING

### MOSTLY As: MODERATELY STAR STRUCK
You sometimes have your famous guy on your mind a bit too often, but you keep the reality of the situation in check. Occasional daydreaming about your crush is harmless, as long as it doesn't interfere with your other important activities. You see the big picture and seem to realize that there are thousands of fans out there, just like you. You don't let your crush come between you and your everyday life, so it seems as though you can have your cake and eat it, too. You can keep your crush, but don't get too starry-eyed!

### MOSTLY Bs: YOUR STAR HASN'T STRUCK
You don't spend much time daydreaming about celebrities and fame. You're more into what's happening around you and have many outside interests. Sure you can't help but admire some of those Hollywood hunks, but you'd rather focus your energy on getting that cute guy in your class. Once in a while, writing a fan letter can be fun. You might try writing to your favorite actor sometime, just for the fun of it! You never know, you might get a reply!

### MOSTLY Cs: STAR STRUCK TO INFINITY AND BEYOND
You've got it bad for your Hollywood Heartthrob. You know almost every detail about him. He's on your mind much of the time and you'd rather stay home and watch him on TV than go out with your friends. You must realize how many thousands of fans adore your crush, too. While you're waiting for the slim chance that you two might someday get together, you're letting your life pass you by. Your family, friends, and schoolwork must take precedence over him. Next time you have to choose between going out with friends or watching your crush on TV, try to compromise. Set your VCR to tape the program, go out with your friends, and save the videotape to watch on a rainy day. Why concentrate solely on a celebrity when that cute guy just winked at you from across the room?

# He Likes You! He Likes You!

## Now What?

### HELP! THIS GUYS LIKES ME BUT I DON'T LIKE HIM!

So you just found out this guy you know likes you, and you don't share those feelings for him. Maybe you think he's a cool guy, but you'd just rather stay friends and keep things simple. Or, maybe the very idea of him makes you want to head for the hills…screaming.

It doesn't make that huge of a difference. Either way, you need to acknowledge that it took guts for this guy to put his feelings out there. The last thing you should do is make him feel ashamed about telling you. How can you admit you don't like him without making him feel like a reject? You can't. He is going to feel disappointed and rejected no matter how you say it. But there are certainly softer ways than others to deliver the news. Your best bet is to put yourself in his shoes. What would you need to hear to cushion the blow?

Ted, 14, had this to say: "If you don't like a guy, you should tell him you'd rather be friends. We all know that it's code for 'I don't like you in *that way*,' but it's a lot nicer than telling a guy you don't care about him or you think he's a geek."

James, 14, adds, "Be honest. It stinks to hear that she's not interested, but it's much better than having her play mind games with you. Once a girl told me, 'I don't really want to go out now, but maybe next month.' So I waited and waited and asked her out the next month and she said no again. I wished she'd just said she wasn't into it the first time. You've got to be real with a guy."

Mickey, 15, confirms this. "Don't go on and on about it. He's going to feel like enough of a jerk without you going into detail about why he's not cool enough for you. If he wants to know why you're not interested, he'll ask. And don't try to force him to be friends with you after, either. He might feel too embarrassed."

We agree with these guys and suggest saying something like, "I'm flattered and I think you're a great person, but I'd be more comfortable being friends with you" or "I think you're a great guy, but I don't really have romantic feelings for you. I hope we can be friends."

If you have no interest in even being friends with this guy (as in, you've always thought he was a complete jerk), try "I know how hard it is to tell someone your feelings, but I'm just not interested in you that way." That's all you have to say. If he asks you why or badgers you or makes you feel bad, just say, "That's the way I feel." End of story. You don't have to apologize.

A note to all those who think it's kinder to lie than admit you're not interested. It's really not kinder—and it can backfire on you. For instance, if you tell him you're not allowed to go to the movies with guys, and then he sees you with some guy at the theater two weeks later, you're going to look—and feel—like a moron. Same deal if you tell him you'd rather go to the mall with your friends, and then he sees you with another guy. Better to follow the advice from the guys above and stick to the truth. You and he will both respect you a lot more.

## IF YOU DO LIKE HIM BACK

So you have a huge crush on a certain someone and find your thoughts drifting back to him all the time. Now, overnight, you find out that he has romantic feelings of his own reserved for you. While the news is awesome (more than you dared hope for), you're wondering about all the expectations—yours, his, and all your friends. How are you supposed to start a normal chat or goof around with him when you both know that the other is thinking, "I know that you like me. Why don't you just say so?"

"It's not natural," Jessie, 14, says. "Like with Kevin and me, I knew he liked me, and I wanted him to know that I liked him too. But once I told him, I couldn't even look at him. It was like I didn't want him to have this power over me—knowing how I felt. I knew it would change everything, and it was so much easier when we were friends and I could just go up to him and joke around."

For the record, don't think guys get off scot-free, either. Most guys are just as embarrassed, if not more so, when they find out how you feel. As ultra cool as they try to seem, you can bet they are just as nervous once the beans are spilled.

Alan, 14, had this to say: "Last year, this girl from class told me she liked me, and it was cool and all. I mean, she was cute. But once I let it be known that I liked her too, neither one of us knew what to say. We both just sat there blushing. I felt like an idiot."

This isn't to say that you shouldn't admit your feelings or respond to his because you don't want to face potential embarrassment. That awkwardness is sometimes a necessary bummer many

**Dear Carol:** I like this boy and he likes me so we are about to start going out. The problem is that a lot of my friends like him and they might be mad if I go out with him. Should I go out with the boy I love or should I keep my friends?
—LOVE OR FRIENDSHIP

**Dear L. or F.:** It's not an either/or. You can have a boyfriend and keep your friends—you just have to be sensitive about it. Here's what *not* to do: 1. Act stuck-up and make everyone else jealous by boasting about him and "rubbing it in." 2. Dump your buds in order to spend all your hours with him. Here's what you should do: 1. Act the way you always do. 2. Continue making time for your friends and talking with them about what's on their minds. They may occasionally envy you (they're human), but they won't hate you.

of us face initially, and it can even add to the excitement. If you guys have stuff in common and enjoyed hanging out before, the embarrassment part will probably fade.

But if we're talking about one or both of you being downright humiliated and afraid to speak to each other, you may have to rethink whether you're really ready to put your feelings out there.

Sometimes girls feel more than shy or awkward when they hear a guy likes him. They feel downright scared about what's to come. This usually happens when girls feel the feelings, but aren't ready to act upon them. They worry they will be expected to go on a date as soon as the guy knows they're interested, or kiss him at a party, or start talking on the phone every night of the week. It's enough to make a girl keep her lips sealed.

Says Sandra, 13, "When I found out Billy liked me, I was so psyched. I'd liked him all year, and I couldn't believe he felt the same way. But when Billy wanted to know if he could call me at home, I suddenly freaked out. I mean, what would we talk about? Was he going to expect me to be all gushy on the phone? That's just not me."

Jada, 14, says that after finding out a boy from class liked her, she felt terrified. "It's not that I didn't like him too, it's just that I'm not ready to deal with all that stuff yet. My friends want me to go on a date with him so they can hear all the gory details, but I don't even know if I really like him. I think my friends like him more than I do."

The most important thing to remember is that you don't have to do anything upon hearing the news he likes you. You don't have to talk on the phone, date him, or do anything else considered couple-like. You don't have to do a darn thing—and that's true even if you like him. It's not about trying to impress your friends or prove you can have a boyfriend. It's about figuring out what you're ready for, and then staying true to that.

Alyssa, 13, knows how easy it is to forget this. "I went out with this guy Brad because he was the cool guy in school and all my friends pushed me to do it. I should have just told him that I liked him but that I wasn't ready to date."

If this is the case, the best way to tell him is to be straightforward. One suggestion: "I really like you, but I'd rather just be good friends with you until I feel ready to date." You don't have to explain or clarify why you aren't ready, nor do you have to give him a time when you'll feel differently. (How are you supposed to know?) Granted, he may be a little hurt or disappointed, but that's his right. And understand that it's temporary.

As for what he'll do next, he will either wait for you until you are ready, or he won't. You can't control how he feels or acts, so why waste your time trying? Instead, concentrate on just being you and staying true to your self and your needs. You've got good instincts, and when you're ready to move from admitting your feelings to actual dating, you'll be the first person to know. If he is no longer available or interested when you are finally ready, then he's not the guy for you. Someone else will come along.

What if you find out that he likes you, and you decide that you are ready to spend time hanging out and getting to know him better? Then you must feel wonderful! You know to take things slow and go at your own pace. You know to keep checking in with yourself to make sure things still feel cool and right. And when other girls go to you for support and advice, you'll be able to share your experiences, both good and bad, with them.

# 39 WAYS TO GROSS OUT YOUR DATE

We feel it is our duty to come up with new and imaginative things to do on a date. As long as you never want to see him again, that is.

1. Guard your plate with fork and knife and act like you'll stab anyone who reaches for it, including the waiter. 2. Collect salt shakers from all the tables in the restaurant, and balance them in a tower formation on your table. 3. Wipe your nose on your date's sleeve. Twice. 4. Make faces at other patrons, and then sneer at their reactions. 5. Repeat every third word you say. 6. Read a newspaper during the meal, ignoring your date. 7. Stare at your date's neck, and grind your teeth. Ask if he's a slayer. 8. Twitch spastically. If asked about it, pretend you don't know what he's talking about. 9. Every five minutes, circle your table with your arms outstretched while making airplane sounds. 10. Order a bucket of lard. 11. Ask for crayons to color the placemat. This is especially fun in fancy places with linen tablecloths. 12. When ordering, inquire if the restaurant has any live food. 13. Without asking, eat off your date's plate. Eat more of his food than he does. 14. Drool. 15. Talk with your mouth full and spray crumbs. 16. Scarf down everything on your plate in thirty seconds. 17. Excuse yourself to use the restroom. Go to the hostess and ask for another table. Order another meal. When your date finally finds you, ask him, "What took you so long in the restroom?!" 18. Ask the people at the next table if you can taste their food. 19. Beg your date to tattoo your name on his bicep. 20. Order something nasty for your date. Act offended if he refuses to eat it. 21. Ask for a seat away from the windows where you have a good view of all exits and can keep your back to the wall. Act nervous. 22. Lick your plate. Offer to lick your date's. 23. Hum. Loudly. In monotone. 24. Fill your pockets with sugar packets, salt and pepper shakers, silverware, floral arrangements—anything that isn't bolted down. 25. Slide under the table. Take your plate with you. 26. Order a baked potato as a side dish. When the waiter brings your food, hide the potato, wait a few minutes and ask the waiter for the potato you never got. When the waiter returns, have the first one back up on the plate. Repeat later in the meal. 27. Throughout the meal, speak in pig Latin. 28. Take a bathroom break. When you return to the table, throw a spare pair of underwear on one of the chairs. Say they need airing out. 29. Bring 20 or so candles with you. During the meal, arrange them in a circle around the table. Chant. 30. Order your food by colors and textures. Sculpt. 31. Insist the waiter cut your food into tiny pieces. 32. Accuse your date of espionage. 33. Don't use any verbs during the entire meal. 34. Break wind loudly. Add commentary. Bow. 35. Feed imaginary friends or dolls you brought with you. 36. Shoot hoops with shrimp into his water glass. 37. Every time your date opens his mouth, interrupt and start a new conversation. 38. Belch. Score it according to the Olympic standard. 39. After kissing him, explain you're doing a study on the spread of mononucleosis.

# The Girls' Life

## Guide to

# School

# She's All That—Or Is She?

## Popularity Myths Revealed

Every girl wants to be popular. How do we know? Because feeling you're liked is one thing all people—young and old, male and female—have in common.

But why is it so important to some girls to be in the "most popular" clique? Why do girls tear themselves apart trying to climb the popularity ladder? In the big scheme of things, why does being popular matter so much?

Here's the trickiest question: Why does one group get to be on top? Why are they so great? Do they have some special thing the rest of us don't? In order to find out, we talked to "popular" girls and asked them what the deal is. What we found out is this: There are a lot of myths about being popular.

**Myth #1—People like you more.** Wrong. Popularity means you're well-known, not that people like you. And even if popular girls seem to have more friends, it doesn't mean they have lots of real friends. Since popularity is based on reputation, girls often spend more time knowing a lot of people a little, rather than having a few really good friends. Said one girl, "I don't know what would happen if I ever really needed one of my friends to stick up for me and take a stand against someone else in my clique. They mostly look out for themselves."

**Myth #2—You get to have more fun.** Oh yeah? Everybody thinks popular people go to the most fun parties, have the best time at the mall, hang out and share the best gossip. Wrong. Our group of popular girls report a much different reality. "I'm supposed to be funny, pretty, look nice and be in a good mood all the time," reports Justine, "I can't just not talk to anyone one day if I don't feel like it." Lindsey also didn't have very much fun. "When you hang out with the popular people, you hang out with the popular people. That's it. I wanted to hang out one day at the beach with this girl I used to be really good friends with before them, but my other friends freaked. It was them or else."

**Myth #3—You need to have the best house and best stuff.** Like that's so important. Sure the kid with the pool will be everybody's best friend in July, but loyalty is not part of the popularity game. The girl who lives in a small house with a mom who makes everybody feel special can be just as popular as a girl with a mansion. The bottom line? As one girl sniffed, "You can't buy your way in."

**Myth #4—You can make yourself more popular.** Uh-uh. The word from popular girls is, don't bet on it. Making friends with all sorts of people is a great idea and good fun, but trying to break into the popularity penthouse is a waste of time. Why? One popular girl couldn't even believe we had to ask. "If we let anybody hang out with us, that would ruin the whole point of being popular."

**Myth #5—Popular girls are happy.** This is the saddest myth of all. With a few exceptions, most girls we talked to are really insecure underneath. In order to stay popular, you have to leave some people out, making them feel they don't fit in. Defending your territory and making sure no one is taking your place in the clique is exhausting and warps your self-image. One girl we talked to actually wished she could move to another state and start over as a less popular girl. "Once you start," she said, "you just can't stop and go away quietly."

**Myth #6—The same people will always be popular.** They wish. Again, some people are just so likable, they can't help but always be buds with everyone. But for the most part, popular people are like bell-bottoms—as soon as enough people get sick of them, they end up on triple markdown. It's safe to say that today's seventh-grade queen could be tomorrow's eighth-grade loser.

**Myth #7—Popularity will go away.** You wish. There are few things in this world that you can't escape: death, taxes, and popularity. Realizing that popularity is stupid and vile does not change the fact that it exists. What you can change is how you look at it and how it affects you.

## BEYOND POPULARITY TO TRULY COOL

Want to know who all the girls we talked to secretly admired and wanted to be more like? The truly cool girls. Call them "most popular for the '00s."

Who are the new truly cool? The girls who are self-confident. They don't suck up to popular girls because they know who their real friends are. Truly cool girls set their own styles—no copying. Cool girls follow their hearts.

It takes guts to rise above the status quo. Speaking to be heard and letting your actions, clothes and attitudes show your true self is a bold move. Do this for a few weeks and you might notice something. Not only will you be happier, a lot of other people might follow your lead and start dancing to their own drummer, too.

And you might find that you have become popular with the most important person of all— yourself.

# How Far Would You Go to Be Popular?

1. You are talking to the most popular girls in school when they start saying mean things about one of your friends. You…
   a) yell at them. Who cares about being popular?
   b) walk away. You're not going to diss a friend, but you cannot help it if the popular girls do.
   c) start laughing along with them. Face it—sure your friend is nice, but she isn't going to get you in with the cool crowd.

2. You and your mom are planning a mother/daughter day. She has been talking non-stop about it. You have never seen her so excited. When a popular girl calls and asks if you want to go to the movie with her that same day, you…
   a) say, "Sure, I'm not busy," then ask your mom to drive you to the movie.
   b) say, "Gee, normally I would love to go, but today I am going out with my mom."
   c) say, "I really want to, but I am going out with some other friends today." You are not about to tell her you are going out with your mom.

3. You and some popular people are at the mall when one of them steals an expensive pair of earrings. You…
   a) ask her to put them back but make sure she knows you are not going to tell on her.
   b) don't say anything about it. You figure it's the store's fault for not paying attention.
   c) yell at her in front of everyone, making such a commotion that the store manager comes to see what is going on.

4. Your dad has made you swear not to touch his beloved new computer. When a cool girl is at your house and asks to use it, you…
   a) say, "No way. My dad will kill me if it gets touched." That's the truth!
   b) say, "Oh, I am so sorry, but it broke this morning. How about watching a movie instead?"
   c) say, "Oh, sure. Do whatever you want," silently hoping your dad will never find out. If he does, you will be grounded forever.

5. You miss the 'N SYNC special studying for a math test. A popular girl (who would never talk to you otherwise) comes up to you before the test and asks you to help her cheat. You...
   a) tell her one measly little lie that you didn't study. That way, you won't have to cheat.
   b) yell, "Um, I missed the N'SYNC special to study for this test. I don't *think* so!"
   c) tell her she can cheat off of you anytime. After all, she *is* popular.

6. It is your best bud's birthday, and a popular girl at the party invites you to leave and go for pizza. You...
   a) say, "I would love to, but it is my best bud's party. I heard they are going to have fun games. Why don't you stay for a while?"
   b) say, "Sure. This party is a drag."
   c) say, "Why would I? It is my best bud's party. And she invited you. It is only kind to stay."

7. You pride yourself on never lending anyone money. You even turned down your best bud when she had no lunch. A cool girl comes up to you and asks you for $20. You...
   a) say, "Of course. Here, take $40."
   b) say, "Oh, I am sorry. I only have $5," even though your wallet is full of money.
   c) say, "Oh, I can't. You see, I never lend anyone money under any circumstances."

**SCORING:**
1. a. 3, b. 2, c. 1
2. a. 1, b. 3, c. 2
3. a. 2, b. 1, c. 3
4. a. 3, b. 2, c. 1
5. a. 2, b. 3, c. 1
6. a. 2, b. 1, c. 3
7. a. 1, b. 2, c. 3

**7-11 POINTS:** Well, let's just say you could be nicer. You must learn that being popular is not so important. You seem to think you can drop everyone in this world and then pick them back up when you need them. I suggest you hold on to those who care about you. In the end, they will be there for you.

**12-16 points:** You want to be popular, but you would not step on other people on your way up the social ladder. You understand the importance of friends and family. Still, you are willing to fib to be popular.

**17-21 points:** You go, girl! You stand up for yourself when anyone comes between you and your morals. Your loyal personality will gain trust and love from people who deserve it. You understand that being popular is not the most important thing in the world.

—BY KEREN KATZ, 12, AND MANDY GINZBURG, 12

# Shy-Busting Solutions

*"Ever since kindergarten, I've been known as the 'quiet girl.' My parents get mad every time I meet someone because I don't have much to say. I won't go to a party alone; I have to go with a friend or my mom! When I'm shy around cute guys at school, they make fun of me. I wish I could, but I can't help being shy."*

For some people, the art of conversation is never a problem. There are those who always seem to know just the right thing to say at just the right moment. But many girls get tongue-tied in social situations. Sure, you can hang loose and be yourself when you're around family and friends, but what about when you're out?

Unfortunately, keeping to yourself can be social suicide because some people get the wrong impression. Quiet girls often wind up being labeled snobby or stupid. "A lot of my classmates think I am dumb," says Lori, 12. "The reason is I am really shy. I don't have a lot of friends because of it. I would really like to overcome my shyness."

For some girls, mustering up the nerve to talk to their Beanie Babies is tough. "I used to be soooo shy," confesses one girl. "I mean, I was even afraid when attendance was called. One night while lying in bed, I thought to myself, 'Girl, what are you doing with your life? Get up and get going. That night, I took my own advice. Now a year later, I'm so popular that almost everyone at school knows my name. Not that it isn't okay to be shy, but if you don't come out of your shell, you may never meet your lifelong best friend or some cute guy."

You can barricade yourself in your bedroom and become known as the class recluse. But we have some better suggestions. If you weren't blessed with the gift of gab, we have some great bashful-bashing advice that's sure to help.

## WHY YOU'RE SHY

If you look down at your shoes every time you're forced into a conversation with someone new, chances are it's probably spurred by negative thoughts. Feelings of inadequacy ("I sound stupid") or a fear of being rejected ("He probably thinks I'm a total jerk") can totally sabotage your attempts to be social.

Maybe you're afraid you'll say or do something embarrassing, like trip over your shoelaces. "I can be really shy around people," says Toni, 11. "I think this is because I don't want to make a bad impression. When I'm around boys, I tend to be a little clumsy. I guess it's because I'm nervous."

Many adolescent girls lack self-confidence and feel awkward because they think they're too short, too tall, have braces, wear glasses…. Add your worst hang-up to the list. But whatever the reason, you can overcome shyness, like this girl did: "I used to be shy, and then I realized it wasn't getting me anywhere. I found out that shyness is just a state of mind. If you build up your self-confidence, you can wave shyness good-bye!"

## SHY-BUSTING SOLUTIONS

Even if you're usually not the shy type, maybe you freeze up in specific circumstances. "Okay, I'm not shy at all," says Meredith, 13. "My friends say I'm the most outgoing person they know. But when I go to a dance, I clam up."

Says Sarah, 11, "I am only shy when I meet someone, especially when it's a cute boy!" Similarly, Amanda, 12, says, "I'm usually only shy around adults."

Whether you're terminally shy or your fears only creep in on occasion, there are ways to tackle the timids. The trick to *being* a social butterfly instead of *having* them in your stomach is to keep your insecurities in check. Everybody has certain levels of fearing humiliation, but some girls blow this so out of proportion that it cripples their conversational skills. But fear not, for you can overcome.

**Quit focusing on yourself.** So much shyness is about people obsessing over how they are acting during a conversation. Every blink of an eye or twitch of a nose suddenly seems to be obvious. Forget about it. Unless you're Gwyneth Paltrow, nobody is analyzing your every move.

And so what if you make a few goofs? You're probably the only person who notices anyway—or cares.

**Fake it.** To get out there and break the shy habit, try tapping your inner drama queen—with script, rehearsals and action. Don't be too weirded out about practicing your lines, gestures and movements in front of your bedroom mirror. Before going to any gathering, make a mental list of three topics you can bring up so you'll have something to contribute to the conversation. Without trying to be a standup comic, be able to tell a few good jokes.

And anyone who's ever taken acting lessons knows how important breathing is in helping you to relax and get rid of stage fright. Try not to take quick, shallow breaths. Take long drawn-in breaths, inhaling through your nose and exhaling through your mouth. You probably should practice this at home, too. The last thing you need is to hyperventilate at the holiday dance.

**Be a good listener.** A good way to strike up a conversation with someone is to get him to talk about himself. Everyone loves to talk about themselves because we're all at least a little bit egocentric. Show a sincere interest in his life by asking about his hobbies, family, pets, and so on. Keep it natural, and just be yourself.

If you find yourself at a total loss for words, compliment a girl on the sweater she's wearing or say you like her new haircut as an icebreaker. She just might take it from there. If she walks away, don't crawl back into your shell. Tell yourself that maybe she just had to go pick that spinach dip out of her teeth or perhaps she's shy just like you. And even if she was bored? So what? Why would you want to be friends with someone who won't even give you a chance?

**Keep the conversation on a two-way street.** Try not to get nervous and babble nonstop. That's not a conversation—you're delivering a monologue. A conversation is back and forth banter. Keep the ball rolling as one idea flows into another. She's telling you about her piano lessons? When she pauses, tell her you play guitar. Then listen while she tells you about the time she saw that Barenaked Ladies concert…and so on.

She's on a filibuster? Your silence can be golden. Sometimes it's good to just listen. Pay attention to what is being said, and interject a few verbal cues—"Yes," "Uh-huh," "I see," "Really?"—to let her know you're still hanging on her every word. But keep in mind that a lull in the conversation is okay also.

**Know when to quit.** No matter how hard you try, some conversations will be duds. Look for visual cues that your listener is bored. (Or maybe you're bored.) If he is looking around, tapping his foot, sighing, or showing other signs of restlessness, give it up. Dismiss yourself with something like, "Well, I think I'll go over and try the Jell-o mold."

Stop thinking about how you blew it because it's very likely the other person was just as scared to carry on a conversation as you were. Reach out to other shy people because you know how they feel. "It takes some courage for me to be outgoing around people," says another shy-bee. "I try to make a real effort to talk and acknowledge others. They may be just as shy and will be grateful if I make the first move. I try to talk more because I know that sometimes a shy person may be thought of as a snob."

**Keep working on it.** Read success stories about famous people who overcame their fears, and be inspired. Instead of focusing on how nervous you are about attending Nicole's party next Saturday, relax by taking a yoga class, riding your bike, playing guitar, meditating, or starting a journal. A diary is a good way to practice expressing your thoughts.

Or use your pen to sign up for drama, soccer, or student government. Activities like these force you to be assertive. "I was really shy when I was little, and I had trouble making friends," says Merri, 12. "That all ended last year because I had a really great teacher who would always pick me for social studies skits so I would have to talk in front of people. Now I'm the lead in the school play, and I'm anything but shy. I'm known as the girl who never shuts up!"

If your best friend is begging you to join French club with her, then why not? You'll meet others with similar interests and get in on related parties and activities. And who knows, *mon ami*? This time around you could be the life of the party! *Non?*

### HANDLE A DISS BETTER

If a meanie boy calls you "Fishface," do you go home and examine your mug in the mirror, looking for aquatic features? Well, stop that right now. Don't believe for two seconds the harsh things other people say about you. Of course, that's not so easy when the diss is true. What do you do when the class know-it-all feels the need to point out publicly the D you just got on your pop quiz? Just cool the confrontation. Say, "Thank you. How kind of you to notice." Then, whatever you do, change the subject! Whew...

# Gossip

## Why We Do It and Why It Hurts

Imagine this: A friend just told you the juiciest tidbit—she saw Lisa, the class brain, pull out a piece of paper during a spelling quiz. Miss All A's, a cheater! You can't wait to tell your best friend—after all, she suffers those B's right along with you. Do you even think twice about spreading the gossip? If you're like most people, probably not. But you should.

Why? Well, here's the rest of the story. Lisa was pulling paper out of her pocket because she forgot to spit out her gum from lunch. Of course, no one knew that but her. But, by the end of the school day, everyone knew that "Lisa's a cheater." It wasn't until Lisa was hauled down to the principal's office that she even heard the gossip about "how Lisa gets such good grades." While the principal believed her (after she aced the quiz, he made her retake it right then and there), Lisa couldn't believe how all the other girls—many she considered to be close friends—could think the worst of her.

Gossip! While most of us know better than to repeat nasty news, who can help it? No one, it seems. For better or worse, we're a country obsessed with the stuff. Used to be that you had to read the supermarket tabloids to see who was doing what. Now the nightly news reports are as likely to bring you a live feed from the rumor mill as any tabloid. Is it any wonder that when we have a chance to spread news about Lisa, we hold back no more than Peter Jennings does about the latest Presidential scandal? But should we? And what happens when gossip hurts? When the mean talk turns to you?

## GOSSIP'S GOOD POINTS

Believe it or not, gossip can have some merits. For one, it lets us know more about the people around us. While no one should ever take pleasure in hearing about someone else's misery, hearing about troubles, as well as triumphs, makes others seem more...well, normal. When Lisa found out about what her friends had said, she was really hurt. But, she says now, "It made me realize people thought I was perfect. They were so eager to believe the worst because I never let on how hard it is for me to get those grades. Now I study with the other girls, so they see how I struggle with fractions just like them."

Gossip also lets us know how others expect us to act. When people talked about Lisa cheating, many girls got the message that if they cheated, they would be busted by the group too. While other issues—a fight with a friend, a divorce—may be seen as a part of life and get you sympathy, every group of friends has offenses that will cause the pack to talk against you...and you'll only know it when the word gets back to you.

Gossip also supports our very human need to bond with other people and make clear who is in and out of the group. "It's pretty clear," says 12-year-old Constance, "If you are in the clique, you hear what is going on. And you can be a tighter part of the clique if you have news to share." In other words, gossip—like knowledge—is power. And it must be used just as carefully.

## GOSSIP'S DANGERS

Gossip, of course, can cause a great deal of pain, like it did for Lisa initially and for 11-year-old Misty. "My brother died in a car crash, and people started to say he was drunk. He fell asleep coming home from college. It felt so bad to try to deal with that plus the gossip. At a time when I really needed my friends, I felt I couldn't trust anybody. I could never let my guard down." It took Misty two years to tell her friends why she went from someone who laughed a lot to a sad person. "It wasn't just him dying. They shattered my whole world with that one rumor. Many of them can't tell me enough how sorry they are, and I believe them, but I don't think I'll ever feel OK about it."

Gossip also has a nasty way of backfiring. Twelve-year-old Debbie was telling her friend a story she heard about a girl a grade ahead of them who got caught drinking in the bathroom. Not only had the girl not been caught with alcohol, but she was listening right around the corner. While Debbie felt she was just repeating a story, the other girl didn't see it that way. As Debbie knows now, "It's like they said in the old days, 'Shoot the messenger.'"

Because everyone wants to be in on the talk, gossip can even lead to lying. Even people who usually don't lie may find themselves adding just a bit to a story. Says Debbie, "Back in my days as the town crier, I would put a little spin on things. Like instead of someone just getting caught skipping, I would say they got caught by the principal. I don't know why. I guess it just made for a better story. I didn't even really think of it as lying. Creativity, yeah, that's it!"

## WHY WE GOSSIP

Clearly, gossip can result in some really bad consequences. So why do we do it so much? Again, it makes us feel part of the group. It's fun to be able to share something at the lunch table, especially something exciting that not everyone else knows about. It makes us seem more exciting by association. And being able to make judgments about someone—like the group did with Lisa the "cheater"—is also an exciting and powerful feeling. Having someone care what you think of them gives you a bit of an edge.

But gossiping also brings out your bad side. When we asked Lisa's friends why they were so eager to rat on her, many admitted to being jealous and said it felt good, for just a moment, to bring "perfect Lisa" down. "It's gross what we did," says one, "but some people didn't see the big deal. As if by being smart, she deserved it. I see how weak it makes us all look."

### TAKE A BETTER CLASS PICTURE

Why is it your friends' class pictures seem like glamour shots but you look like you're on *America's Most Wanted*? "A lot of people get nervous, and that's when pictures turn out the goofiest," says Roger Erickson, a celeb photographer in Los Angeles. "My best advice is to relax, and wear a black shirt that doesn't have a high neckline. Yearbooks are black-and-white so the more contrast, the better." As for any crazy prints, doing your hair differently or wearing a lot of makeup? Roger says "Forget about it!" Remember to say "cheese!"

## GOSSIP CONSCIOUSNESS

Remember, there is a difference between news and gossip. It's nice to spread a positive word. But watch out for gossip that can be hurtful, even if it is true. Some good questions to ask yourself—"Would I say this to the person's face?" and "What would I think if someone said this about me?"

For those who can't be quite so noble, ask yourself why you want to tell. Sometimes things just come out of your mouth, but other times the real reason you gossip has more to do with you than the juicy story. If you have trouble keeping secrets, think about why. Do you need the spotlight? Do you feel better about your own life when someone else has trouble? If you think the answer might be yes, time to change how you act and leave other people's private matters alone.

## WHEN THEY ARE ALL TALKING...ABOUT YOU!

Sooner or later, we all become the hot topic of conversation. While some people love the spotlight no matter why it is shining on them, others just want people to shut up and mind their own business. Here's some advice on how to handle it:

**Don't wig out.** The worst thing you can do is freak out. People don't always believe what they hear, and the story may not be as bad as you think. Try the casual approach. If the word isn't too bad, just try to laugh it off. Or wait until it comes up in conversation, explain briefly, and let that be the end of it. Try not to sound defensive, and don't attack back.

**Find out what is going on.** Find a friend who knows the story that has been passed around, and ask her exactly what is being said. That will let you know exactly what you're dealing with.

**If the story is true.** It may be best to face it head on. If your parents are getting divorced but you want to keep it just in your family, tell your friends that. You aren't denying what is said, you're just telling people you will not let them talk about it until you say so.

**If the story is false.** You can do one of two things. One is rely on a friend to stick up for you. But that can get tricky. People don't really do that great a job because it takes guts to stand up for someone else—especially someone who is in the hot seat. So that leaves...you sticking up for yourself. Sounds impossible, particularly when you already feel beaten down. But by being firm, cool, and sticking to your guns, you can silence the masses. It takes guts, but the fallout from telling the truth is probably better than the rumor.

**Move on.** Once you say what you have to say, let the whole thing blow over. Remember tomorrow is another day—for someone else to be the talk of the school!

**FINISH YOUR HOMEWORK QUICKER**

We asked one home-school teacher how she motivates her students (since their only work is homework). "Make a to-do list of everything you have due," she says. "Tackle the subjects you like the least at the start so you can check them off your list. Then take a ten-minute break to stretch or eat a snack, but don't leave your work area or you might get distracted. Now all you have left are the subjects you really like, and since that homework is fun to you, you'll finish it faster." This teacher gets an A for good A-dvice!

# Can You Keep a Secret?

Chinese water torture couldn't make you blab, nor could all the money in the world. Still, you're a dam about to burst. All sorts of temptations keep popping up, and the stupid secret is teetering on your tongue. It's driving you nuts! The temptation to tattle usually depends on the circumstances. Did someone trust you with their secret, or did you find out by accident? Is the information low-down gossip or truly important? What would it take for you to tattle? The following quiz will make it crystal clear.

1. When an older sib admits she sneaks out of the house and asks you to cover for her, you:
    a) race to your parents and report the where, when and how.
    b) see what's in it for you. You've been dying to borrow her new CD…
    c) find out where she's flitting off to, and then hold your post like a true soldier.

2. When you arrive at school, the biggest troublemaker in school saunters over and brags about a prank she pulled on your favorite teacher. You:
    a) laugh and tell everyone you know what happened.
    b) tell all. After all, he is your favorite teacher.
    c) keep your lips clamped.

3. You hear your mom and dad whispering about what's really going on with your neighbor's parents. At the bus stop the next morning, your neighbor mentions his dad is on a long business trip. You:
    a) let him know your family is available if his mom needs help while his dad is away.
    b) take him aside and say, "I know everything. You can be honest with me."
    c) ignore him completely. Otherwise, you might say something dumb.

4. Your best friend confides she's probably moving across the country, but swears you to secrecy. When other friends notice you're bummed and ask what's bringing you down, you:
    a) tell them your new boots are cutting off circulation to your toes.
    b) say, "Oh, nothing…" and sigh melodramatically.
    c) tell them you recently received bad news.

5. Jill tells you in secret that she can't stand Amy anymore. When Amy says practically the same thing as Jill, you:
- a) schedule a three-way meeting and help them work it out.
- b) become the middle man. Explain to Jill how Amy feels, and tell Amy how Jill feels. Then call them each at home and fix everything.
- c) see trouble coming and book plenty of after-school baby-sitting jobs to fill your time.

6. Your best friend admits she has a crush on Dave, who's best friends with the guy you like. When you bump into these guys at the mall, Dave asks who your friend likes. You:
- a) unthinkingly blurt out, "You!" and feel your face turn red.
- b) chew your gum and ask casually, "I don't know, why?"
- c) say, "Why don't you give me a call later. Maybe I'll find out…"

7. After you promise to keep his troubles hush-hush, your friend Evan tells you the real scoop on his school detention. But in gym the next day, you hear classmates exaggerating the supposed crime. You go over and:
- a) say, "You are making it sound much worse than it was," and fill them in on the real deal.
- b) say, "Maybe this is just a rumor. Let's not talk about Evan behind his back."
- c) give their account an even crazier spin. Maybe they'll get the point.

8. Your friend Kate is planning a small get-together and asks you not to breathe a word because there are lots of girls she can't invite. Later, you're at the mall with another friend, who begs you not to tell Kate about the cool necklace she's buying for her birthday. Since you're sure she's not on the guest list, you:
- a) lie and tell your friend that you don't think Kate's having a party this year.
- b) ask your friend if she's gotten an invitation to Kate's party yet.
- c) bite your lip. If you can, think of a reason why she should wait a bit before making her purchase (say, Memorial Day sales) and offer it.

## ANSWERS
*Give yourself one point for each correct answer. Add the points and see how you did.*

1. c) As a general rule, rat on sibs only when you fear for their safety—or your own. Oh, and asking for something in return for keeping a secret is called *blackmail*, which is bad news!

2. c) Whether you think the teacher is tops or the worst is beside the point. (Don't even think of tattling for brownie points. Yuck!) As tempted as you may be to see justice, you didn't see what happened. Suppose you inform, then discover they made the whole thing up?

3. a) Finding out a secret accidentally can be the biggest burden of all. You may not even know if the facts are true. If the person involved tells a different version, respect it. Maybe speaking the truth—or even knowing it—is too painful right now. Plus, your neighbor's parents will want to tell their child in their own way and time. Offer only your friendship.

4. a) When we're affected personally, secrets are even harder to keep. If your face betrays emotions, say something true—even if it's not the whole truth. Mentioning something else on your mind will prevent others from getting suspicious.

5. c) Even if neither friend swore you to silence, secrets were implied when they confided in you. Trying to straighten out their problems would mean revealing these secrets. Plus, your plan would probably backfire, leaving them angry at you!

6. b) Yes, it's hard to keep a leash on your tongue when you're nervous. But it's okay to lose your cool, while it's never okay to sell out one friend to make another.

7. b) It's tempting to blab if you think it might help. But, it's not your secret to tell. Each time a story is retold, it changes. So adding to the confusion just fuels the fire.

8. c) Your friends asked you not to tell. So zip your lip, and hope that maybe Kate will find room for one more guest.

## CHECK YOUR SCORE
*Give yourself one point for each correct answer, add up the total, and locate your score.*

### 6 - 8 Super Secret Stasher
Want to know a secret? If we had one, we'd tell you.

### 5 - 7 Moderate Mouther
Work on the situations that pry loose your tongue, and you'll earn more trust.

### 0 - 3 Secret Slipper
Read the tips on the next page on keeping your mouth sealed. If all else fails, try masking tape.

# FOUR REASONS NOT TO BLAB

**Trust.** Since a secret is a verbal contract between you and the teller, blabbing is a betrayal of trust. And we all know how precious trust is to relationships: easy to lose and difficult to regain. So, if you're becoming more and more tempted to spill the beans, stop and consider how much you're putting at risk.

**Invasion of Privacy.** When someone asks you to keep a secret, it's usually because the information is private. You feel special because they chose to tell you. Secrets about deep feelings and family matters usually fall into this category. If you blab, the secret holder feels exposed. Imagine how you'd feel if something you've told only to your diary was suddenly the top news story in your school! You'd probably feel hurt, betrayed, and incredibly angry.

**When Rumors Backfire.** Suppose you spill the beans about Margo moving to Hawaii. You and your friends plan a huge *bon voyage*, offer your services to the family she baby-sits for, and find a sub for the softball team. Now, imagine what happens when Margo doesn't move. You look like a major fool—at best. To prevent a similar catastrophe, remember this scenario before sharing "news" still in the planning stage.

**Do No Harm.** Secrets often involve more than one person, conflicts, and hidden feelings. When you're the bearer of a secret, it's tempting to try to make things better, to prevent bad things or, more selfishly, to make yourself feel important. But as you've probably learned, the chances of reaching your lofty goal after telling someone's secret are about the same as visiting Neptune. In fact, you're more likely to make things worse. If you're tempted to save the world, take a Hippocratic oath to "Do No Harm."

# IT'S TOO LATE—I BLABBED!

You knew it was a bad idea, but the secret flew out of your mouth. You keep asking yourself, "Why?" and calling yourself an idiot. Since you can't un-say it, realize your mistake. Then, apologize. You feel genuinely sorry about what you did, so say so. It doesn't matter if you don't understand why you blew it. Sometimes that's hard to figure out, but you still need to apologize. And don't expect to be forgiven immediately. Your apology doesn't make your mistake disappear. You may have to live with your friend being upset for a while. Earning trust back can take a long time.

# WHAT IF I HAVE A SECRET?

So, you're bursting to tell a secret. First, determine whether you truly want to tell. There's nothing more annoying than those who hint around and then say, "Never mind." Whispering, "I just can't say" practically forces others to beg for the dirt. If your inner voice says "bad idea," write the secret in your diary. Or tell your puppy. If you need feedback, try an overseas pen pal. (Beware—the Net is not secret-safe!)

One of life's sweetest indulgences is spilling the beans to a bud: You think you made varsity, you might be going to Paris, the cute boy in algebra asked a friend about you. When the secret isn't too serious (it wouldn't be a nightmare if it leaked) pick a friend you trust. Choose someone who doesn't dish about others, and whom you've shared secrets with before. Do not tell secrets that might become a burden. Bad news may make her so upset, she'll feel desperate to tell someone else. Also off-limits are secrets about upcoming events that spell future trouble. Telling your bud you-know-who is going to break into school to steal an old test—but mum's the word—will only make her feel helpless. She's better off not knowing.

## SECRETS YOU SHOULDN'T KEEP

If you or one of your friends has been abused, physically or sexually, tell a responsible adult. There are even laws forcing professionals to tell authorities in situations of suspected abuse. These are clear-cut situations. No doubt, tell right away. If you have thoughts of hurting or killing yourself—or a friend has confided that he or she has them—tell a trusted adult immediately. Even though it's a secret, the possibility of harm, or even death, always takes priority. Yes, your friend might be ticked, but an angry friend is better than a dead friend. Besides, after they've gotten help, kids are nearly always grateful that someone cared enough to do something.

Some situations aren't so black-or-white. What if a friend is skipping school and getting into trouble without parents knowing? Or what if your parents ask you not to tell anyone that they're having serious marital or financial problems? Even though you want to obey, you're having a tough time dealing by yourself. Talking to someone your age may be risky. Plus, it's unlikely a friend would have the experience to offer helpful advice. These are situations that call for a trusted adult. Talking to a counselor, therapist, or religious leader is confidential (they're forbidden by law to tell). Or, share the news with an aunt, older cousin, special teacher, or a friend's mother.

Last, if you ever accidentally overhear a buzz word from your parents' room—like "move" or "divorce"—it's okay to talk to them. It doesn't help anyone if you keep it bottled up and then stay awake at nights panicking. Tell your parents you heard a word or two, and let them know you want to be clued in. It may save a lot of unnecessary misery.

Having the perfect secret to share is like striking it rich. As long as you think through who and when to tell, you're golden. And if you decide it's best to keep the secret buried, be sure to throw away the key. You'll be the most treasured friend around.

# Rebuild Your Rep

## It's Never Too Late!

Whether you're starting a new school or just a brand new year, you might be thinking it's time to unveil a whole new you. Maybe you'd like to shed your reputation as "goody-goody," "flirt," "fake," "nerd," or "space cadet." No matter how many times or ways you've strived to lose the old image, it's managed to stick to you like a big, annoying "kick me" sign. But you have the potential to get rid of that troublesome rep once and for all. Follow the tips below, and you'll find out exactly how to replace your old image with one you've always wanted.

### THE ACADEMIC YOU

Last year, you might have been known for writing illegibly, losing assignments, answering questions wrong, or debating any grade worse than an A.

Perhaps your teacher had a pet name for you, like Sleepyhead, Chatterbox or Grouchy. While these nicknames were humorous at first, and maybe even made you feel special, they ended up taking their toll on you and your work.

Perhaps you became more and more like the nickname, since that's what was expected of you anyway. Developing a bad reputation often makes us fail to see ourselves as we really are: girls who sometimes talk too much, fall asleep in class, or scribble our homework—but who also have terrific questions and ideas.

Margi, 13, says, "When I started middle school last year I had a hard time with my locker. One day, I got mad and kicked it. This teacher saw me, and when I was in his class that spring he said, 'Oh, you're the girl with the temper!' And no matter what I did, that's how he thought of me."

While Margi got her reputation from a one-time outburst, other girls are known for more long-lasting, troublesome habits. When Jill, 12, kept forgetting to look over her papers, her teacher took off major points for sloppiness and spelling goofs. "I guess my teacher expected my paper to be a mess, so he seemed to look for my mistakes more than anyone else's," she says.

Having a new teacher can be a great opportunity to start over. But just showing up and introducing your improved self won't cut it. You have to decide how you want to be considered, and then change yourself to fit the new image. Do you want to be known as smart, confident, outspoken, responsible? What would it take for you to be seen that way?

To spruce up her image in school, Ellie, 14, decided to get super organized. As she puts it, "I started a system to write down my homework, and I put stuff in my backpack the night before so I'd never forget it." Suzie, 10, confides, "I was sick of looking dumb when my teacher went over assignments. So I decided to do my reading, no matter what. At first, everybody looked surprised, but I knew all the answers." Caroline, 13, says her teacher told her that she didn't seem to think for herself: "He said all I did was go along with what other people said. But I did have my own opinions. I just had to figure out how to say them."

Once you've come up with a plan and practiced new behaviors, you'll be on your way to an improved image. Give it time to stick. You'll need plenty of practice, and your teachers need time to notice. However, if teachers bring up your old rep, it's okay to remind them of your new self. Rita, 14, had to repeat a year of math. On the first day, her teacher asked, "Didn't you take this class last year?" Rita says, "It was like he was expecting me to fail again." Wisely, she answered, "I had trouble with math last year, but I had tutoring over the summer and I'm ready to go."

Making a lasting change isn't easy. Old habits are hard to break. If you're tempted to go back to your old ways, keep your goal in mind. Ilene, 13, also has good advice: "Don't let yourself get lazy, even once. Last year, I decided to put away every test I got back in the right notebook. Then I got rushed and stuffed 'em anywhere, thinking I'd catch up. But I never did. Stick to your plan exactly."

## THE SOCIAL YOU

For most girls, a top priority is how they're seen on the social scene. September may offer your best hope of experimenting with new styles or escaping a bad rep that's haunted you since you made that one, teensy mistake. Maybe your best friend's secret accidentally popped out of your mouth. Or you couldn't resist starting a mean rumor about a friend who made you angry.

As Holly, 12, reports, "I went a little overboard flirting with this guy at the spring dance, and since then everybody's always accusing me of being boy-crazy." So how did she deal? "I kept a low profile all summer. Then when school started again, I went out of my way to show everyone I had changed. I told my good friends what I was doing so they'd understand."

Holly's plan worked because she truly did change her ways. But it certainly helped that she launched her plan at the beginning of a new school year. First, after the summer break, memories of her behavior at the spring dance had faded. Second, many of her friends had also undergone their own changes. Part of adjusting to the new school year involves getting used to people's new heights, hairstyles, interests, and attitudes. So it took a while for reputations to get fixed in everybody's minds again. It wasn't that Holly's changes were seen automatically, but everyone seemed more open to recognizing her efforts. Third, there were different mixtures of girls in all her classes—new students entered, others moved away—so the chemistry among her friends changed.

As Holly says, "When Trish moved away, Abby and I got to be better friends. And since Pam was in my science class I got to know her better too."

Besides offering a second chance for girls to live down their mistakes, a new school year brings possibilities for social changes.

Wendy, 13, had a best friend since kindergarten. But once she got to middle school, "I didn't want to be known as one of the 'twins' anymore. Everyone expected us to be together. I was sick of it." Other girls are tired of being pigeonholed into one of the known groups, such as the "jocks," "brains," "nerds," whatever. You may want to change the image that's followed you around like a shadow. Or maybe you've decided this year—no matter what it takes—you'll be one of the "cool" girls. But let's be honest. Doesn't almost every girl hope (even a little) to be more "popular"?

## THE POPULARITY PROBLEM

This wish to be popular, to join the "A-list," is what lures many girls onto misguided paths. Some get fanatical, buying new wardrobes, rejecting favorite bands or getting radical new 'dos to project an entirely different image.

Having just moved to a new school, Sarah, 14, decided to go goth. "I got all these black clothes, wore combat boots, and dyed my hair black," she says, "and some of the goth kids were nice to me, but most thought I was a huge poser—which I was. I ended up feeling dumb."

Other girls try to hang out with an older, faster crowd by doing stuff they think will impress

### BE ARMED WITH SCATHING COMEBACKS TO A BULLY'S INSULTS

"I'm rubber and you're glue, so whatever you say bounces off me and sticks to you" has been a tired comeback since the last millennium. "Bullies love to get reactions, so the best comeback is to have no reaction," says Dr. Judy. "If you pretend like you didn't hear the insult, you don't acknowledge the bully." Meaning, if a bully says, "Hey stupid!" and you don't turn around, you're sending a message that you don't think of yourself as stupid. Get it? If the bully persists, say, "I'm busy, do you mind?" Then go about your business.

them, like smoking, drinking, or swearing. Erica, 13, admits, "For a while, I was into tight jeans and skirts. My mom had a fit every time I tried to leave the house. Guys definitely noticed me, but not in a good way. It made me feel weird…like they were expecting other stuff from me."

It's perfectly normal (and great fun) to try different looks. Getting to know various kinds of people is also a good thing. That's one way we figure out for ourselves what sort of person we are, what we like and dislike, and our views on important topics. However, getting into unhealthy habits or pretending to be older are two sure ways to flirt with disaster. Making new friends or being accepted by a different crowd shouldn't require putting yourself at risk.

The key to truly learning about a person is discovering what's on the inside rather than copying a look. Unfortunately, many girls believe donning the most expensive purses, wearing tons of make-up, or being seen at the "in" hangout are the tickets to certain social groups.

But as Lacey, 13, discovered, "Trying to be someone you're not gets you into trouble. I wanted to be in the cool group in seventh grade. Eventually, these girls I was dying to be friends with asked me to go to the mall. I was psyched until we got there and they started stealing clothes. I didn't want to steal, but I didn't want to look like a wimp either. All I could think of was how my life was gonna be ruined."

If you genuinely share interests or have common activities, getting to know people and making friends will happen naturally. No matter how tempting, it's usually a bad idea to try to change your behavior, values, or whole self to fit in with friends. That pesky little voice inside your head saying, "I don't know about this…maybe it isn't such a good idea" is on your side. Pay close attention to any and all uncomfortable feelings. They're clues that getting a new image or reputation has too high a price. As Lacey puts it, "You can be who you are with true friends: They respect you—and don't push you to do things you don't want to do."

Should you decide that you do prefer a whole new group of friends, one final warning: Don't burn your bridges. After a bit of experimentation, you may miss your old friends after all. If you haven't blown them off or dropped them, they'll be happy to have you hang with them again.

## TAKING STOCK OF YOURSELF

While some girls are concerned with how their teachers see them and others care mostly what social group they're lumped with, still others want to focus on changing their rep in their own families—and, most especially, with themselves. Somehow, without even understanding how it happened, we can end up seeing ourselves as lazy, ditzy, forgetful, dishonest—you name it! But we're not stuck with these bad reps. We can change every one of them with a little effort.

First, take stock of what unhealthy or self-defeating things you've been doing. If your constant chattering annoys people, you may try "zipping your lip."

If you're tired of frantically rushing around at the last moment, you might want to keep better track of the time. When you can't get your homework or chores done, detach the telephone from

# LABELS
## *Leave 'Em at the Grocery Store*

What's in a label? Just ask anyone who has ever been called a "nerd," a "goody-goody," a "wimp," a "copy-cat," a "fatso," a "showoff," a "brace-face," a "loser," or any other stereotype.

No matter what anybody says, it hurts to be labeled. The worst part is, nasty labels, no matter how bogus, seem to stick like glue. Once a label catches on, it's pretty hard to live the rap down, even if the charge is totally ridiculous.

So what are you supposed to do if a clique chooses you as their victim and starts calling you a humiliating name? You're not going to believe our answer: Laugh. That's right, just laugh in their faces, and say with a smirk, "Yeah, you guys are right. I am a total airhead, princess, cheapo—whatever."

It sounds crazy, but laughter is a sure-fire way to let the wind out of their sails. Nothing else can shut them up faster. After all, it's no fun for them to tease you if you don't provide the desired reaction. They want to see you squirm or attempt a lame comeback.

So, instead of letting these morons at school get you upset, just shrug your shoulders, smile and give them a superior look that says "Get a life" or "Don't you guys have anything better to do?" This strategy may not work the first time, but pretty soon these girls will start looking for an easier target.

The important thing to remember is not to let the labeler decide how others see you and you see yourself. Don't live down to someone's label. Fight it. Do all you can to prove to yourself that you're the person you see yourself as. And, if it comes down to it, confront others and ask them to see you that way, too.

Then you'll only have one label stuck to you as you go through life—winner.

---

your ear or shut down your video games. After some hard thinking, you may decide now's the time to turn over a new leaf.

For example, you might vow to be more honest (stop making so many excuses for yourself), dependable (do what you're expected to), or assertive (stick up for yourself and others).

Two, make necessary changes. Just like New Year's resolutions made on January 1, a new school year is a great time for new beginnings.

To make sure you succeed, keep your goals realistic, be true to you, and congratulate yourself as much as needed. Best of all, enjoy your new changes. Once you have them, they're yours forever—no one can take them away from you!

# Teacher Trouble

## How to Deal with Conflicts in the Classroom

For hours a day, five days a week, you face teachers who observe you, instruct you, test you, correct you, and grade you. Every teacher has his or her own personality, teaching style, rules, level of patience, oddities, and bad days—all of which, like it or not, you have to adjust to by the sound of each bell. Some teachers you'll like and admire; others you'll despise and distrust. No doubt, you have preferences: a soft-spoken, kindly teacher or a dynamic, entertaining one; a serious, no-nonsense type or a stand-up comic. We'll bet there will also be something hugely annoying about every single one of your teachers. Maybe it's the way the art teacher taps his pencil on his hand, the way Mrs. So-and-So smirks after passing out a quiz, or how the science teacher's hair sticks up on top.

And if that's not stressful enough, each teacher has his or her own teaching style. Your teacher might call on everybody and expect lively discussions, but your shyness makes it hard for you to shine when put on the spot. Or perhaps another likes to lecture without interruption, but unless you get to ask questions, you get confused and distracted. Maybe you prefer to work by yourself, but your teacher sticks you in groups and expects you to accept lower grades along with your less conscientious classmates.

The list of potential clashes between you and your teachers is probably endless. In fact, when you think of them all, it's a miracle you aren't on the outs with at least one teacher on any given day! But despite all this, it's important to remember the most basic fact: It's up to you to make your relationships with your teachers work. You have everything to gain or lose—depending on how you play your cards.

### GIVE IT TIME

The beginning of every school year seems to be prime time for conflict with faculty. Some teachers, it turns out, aren't quite what you expect or, more to the point, what you're used to. In general, it's good to give yourself time to adjust to each new teacher's specific rules and ways of doing things. Helena, 11, says, "My teacher last year was big on open book tests, but my new teacher freaks if we even have a book on our desks during tests."

Similarly, work that earned stellar grades from one teacher may receive mediocre marks from another. As Heather, 13, puts it, "Sometimes, you have to forget about last year's teacher and get used to a whole new system." Whether it's not talking in class, chewing gum, getting a rest room pass, or bringing a sharpened pencil to class, rules are rules. Even if you think they're ridiculously stupid, you have to live with them.

## HOW BAD IS IT?

Aside from dealing with rules, at times you and the teacher may mix like oil and water. The critical thing is to ask yourself: "Is the problem important enough to make an issue out of?" You don't want to address every little annoyance that irks you in some minor way. If your teacher gives you 97% and you think you deserved 98%, try to let it go.

But what about when the teacher has affected you in a big way, such as when your feelings are hurt or you feel mistreated? These situations often call for action. Your feelings are saying, "Hey, you'd better do something about this injustice."

Katya, 13, was humiliated by her math teacher: "I failed the first math test of the year. I was having trouble with algebra, and she held my paper up for the whole class to see. She said, 'See what happens when you don't study.' I wanted to crawl under my desk." Similarly, when Felicia, 12, and her whole class had to stay after school because a few kids were being hyper, she was furious because she had to cancel a dance class. "And I hadn't said one single word!" she argues.

It's especially important to speak out if your distress dampens your enthusiasm for class or interferes with learning. For Katya and Felicia, the decision to speak up to their teachers wasn't easy. Says Felicia, "When I talked to my parents, I realized I couldn't see him every day without losing respect for him for being so unfair." After much thinking, Katya felt she'd be increasingly self-conscious in math class. Both girls knew they had to speak up or they'd be resentful. Getting their parents' support helped them feel less scared about having discussions with their teachers, but it still wasn't easy.

## GETTING GEARED UP

Once you decide to face the problem, avoid unnecessary skirmishes. Wait until you're less peeved so you can think straight, and then talk about it with someone neutral. Winnie, 10, once confronted her teacher without thinking—and suffered the consequences: "My teacher said something that made me mad. When I started to argue, she sent me to the principal and I got in even more trouble."

What do you want to accomplish? Do you want your teacher to stop hurting your feelings or embarrassing you? Do you want him to change a policy you believe is unfair? Are you asking her to reconsider a grade? Whatever it is, don't hint and expect the teacher to guess. Say it outright. It doesn't guarantee you'll get what you want, but the teacher should respect you for being direct.

Pick a good time to speak to your teacher, and use a pleasant, firm and non- argumentative voice. Don't insult or accuse him. And no whining! State how you feel and why, and tell the teacher how you think it could be resolved.

For example, if you're upset your teacher yelled at you for taking too long figuring out a division problem on the blackboard, you might say, "I am working very hard in this class, but I get nervous when everyone is watching. When you yell at me in front of everyone, it makes me even more uptight." Be prepared to elaborate, if asked, and be sure to give your teacher a chance to respond. Don't just say "You hurt my feelings." Tell her how: "I get upset when you call me 'Shorty.' It makes me self-conscious, and I prefer my real name." Rehearse what to say with a parent or older sibling. Ask the other person to pretend she's the teacher and you be yourself. Practice different ways of saying your piece until you feel comfortable.

If you still feel the teacher does not take your concerns seriously after speaking your mind, consider approaching another adult, such as a guidance counselor or principal. Don't feel weird about it. That's why they are there.

## BEWARE OF PITFALLS

It's important to first express strong feelings directly to the teacher so they won't fester and cause further trouble. Have you ever asked a friend why she is failing a subject, and she's responded, "Oh, because I hate my teacher." Huh? How do bad feelings about a teacher turn into bad grades? They don't—unless girls resort to any of the following tactics for handling conflicts with teachers, all of which end up hurting only themselves:

**"I'll just ignore him!"** If you're afraid to stand up for yourself, you may avoid the teacher completely, thinking, "If I don't bother him, he won't bother me." Unfortunately, you lose because you miss out on help you need for your upcoming geography test.

**"I'll be darned if I'll do what this teacher says!"** If you dig in your heels and refuse to turn in assignments or study for tests, you're indirectly saying, "I'm angry with you, and I want you to notice." But your teacher can't read minds and will only see you as unmotivated or lazy. You'll get more upset about bad grades, and "hate" your teacher even more. This is a no-win situation.

**"It's my teacher's fault!"** You might believe the teacher is too hard, too disorganized, too boring, or too unclear. All this may be true, but in the end you're responsible for your work. Rather than staying frustrated, figure out what you can do to make things better.

**"I'll get that teacher!"** Although rare, some girls curse or threaten or call teachers names. This is obviously a bad move that lands students in heaps of trouble. Plus, losing control never makes girls feel good about themselves.

## HELP! RESCUE ME!

Many girls, especially when they're too frightened to speak up to teachers, try to get their parents to do it. Yvette, 14, was outraged when her homeroom teacher marked her tardy. Yvette insisted she was on time and knew her mom would take her side. "My mom really hates it when people accuse her of stuff she didn't do, so I knew she'd stick up for me. But I was sorry I'd said anything the second they started talking. She made a huge deal and it wasn't worth it. Next time, I'll handle it myself."

Think twice before you ask parents to run interference for you. It might feel good at first to be rescued, but it's better to feel great about handling the situation yourself.

## BRINGING IN THE BIG GUNS

Sometimes, though, it is not a good idea to handle a problem with a teacher by yourself. Some more serious situations are best dealt with by parents. When Ruth, 12, was expected to take a pop quiz after two days off for a family funeral, she was understandably upset: "My mother said it really wasn't a problem between my teacher and me—it was a matter of school policy. So she called the principal."

Other issues require you to tell a parent or another trusted adult—immediately. Dawn told her mother her new language arts teacher was complimenting her: "He kept telling me I had a great figure for a 12-year-old." If you feel uncomfortable around a certain teacher, male or female, pay attention to your feelings and tell an adult who can decide what action should be taken.

Armed with these strategies, you can sort out any disagreements that arise. You can decide what is and isn't important, and how to go about expressing your feelings and requests in ways that will encourage teachers to listen. By dealing with conflicts directly and promptly, you'll use your energy for what really matters in school: enjoying learning.

# Start Your Own Club

You've gone down the list at school. French Club and Future Teachers of America are fine for other girls, but they just don't cut it for you. What are you into? Writing? Collecting? Skateboarding? Arts and crafts? Or how about a club with a cause—want to get a group together to do a neighborhood cleanup or cheer up residents at a local nursing home? Why not start your own club?

Whatever you go for, your club needs members, so get on the horn. Tell all your friends, and tell them to tell their friends. Post colorful flyers on bulletin boards at school and the rec center. On the flyer, announce the startup of your club and attach a piece of paper so anyone interested can sign up to be contacted about joining. Ask for names, phone numbers and e-mail addresses.

Once you've got a list of interested kids, pick a place, day and time to meet (backyard fort, basement, park, or maybe the principal will let you meet in a classroom after school once a week). Then contact everyone on your list and let them know the meeting time—say, every Tuesday from 4 P.M. to 5 P.M.

At your first meeting, you should elect officers. You'll need a president to lead, vice president to assist the prez, secretary to take notes, and treasurer to handle the money. Money? Most clubs need at least a small amount of cash for activities. (You might need craft supplies, for example.) Okay, take a vote. Should your club collect weekly dues or hold fundraisers to rake in cash? Yea? Nay?

The most important part of having a club is to plan stuff and set group goals. Your writing club could start out with haikus and progress to short stories. If your club's goal is to cheer up the elderly, plan to make goodie baskets or make a date for visiting adopted grandparents at the nursing center. But don't lose sight of the most important goal of any club—to have fun!

# The Girls' Life

Guide to

# You

# How Do You Feel About You?

## Self Esteem Stories

You've heard the term "self esteem" a million times. It's talked about on Oprah, after-school specials, drug education programs. Some kids have lots of it, others don't. But what is self esteem? Why is it such a big deal?

Self esteem is how you feel about yourself. Girls with high self esteem feel confident, competent, and valued. They like themselves. Girls with low self esteem feel self-doubting, insecure and, often, unloved. Studies show that girls with high self esteem are usually more responsible, do better in school, and face new situations easily. This makes them feel even better about themselves. The reverse is true for girls with low self esteem, who tend to do poorly in school and relationships, and then feel even worse. It's a big circle. The good news is that we all have the power to improve our self esteem.

Self esteem affects every conversation, relationship, and decision you have. If you feel good about yourself, you're more likely to talk to a teacher about an unfair grade or go out for softball. If you have a low view of yourself, chances go up you'll let friends decide your weekend plans or quit violin lessons because they become too hard.

To see how self esteem affects girls, eavesdrop on the following conversation. Ann, Kelly and Nicole just started at a new school. Ann and Kelly, who've been good friends for years, are discussing tryouts for a play. Sitting behind them, Nicole is enduring her first solo bus ride since her best friend dumped her.

"I'm psyched for the play. I can't wait for the cast party," Kelly says.

Ann mutters, "I'm not sure I'm going to try out this year. I'm just not into it."

"How can you not be into *The Wizard of Oz*?" asks Kelly.

Ann shrugs. "I got my swim schedule and I have tons of practices and meets on the weekends."

"So? Play practice is after school."

"Yeah, but I can't deal with everything at once. Besides, I hate trying out. What if I do something dumb?"

"Come on, Ann," Kelly says, "trying out makes everyone nervous."

"But what if I don't get a good part?" asks Ann. "My parents won't even come unless I'm Dorothy."

"Of course they will," says Kelly.

"You don't know them," says Ann. "No matter what I do, they expect me to be the star."

The more Ann and Kelly talked, the more Nicole felt left out. She wanted to offer suggestions on beating stage fright, but felt weird butting in. "They don't want more friends," she thought. "They have each other." By the time the bus stopped, Nicole felt like crying.

Ann couldn't get psyched about the play because of awful scenarios in her mind. Kelly, on the other hand, didn't care if she was the star. She just wanted to have fun. Nicole was so upset about being ignored or rejected that she was afraid to join the conversation.

Why are some girls, like Kelly, self confident, while others, like Ann and Nicole, are down on themselves? If we're not born with self esteem, how does it develop? High self esteem comes from lots of things—how you've been treated, what goals you've achieved, what failures you've overcome. In the stories of Ann, Kelly and Nicole, you'll see how their backgrounds shaped their self esteem, and what each has done since last year's conversation on the bus. You'll learn how each girl overcame a situation that was making her feel bad about herself.

## ANN'S STORY

Since she was six, Ann has swum competitively. Ann's parents always attended meets and practices. They discussed her progress with coaches and reminded her what she needed to work on. Ann appreciated her parents' interest, but she eventually began to feel they were too gung-ho. "I wanted to talk about something else at dinner," she says. The butterflies she used to get before meets turned into full-blown stomachaches. "I hate that look of disappointment on my parents' faces when I swim badly," she says.

As soon as she saw her new swim schedule, Ann dreaded the first meet. She hated practices, and her school work suffered. "I had to give an oral report in English," she says. "As soon as I saw Mrs. Anderson take out a stopwatch, I felt sick. The watch was just to make sure we didn't go over four minutes, but I felt I was being measured to the hundredth of a second." She decided it was a good thing she'd hadn't gone out for the play.

Ann felt stuck until she saw her sister Meg dealing with the same stuff. Meg asked her parents if she could skip a swim meet for a slumber party. They said no—Meg needed to win this race to qualify for a later competition. Ann blew up. "It's her friend's birthday!" she yelled. "Maybe this party is more important to Meg than a stupid swim meet!" As her parents stared in shock, Ann realized she was voicing her own feelings about the pressure her parents were putting on her. "It hit me that I was swimming to please them," she says, "and it took the fun out of it." Ann realized she wanted to stop competing.

When she told her parents, they said she shouldn't be a quitter. The more they encouraged her to continue, the more she refused. When she told her coach, he asked if she'd help teach swimming to some physically challenged kids. At first, Ann

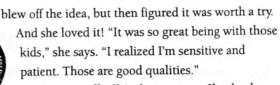

blew off the idea, but then figured it was worth a try. And she loved it! "It was so great being with those kids," she says. "I realized I'm sensitive and patient. Those are good qualities."

Ann put off telling her parents. Slowly, she gathered her courage and took the straight route. "I've decided to do this volunteer work instead of competing," she told them. "Teaching these kids makes me feel great." Ann's parents weren't thrilled, but they accepted it.

Eventually, Ann decided to return to racing—on her own terms. She joined a local swim team that was laid back. After this experience, she feels able to tell people her feelings: "I don't always get what I want, but at least I can ask now.

Once she recognized her real feelings, Ann took steps to reverse her sinking self esteem. Competing to please her parents prevented Ann from doing what she really wanted. She was afraid that unless she won medals, she wouldn't be good enough. Ann needed her parents to value her for who she is—not the champion she thought they wanted her to be. Volunteering helped her see her strengths, which gave her the courage to confront her parents. Ann found a swimming experience that was right for her. It took nearly the entire school year, but by recognizing her needs and talents, doing what gave her satisfaction, speaking up for herself, and resolving a conflict with her parents, Ann's self esteem has soared.

## KELLY'S STORY

For as long as she can remember, school has been Kelly's "thing." She loves reading, writes creative stories, and has a knack for remembering details. Her mom and dad are big on education. "You must be proud of yourself," they said whenever she got a report card. And she was.

So it came as a total shock when she failed a quiz for the first time. Since it was her first geography quiz, she'd had no idea what to expect. "I studied," she says, "but I went blank when I saw the map. I was clueless." She filled in what she could, knowing she was blowing it.

When the teacher returned the quizzes and Kelly saw "58%", she got very upset. Since Kelly was a "brain," everyone compared grades to hers—especially her all-time rival, Jason. When he asked what she got, she pretended it was no big deal. "You flunked?" he asked with a smile. "Too bad." She'd never felt so dumb.

Later that day, the cast for the play was listed, and Kelly had made Wizard. This put her in a better mood. Still, she was wondering what her parents would say about the grade. That night, when she finally told them, she was surprised to find they weren't angry at all.

Jason, on the other hand, became a problem. He was set on making her a wreck. As the teacher passed out the next round of quizzes, he whispered, "Know where anything goes?" She tried to block him out, but it didn't help her jitters.

Kelly got a 75%. After all the extra studying she had done, she was devastated. Her parents took a new approach. They still weren't mad, but they tried to help her figure out why she was having a tough time. They explained that geography tests call for different study methods. Kelly's mom recommended a computer geography game, while her dad taught her memorizing tricks.

But whatever Kelly tried, it didn't work in time for the third quiz. She was stumped again, and for the first time ever, she tried to peek at other people's answers. Finally, she gave up and handed it in. When her friend Ann received a better grade than she did, she felt jealous. "I knew I'd hit a low point," Kelly confides, "I wasn't used to being jealous of others, and I certainly wasn't used to cheating. I was obviously losing it."

Hitting this low helped Kelly return to her senses. "Trying to cheat made me feel worse than getting another bad grade." She decided to beat this problem. First, she bought the computer game her mom recommended and practiced filling in blank maps her dad designed. Slowly, her grade went up. "I had to change my expectations," she admits. "I would have loved a 95%, but when I got an 80%, it was a huge improvement."

The most painful lesson for Kelly was accepting the "bad" parts of herself—like jealousy and urges to cheat. "But as my mom says, we all have feelings we aren't proud of sometimes," Kelly says. "Just because I had nasty thoughts doesn't make me a terrible person."

Even though Kelly had good self esteem, she wasn't immune to a period of self doubt. It took her by surprise, so she felt shaken. But she asked for help and tackled the problem. Kelly didn't let her struggle bring down the rest of her world, and she learned a lot about herself. She had urges to do things she knew weren't right, but recognizing and accepting them made her feel more secure in who she is.

## NICOLE'S STORY

Since she just lost her best friend, Nicole felt weak in social situations. She and Jen had done everything together. Nicole was sure the friendship would last forever. "How was I supposed to know she'd buddy up with the girls on her basketball team?" she asks. Nicole tried to win back Jen, but it was hopeless. She hadn't had to make new friends for a long time, and she was terrified.

Everything felt strange without Jen. It was lonely walking the halls and eating alone. There was no one to pass notes to or sit with on the bus. Everyone else was involved with their own friends. Nicole complained that the kids in school were selfish and unfriendly. Nobody asked her to eat lunch or study together. Her mom was patient, telling Nicole everything would straighten out. She even convinced Nicole to join a youth group. This, however, left Nicole feeling even more depressed, since everyone already knew each other.

What helped finally change Nicole's life was a teacher's comment. When her parents attended the school's open house, Nicole's English teacher told them Nicole was quiet in class. She said whenever she asked Nicole a question, Nicole looked down and murmured. The teacher said it was getting worse as weeks went by. When Nicole's parents reported the news to her, she was shocked: "I've never been quiet in my life!" She watched herself more closely in class and saw her teacher was right.

So Nicole made a conscious effort to use a stronger voice and look at people when she spoke. Classmates listened to her and took her more seriously. She did the same thing at lunch, joining conversations with girls she'd never spoken to. "The first time was terrifying," she says. "I was so worried that they would ignore me when I opened my mouth. But I figured it could not be any worse than sitting there like a statue. When they answered me, it was such a relief."

It was no piece of cake, but making friends became easier. She even went to the school play with a new pal. She realizes her feelings about herself made it hard for her to make new friends. "I told myself that since my best friend dumped me, something must be wrong with me," she says. "I figured everyone already had good friends, and I gave up. I didn't realize I was the one who wasn't friendly. That's why no one wanted to know me."

Nicole's situation is common. Once she decided something was wrong with her, she believed it and acted like it were true. This made her act unapproachable and shy—and people treated her that way. She convinced herself nobody would be interested in being her friend. She behaved in ways that caused the very thing she feared most—not making friends. Nicole took advantage of a teacher's feedback to look at herself in a new way. Rather than blaming others, she recognized her own role in her problem and realized what she could do to change the way she acts. Nicole faced her fear, took a risk, and ended up feeling good about herself.

## RAISING YOUR SELF ESTEEM

**Get to know yourself better.** Listen to your real thoughts, feelings, and needs. Ask yourself, "What do I value about myself?" and "What is important to me?" Determine your special qualities and appreciate them. Recognize that you're honest, compassionate, kind, or funny. Or feisty, outspoken, and opinionated. Whatever you are, you've got unique qualities!

**Stay true to your values.** There will be times when you consider crossing a line, whether it's cheating, lying, or doing something else you know is wrong. During those times, remember that there are always other options. You never have to do something that goes against the standards you set for yourself. So work on picking activities and making choices that fit in with who you are or who you want to be.

**Know your strengths.** Discovering your interests and talents is important. Accept your bad points too. You don't have to be the star of the play or ace every test to feel proud. Maybe you're not musical or artistic or athletic. Some girls feel great about getting along with a sister or making it to the bus stop on time. Others feel good about recycling cans or wearing their retainer two nights in a row. Set realistic goals and work on achieving them. If at first you don't succeed, don't give up—just adjust your strategy. Congratulate yourself when you reach your goals.

**Talk to yourself.** What we say to ourselves is a huge part of self esteem. There will always be people who don't like us and situations we can't conquer. We don't always have control over this. But we do control what we tell ourselves. Whether you interpret situations positively or negatively is up to you—and, therefore, so is your self esteem. When you're in a bad mood, it's easy to think the worst and to talk yourself into thinking you're bad all around. Think positive. Forget "I must be a jerk if she doesn't want to be my friend anymore!" Try "Her loss. It's time to make new friends." Remember past accomplishments, and tell yourself "I can do this!"

**Take nature into account.** Of course, anything is tricky when your body seems so unpredictable. Girls whose hormones, bodies, and even hair appear to change by the end of the day often feel clumsy and out of sorts. You may feel you spend half the day bumping into lockers. It's hard enough to feel cool when you're losing your balance every second. Or you may think you have no friends, and seconds later feel grateful for having such amazing friends. As your mood shifts like the wind, it's often easy to feel downright crazy. The good news is that these feelings are normal. The better news is that they are temporary.

**Add it up.** Self esteem develops and changes over time. You can't feel wonderful about yourself all the time. All that matters is that when you tally up your plusses and minuses, the total sum is a positive number.

**Watch for red flags.** There's a big difference between occasional self doubt and ongoing self hatred. If all you think of is "I just can't do this!" or a ridiculous remark you made several weeks ago, or that everyone seems smarter than you, it may be time to get some help. Dreading getting out of bed and feeling unlikeable are signs of trouble. Thoughts of harming yourself or repeatedly finding yourself in risky situations are red flags that need immediate action. If you feel hopeless about where to start, recognize that it's okay to ask for help. A parent or other trusted adult can find a therapist. It may seem tempting, but don't ask pals to keep your problem a secret. It's unfair to burden them with such a big responsibility. It'll only leave them torn between doing what you asked and doing what is right—getting you the help you need.

# What Kind of Smart Are You?

Think the smartest kid in the class is the one who aces all the algebra tests? Maybe not. Studies show there are many kinds of intelligence. Sure, it's great to be awesome at math and reading, but you can also have A+ smarts in art, music, sports, nature, social situations, or in knowing yourself well. Most girls are actually a combination of two or three types of smart. Take this quiz to learn about your smart strengths. You can circle up to three choices for each question.

1. My idea of a great weekend afternoon is:
    a) curling up with the latest thriller by Lois Duncan. b) rewriting code for my Web page.
    c) sculpting a clay bust of my crush. d) going to an all-ages outdoor music festival with my buds. e) competing in the aggressive in-line skating contest at the new bowl. f) going down to the creek to score some new rocks for my collection. g) going to a party at the new girl's house. h) hanging out in my room by myself and basking in the solitude.

2. When I go to a party, I tend to:
    a) tell the amazing stories of my past summer camp experiences. b) calculate how many pizzas should be ordered to ensure everybody gets at least two or three slices. c) check out what everyone is wearing and how well they're accessorized. d) play the part of disc jockey. e) dance the night away. f) coax everybody outside for some impromptu stargazing. g) make new friends. h) relax on a folding chair and observe the social drama as it unfolds.

3. The perfect gift for my birthday is:
    a) an Amazon.com gift certificate. b) an iMac. c) an easel and some pastels. d) the new Beastie Boy CD. e) a field hockey stick and some shin guards. f) a CD-ROM on oceanography.
    g) tickets to see the latest Julia Roberts with six of my best friends. h) a Heart 2 Heart diary.

4. When a new girl moves into the neighborhood, I know I'm going to like her if she:
    a) says, "Read any good books lately?" b) challenges me to a game of chess. c) unveils a masterpiece she painted. d) plays bass. e) asks me to play some one-on-one basketball after school. f) invites me to tag along on a day hike. g) invites me to her birthday party. h) doesn't pound on my door every thirty seconds.

5. If I'm meeting a friend at the mall and have extra time to kill, you'd most likely find me:
   a) in Barnes and Noble, perusing the fiction section. b) at the computer store, pricing software. c) comparing Rapidograph pens in the art supply store. d) donning earphones at Sam Goody's. e) perfecting my putting skills at the sporting goods store. f) spending my allowance on a butterfly farm at The Nature Company. g) looking for familiar faces in the food court. h) relaxing by the fountain.

6. I'm in the Sweet Tooth candy store. I:
   a) read the descriptions of each confection. b) figure out exactly how much I can afford. c) check out the cool colors. d) sing "Candy Man" to myself. e) open the bins and touch the candy. f) check out all the different categories of candy. g) chat with the lady who works behind the counter. h) buy myself what I want.

7. My favorite school subject is:
   a) English. b) math. c) art. d) band. e) P.E. f) science. g) social studies. h) study hall.

8. More than anything else, my ideal guy would have to appreciate:
   a) the outstanding metaphors in my e-mail. b) that I might beat him at logic games. c) having an occasional lunch in the sculpture garden outside the art museum. d) Mozart. e) ESPN. f) Long walks in the park. g) hanging out with friends—mine. h) sharing our deepest secrets.

9. If I'm working on a group project, I would prefer to:
   a) do the book work and help write the text. b) work out the algebra stuff. c) make a cool poster to go with the presentation. d) create a soundtrack. e) act out the project as a skit. f) research the scientific parts of the project. g) present the project to the class as the main speaker. h) Group projects? Ugh. I work alone.

10. I'm having a sleepover, and we decide to play a game. I'd vote to play:
    a) Scrabble. b) Monopoly. c) Pictionary. d) Simon. e) Twister. f) Trivial Pursuit. g) Family Feud. h) The Ungame.

## MOSTLY A'S: WORD SMART
You're good at reading and writing—you even enjoy them. Plus, you're good at essay tests, cross-word puzzles, storytelling, and word games. You learn best by saying, hearing, and seeing words.

## MOSTLY B'S: MATH SMART
You're a human calculator. People who are math smart are good at solving brain teasers, playing logic and number games, or doing science experiments. You learn best by categorizing, solving problems, and classifying.

## MOSTLY C'S: PICTURE SMART
Do you see pictures when you close your eyes? People who are picture smart are talented artists and have good eyes for fashion. They also are great at jigsaw puzzles, mazes, and reading maps. You learn best by drawing pictures or using visual organizers.

## MOSTLY D'S: MUSIC SMART
Are you always humming tunes, singing, or tapping along to the beat? You may excel at playing an instrument or dream of being in a band. You learn best by putting ideas to music in your head or buying musical tapes that teach math, reading or history.

## MOSTLY E'S: BODY SMART
Making the cut for varsity is a breeze. Dancers and actors are also body smart. Bottom line? You're good at using your hands or body for activities. You learn best by using hands-on materials or by acting out important ideas.

## MOSTLY F'S: NATURE SMART
You probably amaze people by the way you recognize plants, animals, or minerals. You enjoy experiencing and learning about nature. You learn best by classifying items and sorting material into groups.

## MOSTLY G'S: PEOPLE SMART
People always comment on the fact that no matter where you go, you never quit smiling and saying hello to people. You have no trouble mixing with different cliques and love to meet new people. You're probably involved in a lot of extracurricular activities and may be a part of student government. You learn best by working in groups.

## MOSTLY H'S: SELF SMART
You'd rather be far from the madding crowd. You have no trouble hanging out with yourself. Maybe you like to write in a journal, pursue a hobby, or just think. You're the type who has no problem marching to the beat of a different drummer. You know yourself well, and sometimes others come to you with their problems. You learn best by working alone.

Now that you know your intelligence strengths, check out some of the careers that could be perfect for a smart girl like you.

**Word Smart:** librarian, writer, journalist, TV announcer, lawyer, secretary, English teacher. Authors like Maya Angelou are word smart.

**Math Smart:** accountant, mathematician, computer analyst, bookkeeper, pilot, nurse, scientist, astronaut. Scientists like Marie Curie are math smart.

**Picture Smart:** architect, graphic artist, interior decorator, photographer, artist, fashion editor, pastry chef, sculptor. Artists like Georgia O'Keeffe are picture smart.

**Music Smart:** disc jockey, musician, music therapist, songwriter, studio engineer, choral director, conductor, singer, music teacher. Singers and musicians like Jewel are music smart.

**Body Smart:** physical therapist, recreational worker, dancer, actor, mechanic, carpenter, physical education teacher, choreographer, professional athlete, jeweler. Athletes like Monica Seles and Wilma Rudolph are body smart.

**Nature Smart:** naturalist, park ranger, botanist, marine biologist, zoologist, forest ranger, entomologist, wildlife photographer. Jane Goodall, who studied chimps, is nature smart.

**People Smart:** manager, school principal, sociologist, counselor, clergy woman, public relations executive, politician, salesperson, entrepreneur, social director. Secretary of State Madeleine Albright is people smart.

**Self Smart:** psychologist, detective, counselor, headhunter, agent, therapist. Advice columnists like our own Carol Weston (Dear Carol) are self smart.

# Stressed?!?

## Get Organized for a Calmer You

A lot of girls desperately want to get organized. But where to start? Other girls complain that, despite feeling organized, there's hardly ever enough time in the day to do everything.

The reason to get organized is to get control over your life. The best way to do this is to learn to manage your time well, so you can do everything you need to do with as little stress as possible. Don't forget to save time for one key thing—fun.

### "I FEEL ORGANIZED, BUT I NEVER SEEM TO GET IT ALL DONE. OR HAVE FUN DOING IT."

There are some people who are born to follow schedules. They know when to be where and with what in hand. But even the most dedicated clock watchers will run out of time if they don't learn to prioritize. Instead of doing what is most important, a lot of people tend to do whatever is next on their list.

If you find yourself being pulled from one thing to another without a moment to catch your breath, call a time out. How exactly do you spend your time? Are you doing only the tasks you don't dread (other than homework, that is)? Are there new things you'd try if you could find a spare moment? If you answer "yes" to either of these questions, it's time to examine your priorities.

First, figure out the activities you want to do. You may be surprised to find they are not the same as they used to be. If swimming was your thing two years ago, but you now find yourself dreading the pool, it could be time to give up swim team. Those two extra hours will allow you to take up soccer, perfect your watercolor technique, or just put your feet up and read a good book.

When setting priorities, it's important to look at short- and long-term goals. You probably already know how to set short-term goals. Your goal for this week, for instance, may be to get that book report done. Time needs to be set aside, say an hour a day for a week or all day Saturday.

But long-term goals should receive just as much thinking and planning. Whether it's writing your first novel or learning to jump a horse, schedule baby steps to tackle big projects. Week one, you may decide to write one paragraph or pick a riding class. Week two, you could write the first chapter or get all your tack. The key is to break giant goals into manageable chunks.

Another trouble spot for seemingly organized people is underestimating how much time it will actually take to complete the task. It may take only twenty minutes to get the book you need for your report, but don't forget about the time you will spend finding your library card, getting to and from the library, looking the book up, etc. Unless you look at the whole process of what you need to do, you'll lose time and fall behind.

Getting behind is especially frustrating for people who consider themselves on top of things. And frustration can suck the fun and energy right out of the day. The second you feel yourself panic, sit down and take a deep breath. Then set mini goals based on your top priority. "OK, I'll spend the next ten minutes finding my card so I can go to the library." The key is to stay focused on one thing at a time. Face it, if you don't get out of the library in time for aerobics, it's no biggie. Getting your report done is the important thing right now.

But let's say it isn't the 5 P.M. kickboxing class you have to blow off. You have play practice coming up, and if you miss it, your Juliet days are numbered. This is a good time to ask an adult to step in. Why? One, your parents or a counselor will be able to better explain your situation (no one can create a good time plan when they are too frazzled to string a sentence together). Two, they can help you figure out what happened so you don't get too far behind again. Also, if people see you are trying to follow a list of priorities, they are more likely to respect how you spend your time...and you. But "Sorry, Mom, I can't do the dishes because I booked *MTV Total Request Live* from 6:00 to 6:30" won't cut it.

**"I DON'T KNOW WHERE THE DAY GOES. I HAVE TONS OF STUFF TO DO, BUT I CAN'T SEEM TO GET STARTED OR I GET BOGGED DOWN. THEN I GIVE UP AND IT STARTS ALL OVER THE NEXT DAY."**

Procrastination is the single biggest time waster of them all. But the way to get over it is quite simple. To quote Nike, "Just do it." The longer you put things off, the harder it is to motivate yourself to get the job done.

If you're one of those people who find it impossible to get moving, try the following tricks:

First, take five minutes to get simple tasks out of the way. This will give you a quick energy boost and some momentum. Next, think through everything you need to do, in steps. Write down each step and imagine yourself completing it. Focus on how proud and relieved you'll be knowing this task is behind you.

Then, get started. Once you actually begin working, you're far less likely to stop. Some people benefit by taking occasional breaks, but limit yourself. Stretch, run around, grab a snack. Do whatever it is you need to clear your brain. But keep a timer handy, and set it for five minutes. Once you hear the buzzer, it's right back to work. Do not, we repeat, do not reset the timer.

Also, stay away from energy killers like TV and the phone. If you're lucky enough to have a friend who'll give you a quick pep talk, go ahead and call. Just don't lose sight of why you called in the first place.

When you do get the job done, reward yourself. And notice how satisfied you are. Remember this feeling next time you find yourself avoiding something, and remember that you've conquered procrastination before and can do it again.

**"ORGANIZED? I CAN'T EVEN MAKE MY BED."**

For those who rarely (if ever) experience the joys of sticking to schedules and meeting goals, you'll need a basic plan of attack. First, figure out your schedule. Keep a diary for a week, and write down everything you do (well, almost everything). Obviously, patterns will emerge as

**Dear Carol:** I smoke and wear tons of makeup and I know that's not really who I am, but it's hard to change.—BAD GIRL

**Dear Girl:** It is hard to change...but it's not impossible. I applaud you for wanting to change, and I know you can do it. If you were moving or starting at a new school, you could begin with a fresh slate. But even if you're not changing schools, you can still update your style. Behind that makeup and smoke is a good person who wants to come out. Come on out! Think about what you are good at. Soccer? Singing? Science? Spanish? Build on those strengths. Lose the makeup and replace it with a smile\emdash even if it feels kind of forced at first. Ask guys and girls friendly questions like "What are you doing for vacation?" or "Wasn't that test hard?" It may take them a while to recognize the new you, but they will. So hands off the cigarettes and congratulate yourself on having the guts to change.

you pencil in classes, practice times, favorite shows, meals, household chores, etc.

Once you see how you spend your time, figure out how to use it more wisely. Write down how your ideal week would go, hour by hour. Then try to come close to that schedule the next week. Keep checking in with your time diary, and if you find you're blowing your ideal day, write down what interrupted you.

At the end of the week, look over all those unplanned events and decide which time wasters you can kick. It sounds over simplified, we know, but, week by week, you'll be able to actually get more and more control over your life. This is basically what managing your time is about.

Once you have a plan, you can advance to some other tactics discussed before, like goal setting and prioritizing. And like all people looking to make life changes, enlist help from friends, teachers, and parents. They can encourage you and help keep you on track. Just make sure they aren't so used to labeling you the "disorganized one" that they don't treat your efforts seriously.

Last, think about why you're having so much trouble staying organized. Sometimes, well-meaning parents still insist on planning every little detail of your life, even though you're way past needing this. If you're in this situation, now is the time to explain kindly that you appreciate their interest in what you do, but you need to (mostly) be in charge.

Also, consider the possibility that other problems are defeating you. When people get tense, nervous, or upset, they sometimes feel disorganized. What's really happening is that your brain is telling you, "Hey, something is wrong here." If you feel there might be a bigger problem than just clutter, it's time to face it. If you're not sure what the problem is, consider getting some outside help to figure it out. Dealing with the bigger issue can help smooth out the rest of your life.

Now that you've mastered organization, spent your time wisely, reached your short term goals, and made progress on long term ones, what to do with that extra time and energy? Anything you want—which could be nothing at all.

# What Does Your Room Say About You?

Your room—the one place you can kick off your shoes, relax, and totally be yourself. But what does your room reveal about you? Are you a major brainiac? The century's biggest socialite? A way artsy gal? Take our quiz and find out.

1. Going into your room is like:
   a) entering the Smithsonian. It's totally neat and tidy, and everything has its place.
   b) walking through a mine field. It seems pretty organized—'til you open the closet, a drawer, or peek under the bed.
   c) being on a construction site. You have to dodge the piles of clothes just to get to your bed.

2. You have a TON of homework, so you:
   a) head straight to your desk and hit the books. You probably even have some sharpened No. 2s in the top drawer.
   b) flop down on the bed and pop open your math book. If you've gotta do fractions, you may as well be comfy.
   c) spread your stuff out on the kitchen table. There's no decent place to study in your room.

3. Of course, you've gotta have tunes to create just the right atmosphere. When your pals come over to hang, you're most likely listening to:
   a) something from the alternative station like Beck, Goo Goo Dolls or Third Eye Blind.
   b) Britney, 'N SYNC, Backstreet Boys   you never let a Top 10 CD pass you by.
   c) anything. No one's ever quite sure with you—one time it might be your old Pearl Jam CD, another time it might be the Beasties or even some old disco stuff!

4. If you could paint and decorate your room in any color, it would be:
   a) white. You like clean and simple.
   b) anything bright—primary red, blue, green or yellow, or maybe even lime green or hot pink.
   c) more muted, lighter shades like seafoam green, baby blue, lavender or rose.

5. Your bed is:
   a) the place you sleep. It has sheets, a pillow and a warm blanket. What more do you need?
   b) piled high with your most cherished stuffed animals.
   c) accented by lots of colorful overstuffed pillows and a comfy down bedspread.

6. Your parents are gonna let you redo your room and promised the sky's the limit. You:
   a) go for very functional modern stuff a la IKEA.
   b) dress your room up like Rachel and Monica's apartment on *Friends* mixing cool antique pieces with Pottery Barn-like accents.
   c) go retro with blow-up furniture, beads, '60s bubble clock, and black light posters.

7. If you could choose one word to describe the way you feel in your room, it would be:
    a) calm.
    b) happy.
    c) inspired.

8. When you go into your closet to grab a shirt:
    a) it's easy to find what you want because it's in the shirt section right behind the dresses.
    b) you rummage through the hangers 'til you find what you're looking for.
    c) you fish around on the floor, but can't find the tee you wanted.

9. The lighting in your room is:
    a) an overhead light and some strategically placed reading lamps.
    b) natural. You like the shades open to let the sun shine in.
    c) dark and moody, with maybe a lava lamp.

10. The first thing you smell when you walk into your room is:
    a) vanilla flavored potpourri.
    b) CK One.
    c) sandalwood incense.

11. When your friends come over, they tend to:
    a) hang in the den—it's way more cozy there.
    b) drape themselves over your bed.
    c) push your clothes out of the way and make themselves comfortable wherever they can.

12. Wall decorations tell quite a bit about a person. Your walls are full of:
    a) a couple of framed prints by your fave artists.
    b) collages with pics of your family and friends.
    c) posters of the U.S. Women's Soccer Team

## MOSTLY As: SERIOUS AND STUDIOUS

Conscientious and organized, you like to know where everything is at *all* times. You're a good student, practical, and a no-nonsense kinda gal. But, c'mon girl, sprinkle a dose of fun into your life! Add a splash of color with a red or purple bedspread, a couple of brightly-colored pillows, or by "painting out" one wall. Brainy girls choose a bright color, like yellow, blue, or red, and paint one wall of their room with it. Then add a fun, colorful border just under the ceiling all around the room. It will really brighten and open up the room.

## MOSTLY Bs: FUN AND FRIENDLY

You're outgoing and sociable, and everyone loves hanging out in your room. It's nice and comfy with great energy. But try not to go overboard on the "cutesy." A few well-placed knick-knacks, like wacky vases or cool old dolls, can show off plenty of personality. Another way to tone down the busyness of a room is to use simple, tailored bed coverings. A nice duvet cover, dust ruffle, and lots of pillows in light pastel colors can redirect the focus of the room.

## MOSTLY Cs: COOL AND CREATIVE

Because you're imaginative and inventive, atmosphere is everything for you. The mood has to be perfect for you to let the creative juices run wild. Your taste is varied and eclectic. Sometimes, though, you tend to be a bit scattered, and you're not as organized as you'd like to be. Result? A messy room. Shelves and containers from the organizer section of any department store could help you get your stuff together. Also, have plenty of light: task lighting is very important. Overhead light, good reading lamps and a desk lamp will not only brighten up your room, but will also help you see. May we also suggest a good working surface? Like a clean desk (hint, hint) and calm, neutral colors to inspire your imagination.

# Look Out Bill Gates!

## Starting Your Own Business

Allowance or no allowance, we could all use some extra spending dough. There are the cool shoes in the mall window just waiting for you. Or that ridiculously overpriced concert you're dying to go to. Or maybe you just want to watch your bank account fatten. No matter what your motive, there's a simple solution: start your own business.

It's not that hard, really. Just because you don't know the meaning of words like "franchising" and "conglomerate" doesn't mean you can't put together a successful business—and have a good time doing it.

When you think about it, there are only two possibilities: You can offer a needed service to clients or create and sell a product that's in demand. That doesn't mean business will be a breeze. You'll have to be creative, patient, and one hundred percent dependable. In other words, you can't stop running your business one day to watch a *Real World* marathon on TV, especially if customers are counting on you.

As you're reading, keep reminding yourself of this important fact: The most important part of starting a business is choosing something you'll enjoy. Otherwise, why would you want stick to it?

### FIND AN IDEA

You've got to pick a service that you not only like doing but are good at. If you burn waffles in the toaster, you're probably going to be a lousy caterer, no matter how much you love the kitchen.

Happily, most activities we're good at are the ones we enjoy. So jot down some of your favorite hobbies: gardening, taking care of animals, cleaning, baking, going through junk, drawing, whatever. Then write down how each hobby might be profitable. Take drawing, for instance. You might not be able to sell your sketches right now, but that doesn't mean you can't design your own T-shirts. Baking isn't just good for one-time bake sales—you can sell your cakes and cookies to locals who don't have time to bake for their own parties. If you have a green thumb, provide lawn and garden care for some neighbors.

Circle the ideas you think might be needed in your area. For instance, walking dogs is a great city idea, but shoveling driveways for people who live in high-rise apartments is out. Feel free to ask friends and neighbors if they'd be into your idea. Hey, you never know—they could become some of your first customers.

## ASK TONS OF QUESTIONS

Only by asking yourself practical questions will you know if your plan is truly do-able. Think about prices, for example. If you want to sell a product, how much will it take to make it? What selling price would make it profitable? How much would you have to invest to start your business, before any money comes rolling in? How would you get that money? If you plan to offer a service, say, cleaning garages, what do you think a reasonable fee would be? Is there local competition to think about, and how much are they charging?

Also ask yourself whether your service or product is needed. What's the point of offering pet care in an apartment building that restricts pets? Lemonade stands are cute, but that's about all they are. Okay, and will you need others to help? Who would help you? How much would you have to pay them? After paying them, will you still be making a profit that is worthwhile to you?

## SELLING YOUR PRODUCT

**1. Start with a goal.** Let's say you plan to create and sell bead bracelets. Your business plan might be, "I plan to make bead bracelets and sell them for three dollars each. I hope to sell at least five to ten a month so I can pay for a new CD player by this August." Easy as pie, as long as you keep all of your expectations realistic.

**2. Write down reasons your product will be desired.** "All the girls in my school wear loads of beaded jewelry, but it costs a lot at stores. Plus, most girls don't want to make them at home. I'll even let them pick the color combinations."

**3. Determine exactly how you will make your product.** "I will go to the local craft shop twice a month and get clasps, hooks, wire, and beads in lots of colors. I'll pay for this stuff with my allowance or money loaned to me from Mom and Dad. Then I'll spend at least one or two hours a night making bracelets."

**4. Figure out your competition and how to beat them.** "No one at school is making them, but there is a store at the mall that sells beaded bracelets for six dollars. My three dollar bracelet will be an awesome bargain. Plus, my bracelets, unlike store bracelets, will be made to fit the girls perfectly since I will measure their wrists beforehand."

**5. Decide whether you want to ask friends to help.** Either "I'll ask my friend Emily to help and offer her one-third of the profits" or "I think I'd rather try it myself so I won't have to split the profits. If it turns out I need help, I'll ask later."

**6. Consider how you're going to get the word out and get noticed.** "For starters, I'll make a whole bunch of bracelets and wear them around school so everyone can see them. I'll also ask a few friends to start wearing them. Maybe I can even start a trend. If it's okay with my principal, I'll show off my bracelets in front of the lobby after school and put up some signs in the girls' bathrooms and locker rooms announcing when my sale will take place. I'll even spend some time after school going around the neighborhood showing off my bracelets."

**Dear Carol:** I'm 11 and I love to act goofy with my friends. But lately, I've also been wanting to try harder to look better. I've even been buying nail polish. I also want to babysit to make money. But I'm afraid that if I do all that, they might think I'm acting like the snobby kids we don't like. —SILLY

**Dear Silly:** You can be goofy *and* wear nail polish. Your friends may be surprised if you alter your style or start babysitting, but so long as you don't suddenly act snobby, they shouldn't object or feel threatened. Friends don't mind if you grow up—they just don't want you to grow away.

## SELLING YOUR SERVICE

**1. Again, figure out your goal.** "I will have people pay me to hop on my bike and go get them food, videos, stamps, and other small conveniences."

**2. Write down reasons your service will be desired.** "Older people and busy working folks would love to pay someone to buy a few items for them. There are also plenty of people who forget things at the supermarket and will pay me to go."

**3. Advertise.** Put up flyers in the neighborhood and around your apartment or by your house. Place some in grocery stores and video stores, if managers give the go-ahead. Include your name and number. Do not write down your address—it's not safe. List items you're willing to retrieve (perhaps any that fit in your bike pack), times you're available, and how much you charge. We suggest two or three dollars per trip (there and back), more if the store is far away.

**4. Name the competition and how you'll beat them.** "There's no one offering this service in my apartment complex. Some grocery stores deliver but only if the customer orders more than ten dollars worth of groceries. I'll make the trip no matter how much they spend, as long as the stuff fits in my pack."

**5. Figure out if you want to hire others or go solo.** "I'm going to ask my friend Beth if she wants to join me. I'll have to give up some money, but she'll be able to do runs when I go on vacation or get sick. Anyway, it'll be more fun."

**6. Ask yourself if there are ways to bring in more cash.** "I will schedule trips so I can pick up items for a few customers at a time. If things are slow, I'll keep adding more services to my list."

## MORE BUSINESS IDEAS

If you're psyched about getting to work but having trouble sticking to one idea, here are a few proposals. Remember—if you create a good business plan and then your job flops or you hate it, you can quit.

Also, the goal is not to become a 13-year-old Entrepreneur of the Year, although hats off if you do. The idea is to get some experience with business, make some cash, and take pleasure in what you're doing. Maybe you'll decide you're not ready for a business right now. That's fine. Or maybe you'll learn from past mistakes and find a job that's more suitable. Or just maybe you'll find a job you adore and make more cash than you ever thought imaginable.

**Parties for pay.** You and a pal can throw parties for neighborhood children. Make and send invitations, decorate the party room, think of games, create a magic or talent show for them, and clean up afterward. Charge twenty dollars (ten dollars for each of you) for a two or three hour party. Ask parents to pay for all expenses, including postage for invitations. They are paying you for the entertainment and cleanup—make this clear. Also let them know if you need cash up front.

**Seasons greetings.** If you have an artsy side, design your own greeting cards. You'll have to buy plain, solid-colored stationery (buy sheets of paper and matching envelopes in bulk). Fold the paper in half, and decorate the front with paint and colored pencils. Create funny covers with words inside to match, or design beautiful sketches on the cover, and leave the inside blank. Decorate the backs of the envelopes to match. Sell bundles (ten to fifteen sheets of paper and envelopes) tied with ribbon for nine dollars each.

**Feeding green.** If you're not very creative or don't you want to spend lots of energy, there's still a job for you. Water plants when neighbors go on vacation. Find out how often, when and how much they have to be watered. Feed their fish while you're at it. Charge fifteen dollars a week. Charge a little more to feed and walk pets.

## STAYING ON TRACK

Whether you open a savings account or not, it's important to keep track of how much money is going in and out of your business. How else will you know whether your business is successful, needs budget cuts, or is ready to expand?

**Keep two ongoing lists.** Call one "Money Out" and keep track each time you take money out of your business, the date, and cause. If you and your friend are in business together, make sure whoever takes money out of the account initial the entry—every time.

Call the other list "Money In" and list the amount of money as soon as it comes in, the date, and source of money. Keep these lists and the money (if not in the bank) in a closed container in a safe, private place.

Once a month, subtract the total of your "Money Out" list from the total of your "Money In" list to determine your profit. That's how much money should be in your box. If there's more, you forgot to write down one time you made money. If there's less, you forgot to write down one time you spent it. Of course, there should be money in your box—or you've made zero profit. Save all of your paperwork.

Next, set aside some of your profit to pay for the upcoming month's "Money Out" items, which you will need until money starts coming in again. What's left is yours—and your partner's if you have one. Do whatever you wish with the profits. Congratulations, you've just earned your first paycheck!

# Babysitting

## It's More Than TV Dinners & Talking on the Phone

Think babysitting is just about showing up, putting tots to bed early, vegging out with the satellite dish and raiding the 'fridge? Nice try! There's a lot to know when it comes to babysitting—especially if you want to build your rep, keep steady work, and rake in the green.

### ARE YOU READY?

Messy diapers and sticky fingers all over your homework. The teary two-year-old who wants her sandwich cut into triangles—not squares!—and the hyper four-year-old bopping out of bed (for the fourth time) when you've finally settled in. Don't be fooled, babysitting is hard work.

While you may feel more like a traffic cop ("Sit there. Eat this. Don't do that!"), good sitters should be a lot more—friend, teacher, chef, even body-guard. Do you have what it takes to be successful?

For starters, you must enjoy being around kids. That doesn't mean you have to adore sitting with little Johnny in front of *Sesame Street*, but parents hire sitters who like being with children. "It's important to me that Jessica likes playing with my daughters," says one parent. "My girls look forward to the time they spend with Jessica. So I can look forward to enjoying my time out."

Okay, you say. You have the attitude. You're ready to play cat's cradle or catch, make snacks for the "hungries," and read *The Little Engine That Could* thirty-three times. But truth is, truly great baby-sitters aren't just good with kids, they're good for kids. Baby-sitters are responsible for the happiness and health of their charges.

Finally, baby-sitters must be able to get along with their employers—the parents. Mrs. Jones may like her kids tucked in by 8 P.M., while Mr. Smith figures somewhere between 8:30 and 9:30 is cool ("whenever you can get the rascals down"). Ms. White says the kids can have anything their little hearts desire for dinner, while Mrs. Williams insists on tofu and veggies. All parents have different house rules. The babysitting biz requires you to be flexible.

## DRUMMING UP BUSINESS

Before you start eyeballing that new spring wardrobe, you should probably line up some jobs. Some lucky girls inherit sitting jobs from older sisters who move on to bigger and better things ("Would you like fries with that?"), but most of the time you'll be on your own. Get the word out to neighbors, relatives, friends of the family, and teachers. Sitting for familiar people is a smart way to get started. Once you expand, the tips below will help you.

**Advertise.** Put an ad on the bulletin board at your church or synagogue. Your school newspaper might have a section for employment notices. Ask if you can post flyers in your doctor's office.

**Talk to your baby-sitting friends.** Ask them to recommend you next time they get a job offer they can't accept. Of course, this works both ways.

**Check out child care programs.** Your neighborhood elementary school may have an after-school care program for children of working parents. Programs at local park and recreation centers can often use your help working with small-fries. Volunteering can introduce you to lots of prospective clients.

# GETTING STARTED

Parents prefer hiring sitters who've had plenty of experience, but you have none. How can you get some fast?

1) Take a baby-sitting class through the Red Cross, YMCA or local hospital.
2) Check your local library for books and videos about babysitting.
3) Accompany an older sister or brother (with permission) to learn the ropes.
4) Work as a mother's helper. The pay is less because the parent is home, but it's a good way to build skills.
5) Volunteer at a childcare center.
6) Tell prospective employers why you'd make a good sitter.
7) Create a resume. Include your name and number, experience, skills (such as crafts or storytelling), availability, and a few references.

## MONEY MATTERS

"I take what they give me," admits Jackie, an experienced sitter. Setting rates with employers can often feel awkward. What if you announce your rate, and they look at you like you're insane? Or agree so readily you know you charged too little?

Prices vary, depending on where you live, your age and experience, number of children you're responsible for, how late parents will be out, and whether you will be expected to perform other services, such as pet care. Do some detective work to be sure you're setting reasonable fees. What do your friends charge? How much do babysitting instructors suggest?

Once you decide what you want to charge, talk to parents before accepting the job. Ask questions about your responsibilities first. It'll calm your jitters, let you know how hard the job will be, and impress potential employers with your professionalism. Then state your price (do not ask it like a question, eyebrows raised), and see how they respond.

If they feel your price is too high, they'll be the first to say so. Then you have three choices. You can refuse the job in hopes of getting others, compromise for now, or accept less from this particular parent. "I am more willing to take less for the twins around the corner who are well-behaved than for the brother and sister next door who are always fighting," reasons Jessica. And when you have more experience and the parents feel more comfortable with you, you can always ask for a raise.

As a business person, you should think about each job offer. If you think your prices are fair and are unwilling to accept the figure your future boss just offered, politely refuse the work. Good sitters are worth their weight in gold, and you have the right to expect fair payment.

## DOING THE JOB RIGHT

Congrats—you've landed your first job! Begin with a short (no charge) pre-sitting "housecall." Kids are more comfortable with someone they've met and you'll feel more confident. It'll also give the parents time to show you around the house, without worrying that *Chez Paris* will give their table to somebody else.

## CHECKLIST OF IMPORTANT INFORMATION TO LEARN

**Phone numbers.** Post the following numbers by the telephone: where parents can be reached; emergency numbers including the doctor, police and fire departments, hospital, poison control center, and the number of a trusted neighbor. Ask if they have caller ID so you screen calls. Know the address and phone number of where you're at, in case you have to give them in an emergency.

**Locations.** During the house tour, find out how locks work, where phones are (not that you'd be calling your buds or anything), emergency exits and fire extinguishers, first-aid supplies, thermostats, and security systems. Check also whether there are off-limits areas.

**Routines.** Establish bedtimes and learn routines. Do this in front of the children to ensure calm when you tell little Matt you're going to play one last game of Candyland and it's lights out! If Britt must have two cookies, her Barbie pajamas, and a light on in the hall before she can fall asleep, you need to be forewarned.

**Rules.** Most parents will mention anything they feel strongly about, but good sitters ask about rules regarding snacks and cable viewing, and how parents want them enforced. Know how they feel about use of the phone (which should be limited), and refrigerator privileges (unless you crave strained peas, you may want to bring pizza or microwave popcorn for later).

**Pets.** If the Jones' family menagerie includes pets you're allergic to or fear, figure out a game plan ahead of time. Maybe Sparky or Mittens should stay in the bedroom or basement. If the Wild Kingdom is okay by you, find out how Spot does his business and if Blackie gets some late-night Meow Mix.

**Safety first.** Parents are counting on you to spot potential dangers—and handle them. Here are ways to avoid putting that info to use:

★ Know where potential household hazards are, such as electrical outlets and cords, stairs, appliances, and radiators.

★ Ask parents if all medicines and household cleaners are locked up.

★ Never leave children alone in or near a full bath or on a changing table, bed, or sofa.

★ Keep your eyes peeled for small objects children could choke on.

★ Supervise outside play carefully. Watch children on yard equipment, and don't count on them remembering safety rules like "ride your bicycle on the sidewalk."

Your safety is as important as the children's. Accept job offers from people you know or who are referred by a friend. When the parents drop you home, make sure they wait until you are safely inside before driving away. If you need another way home for any reason, like if the dad comes home drunk, call your parents. If that seems embarrassing, develop a code with your folks that means "Come get me." Tell the employer your mom has to run an errand and she'll pick you up.

## READY, SET, PLAY!

You're alone with the kids. Now what? Lindsey, an old pro, suggests starting in kids' rooms. Many kids have collections to show off and favorite activities to share.

The house is a snore? Pity the kids and use what you have. Drape a sheet over a table and make a castle. Staple paper together to make coloring books. Hunt for red things. Be creative!

Jessica brings a "surprise sack" to help pass the time. Some possibilities include books, puppets, balls, cards, puzzles or games, and simple craft projects.

## A JOB WELL DONE

You'll no doubt start your babysitting career motivated by quick cash. But you may soon find the independence, confidence, and friendships you earn to be just as valuable. Besides, what other job pays for finger-painting and chasing bubbles?

# Spender or Saver?

## Discover Your Money Profile

Are you saving smart or spending stupid? Whichever you are, we can help you max your cash. Read on and match your answers to each question with the real life resolutions right below them.

### HOW YOU SPEND

You *had* to have those killer new shoes. You:

a) were desperate so you paid thirty dollars more to get the designer version at the mall.

b) went to the knock-off cheapie shoe store and found a pair that looked just as cool, for twenty-five dollars. Who cares if they only last as long as the trend.

### Resolution for a): Silly Spender

When you want something, you have to have it yesterday! Here are a few resolutions for you:

**1. I'll push myself to be patient.** You're the girl who's gotta have that new skirt to survive. Hold up. Sneak a peek at what you're spending and wait a month for your favorite style to go on sale.

**2. I'll stop spending spontaneously.** You saw those jeans and you bought on the spot. It felt like you'd die if you didn't spend. But it's not worth the money if you can't go for pizza with pals because you spent all of your dough.

**3. I'll shop around for better deals.** You'll find a better deal if you take a sec to look somewhere else. Besides, think of all the awesome things you could have done with thirty-five dollars! A new sweater or pair of shoes could be yours!

### LEARN WHERE THE FREE STUFF IS AT THE MALL

Sure, the folks at Hickory Farms are generous with the meat-on-a-toothpick and dried out cheese that smells like your dad's shoes. But did you know department store cosmetics counters have sample perfumes and lipsticks? Just walk up to a saleswoman who's not crazed with multiple customers and say, "I'd like some sample products and your business card because I'm planning to buy enough for a new look this year." Then make yourself over for free, and buy only what you love.

## GO AHEAD—BREAK THAT PIGGY BANK!

Put all of your money into a real savings account. Here's how:

1. Make sure the bank doesn't charge a monthly fee for your savings account. You should be able to get a free student account without any trouble.

2. Some banks charge a three dollar fee if you don't deposit money every month. And they don't always tell you that when you open your account. Find a place that won't charge you. After all, there will be months (like December) when it just seems impossible to save.

3. Ask them if there are any penalties for withdrawing your dough. Try to find a bank that lets you withdraw without charging you to do it!

### Resolutions for b): Perfect with Pennies

You pinch pennies as well as Grandma. Someone in your family probably taught you to be thrifty with your money. Here are some ways to save a little more!

**1. I'll put away more of the money I save.** Okay, you saved thirty-five dollars hunting around for cheaper jeans. Now feed some of it to your piggy bank or stick the money in your savings!

**2. I'll buy some stuff at the thrift shop.** You always scope for cheap goodies in stores. How about going-where the stuff's *always* on sale? You can find stylin' old school jeans for you and cool presents for your pals. Buy an Atari and have a party! Pac Man anyone?

**3. I'll buy something fun for myself.** Yep, we're giving you permission. You're so careful with money that you rarely splurge on yourself. When you do, you feel bad. Don't. Every so often it's perfectly okay.

### HOW YOU SAVE

Holidays were good to you! Along with a sack of presents, you raked in a hundred dollars. You:
a) took the money to the mall! Yippee!
b) took the money to the bank. Yippee!

### Resolutions for a): Sorry Saver

Some people can't pass up a good shopping spree. But you're minus a savings.

**1. I'll save a tiny stash of cash.** If you've never saved money, it's not like you'll be able to chuck the whole hundred dollars in the bank. So start small. Tuck a few bucks under your bed every time you babysit or have a birthday. You'll have savings faster than you can get that money to The Gap!

**2. I'll get a real savings account.** You know the place that cashes checks and has one of those machines that upchucks the bucks? That place is called a bank. And it's a good idea to put your money there. Just think, if you put in one dollar every week, you'll have fifty-two dollars in a year.

**3. I won't blow my money in one big shopping scoop.** At least slow down. One hundred smackers is a lot of money. Don't slap it down all in one place—or in one day. Don't you need those new sneaks soon anyway?

### Resolutions for b): Super Saver

You'd save your gum wrappers if they were worth a penny. Here are a few more things you can do to save money.

**1. I'll look into getting a checking account.** You're so good with money, you might as well start establishing an awesome credit history now. (And a savings account, but you probably have one!) You may need a college loan when you're eighteen. Or maybe a car. If a bank has known you for a few years, it's more likely to let you borrow it's bucks. (Ask a parent to help you get started.)

**2. I'll scope my parents for more moolah.** If they're into saving money, ask Mom and Dad if they'll consider putting you on a matching program. That means for every dollar you put into your piggy, they'll put in a dollar more. If the 'rents say no, see if they'll put in a quarter for every dollar. Hey, it's worth asking!

**3. I'll invest my stash.** You really can do it right now. Buy things that are likely to be worth money later. Like baseball cards or antique dolls. And if you really want to invest in stock, that's a real possibility too. Write individual companies, like McDonald's and Disney and tell them you're a kid and you want to buy just one share. Usually they'll sell it to you.

### HOW YOU BRING IN A BUCK OF YOUR OWN

You're low on dough and completely desperate. If you don't score more money soon, you'll *never* have those new swim goggles you need. You:

a) ask for a big fat raise in allowance.

b) see if the lady you babysit for will tell all her friends about you.

### Resolutions for a): Buck Beggar

Sheesh, the least you deserve is a bigger allowance. Right? Wrong.

Your 'rents aren't made out of cash and may resent you asking them. Here are some things to tell yourself instead.

**1. I'll make money on my own.** If you can mow a lawn, shovel snow or take out people's trash, you can make moolah. Ask people around the neighborhood if they need help with odd jobs. If you see kids, ask about being their babysitter.

**2. I'll stop asking for so much money.** Handouts are the easiest way to get a quick buck. But don't make parents mad by begging for extra dough. If you have to ask, offer to do more chores and earn the money.

**3. I'll stop spending so much, period.** If you didn't spend you wouldn't need a raise. Cut back on the candy and other things you can live without.

**Resolutions for b): Bringin' in the Bread**

If anyone needs a hand, you're there to lend it—for a price. Business means bucks so here's what to tell yourself in order to make a few more.

**1. I'll work at home.** Your parents know you're a worker and might be willing to give you more responsibility. Offer to do the laundry for a raise. Or start walking the dog. Spending more time with Fido might actually be fun.

**2. I'll be realistic.** You only have two hands and they don't need to work all the time! It's fine to take on more babysitting jobs as long as you can handle your homework. Don't feel bad saying no to a job. Your personal life is important too!

**3. I'll keep up the good work!** Dealing with your money isn't your major malfunction. So don't change too much. You're already awesome with your bucks!

# Get Involved!

## Volunteering and Making a Difference

Community service? Sounds like a hard job for people with nothing else to do with their time. What's the point? It would be like doing (gasp!) work and not even having a new sweater to show for it. But there's a lot more to volunteering than most people know. I'm a typical, semi-active fifteen-year-old who doesn't particularly like to work, especially for, ahem, free. So when my dear mother suggested it, I wasn't too thrilled. But she warmed me up to the idea and the more and more I thought about it, the more fun it seemed.

I don't exactly get cold, hard cash, but volunteering has great payoffs. Of course, it goes without saying how awesome it makes you feel to help others, but there are also practical reasons for volunteering. First, it's a great way to get experience for future jobs. You may have some yard work on your resume, but showing you organized a team of workers to paint over graffiti is pretty impressive. Your future afterschool and summer employers want to know you're responsible, have initiative, work effectively, and can motivate others.

And besides bosses-to-be, school admissions officers look for these qualities as well. Many schools now require community service as an entrance or graduation requirement, but even if your school of choice doesn't, volunteer work on your list of activities sure won't hurt.

But here was my big concern—would it be a total drag? And the surprising answer is no. The trick is to find something you enjoy. At first, there was nothing I really wanted to do. But then I heard about a Brownie troop that needed a helper. I was hesitant since my recent babysitting adventures had left me wanting to pull my hair out, but it was actually great. Twenty-five seven-year-olds can tire you out but, boy, I love those girls.

I've actually been promoted to assistant leader for Troop 1176. I go to meetings and field trips and this past summer we went on a camping trip. What an experience!

### THROW A GROOVIER SLUMBER PARTY

"First, pick a theme and make your own cute invitations," says an event planning director. "The magic to a great party is lots of snacks, good music and having the whole night of activities completely planned. I used to have makeover parties and we'd dye each other's hair with Kool-Aid or henna. And I once had a Pink Potluck Party where everyone had to bring food that was pink. But my favorite was my cooking party where we all helped make three different kinds of pizza." Yum!

We hiked, canoed, and swam. We went fishing and caught more trees than carp. There were tears, injuries, arguments, and even an asthma attack. It was a lot of responsibility, but I can't wait until next summer when we go back.

And I didn't stop there. Whenever I get a chance, I tutor younger kids at school. Some kids fall behind, and there just aren't enough teachers for everybody to have individual instruction. Then I found out the local ice rink needed helpers for skating lessons so I teach a group of beginners. It's so much fun to see the kids stumbling across the rink, having the time of their lives.

I never knew how much help one person could be. If you look around, there's probably community service right under your nose. You don't need to turn into Girl Wonder overnight, but if you're bored and have the urge to help, go for it. Someone will really appreciate it, and it sure beats sitting in front of the TV! Here are some things to remember before starting.

## YOU WON'T BE ALONE

Before you think you're too young to make a difference, consider this: Nickelodeon's Big Help campaign attracts over eight million kids pledging over eighty-five million volunteering hours. That means kids have saved not-for-profit organizations millions of dollars! That's money that can feed hungry people, build homes for the homeless and support the arts. So if you don't think you'll make a difference, you're wrong!

So where do you start? Look right in your community. That nursing home down the street would love you to make friendly visits to a senior citizen. The pet shelter needs people to walk animals. Candystriping (a name given to hospital volunteering because the uniforms are red and white striped) is popular for girls who see themselves as future doctors. Libraries, schools and outreach centers are all waiting for your call.

Many schools have programs to match volunteers with projects that interest them. If yours doesn't, check with your church or synagogue.

**Funner with friends.** My friends and I love to volunteer together. Lots of places are happy to put you and your buds on the same project or schedule you on the same days.

Are you already volunteering but know your friends, as much as they would like to help, are just too busy? Don't count them out just yet. Some times of the year are busier than others, and your organization can probably use temporary volunteers. Ask your coordinator what days they could use volunteers and ask friends to join you then.

**Making time to help.** Do you run from soccer to flute to ballet, only stopping to grab a bite to eat? When deciding where to offer your talents, take into account how much time you have to give. Some projects can be done whenever (say, stuffing envelopes for a museum fundraiser), but others need you to commit to a certain time. If you're super busy as it is, consider doing one time projects. Spend an afternoon cleaning a park, or devote the two weeks you have between soccer and basketball to organize a coat drive for needy kids. Even if you don't have tons of time, you can still help in a big way.

**Put your talent to work.** Once you make the decision to volunteer and find the time, the next problem just might be picking from all the choices you have! No matter what your talent or interest is, there is a way to use it to benefit someone else. Love cooking? Volunteer at a soup kitchen. Great at sports? Help coach a tiny tots softball team. Are you a math whiz? There is a kid at your school who needs a tutor. Everyone from budding artists (organize an art supply drive for a low-budget school) to writers (read stories to kids at the public library) to computer geniuses (teach basic skills to people just entering the work force) can use their gifts to help others.

**Let your family help you help others.** While you may need the 'rents to give you a ride to your volunteer job or pay for some extras (those bags of chocolate chips for your bake sale add up), don't count out tackling bigger projects as a family. I know families who "adopt" other families around the holidays—families that might not have a Christmas dinner or any presents or even a tree if someone didn't help. And if you have a great idea about how you want to volunteer but know you need adults to cut through the red tape, get you an interview with a recruiter or fill out some complicated paperwork, moms and dads (or even aunts and uncles) are great for that. And, hey, it's a great way to spend some quality time together. —BRITT BELLINGER, 15

**Dear Carol:** Help! I have a terrible problem. I lie too much. People say, "Be yourself," but I always want to impress people. Whenever I meet new people, I start lying and I can tell that they believe me most of the time. —LIAR

**Dear Liar:** More important than impressing people is making friends, and friendships thrive on trust. Since you know lying is a problem, make today the day that your start telling the truth. You say people believe you most of the time. But that means that occasionally they see right through you—and your claim to be a descendant of a Russian heiress or a movie star's secret flame. Save your dignity by reining yourself in, and save your imagination for a creative writing workshop. (Note: If a buddy says, "Does my haircut make me look like a dork?" and you think it does, say, "No." That's not being dishonest; that's being polite.)

# How Well Do You Cover
# Embarrassing Situations?

1. You're walking down the street and your crush sees you fall flat on your face. You...
   a) blow it off. It doesn't matter if you're a klutz. If he really likes me he won't care.
   b) get up giggling and say, "I meant to do that."
   c) pretend you are sick the next day, and for the next two months avoid him in the halls.

2. You're bra shopping with your mom and your crush sees you. You...
   a) make a fuss, pretending your mom's picking one out for herself.
   b) duck behind a clothes rack hoping he didn't see you.
   c) casually continue as if he weren't there.

3. You're daydreaming about your crush. Not knowing it, you walk into the boy's locker room and there's your crush in his boxers. You...
   a) pretend you have amnesia and say "Where am I? I'm confused."
   b) turn beet red and run into the wall on your way out.
   c) stand there in a daze, then start giggling.

4. You're with some of your buds at the pool and you see your crush there so you go over and say hi. As you're talking you keep backing up and back right into the pool. You...
   c) come up sputtering for air in four feet deep water (and you're five feet tall).
   b) stand up and say, "I meant to do that."
   c) jokingly pretend your friends pushed you. (They're on the other side of the pool.)

5. You're talking childishly to your crush on the phone. Your brother puts you on speaker as your parents walk in the door. You...
   a) hang up immediately and apologize the next day.
   b) keep talking; you have no idea.
   c) know what your brother's doing, so you say something you NEVER would in public.

6. You're caught in a parking lot with your dad singing an oldies song. You...
   a) sing along with him. You always sing together.
   b) duck behind the nearest car pretending you're not with him.
   c) continue walking with him without saying a word.

7. You hop off the bus as your dad pulls up. He rolls down his window and shouts loudly, "Hi Princess! How was your day Sweetie?" You...
    a) get back on the bus. This isn't your stop.
    b) run as fast as you can home. You don't know this weirdo.
    c) yell back, "Hi daddy! My day was juuust peachy!"

8. You're at your first school dance and everyone's giving you funny looks because there's a roll of toilet paper trailing behind you. You...
    a) run into the bathroom and wait for the comfort of your friends.
    b) pick it up and blow your nose.
    c) say, "Hey you never know when you're going to need it!"

9. It's your first date. When he walks in, your dad says, "Okay kids, where are WE going tonight? You...
    a) run out the door with your date and later apologize about your psycho uncle.
    b) tell him your dad was repeatedly dropped on his head as a child.
    c) make some introductions and quickly leave.

10. At the pool, your bikini top flies off in front of the most popular girls at school. You...
    a) take a deep breath and pretend to sink.
    b) grab your top, quickly go under water and put it on.
    c) cover yourself and run to the bathroom crying.

## SCORING
1. a-3, b-2, c-1
2. a-1, b-3, c-2
3. a-3, b-2, c-1
4. a-1, b-3, c-2
5. a-3, b-2, c-1
6. a-3, b-1, c-2
7. a-3, b-2, c-1
8. a-3, b-2, c-1
9. a-3, b-1, c-2
10. a-2, b-3, c-1

**25 - 30 points:** You cover up bad situations quickly and with humor. They may not always be the best, but you can't expect too much. You are not easily embarrassed. Congrats.

**15 - 24 points:** You're doing okay but you could use a little work. Keep at it. Not everyone's good at this stuff.

**9 - 14 points:** You are easily humiliated and don't handle embarrassing situations very well. You need a lot of work.

**0 - 8 points:** You are VERY easily embarrassed. Take a dive and try to cover up better. You have a hard time handling these kind of things, but that's life.

# Express Yourself

## The Joys of Journaling

Here's a simple way to have fun, improve your writing skills, and learn about yourself journaling. The great thing about a journal is that it's filled with personal choices. Your journal can be a place to record daily happenings, a creative forum, an outlet for your emotions, and a place for poetry, lists, quotes, artwork, and anything else you choose. Your journal can be a fancy leather diary, a binder filled with loose-leaf paper, or an inexpensive spiral notebook. You can write in your journal every day, on special occasions, or just whenever the mood hits. You can keep your work private, or you can share it with others. Every journal (and journal keeper!) is unique. Here are five journaling activities to get you started:

**1. Write about your personal philosophy.** Don't have one? Well, it's time to get one. Sit down and ponder some of life's most difficult questions in your journal: Who am I? Is my life meaningful? What is my role? What are my goals, and how can I achieve them? You don't have to know the answers immediately; in fact, you don't have to know any answers at all. The main point is to think deeply about each question, and open yourself up to new possibilities. Don't censor what you write—just let the words flow.

**2. Keep a dream journal.** Dream journals are one of the most fun types of journals and are also very useful windows into the subconscious. Dreams often contain rich symbolism and hidden meaning. A dream journal is a place to tap into the hidden meanings of your dreams. First, place your journal beside your bed along with a pen or pencil. Repeat in your head the phrase "I will remember my dreams" before you go to sleep at night. As soon as you wake up the next morning, while still in your sleeping position, try to recall your dreams from the night before. Don't be discouraged if you can't remember your dreams at first. Even if you can only remember fragments, write them down. Your dream will probably become more and more vivid as you write. Also, don't worry about grammar or spelling during the writing process. There are many useful dream dictionaries that can help decipher the messages in your dreams. An especially good dream guide is *Dreams Can Help* by Jonni Kincher.

**DECORATE YOUR ROOM WAY COOLER... FOR NO MONEY**

Is your room a shrine to everything you loved in first grade? Making your room look more like you starts by packing away the toys you don't play with anymore. Next, display snapshots of you and friends in the crease of a dresser mirror, on the night stand, in collage frames on the walls. Another middle-school decor tip: Tear out pictures you like from magazines (trim the jagged edges) and tape them on a wall in a cool collage. And don't overlook yard sales. Sure that wood dresser is ugly, but just about anything looks great after a few coats of white paint. Then, pick some flowers for your night stand. How Martha Stewart of you.

**3. Write a letter...to yourself!** Once a year, on a special occasion like your birthday, write yourself a letter. In this letter, reflect upon the past year, state your goals for the upcoming year, and simply remind yourself of who you are and what you want from life. The following year, read your last letter and write a new one. This is a great way to keep track of how you and your goals have changed. There are many other types of letters you can write to yourself. Write one to be opened upon graduating from high school or when you get your first job. The next time you are peeved with your parents, write a letter to yourself that can be opened when you become a parent. In the letter, record all the things you like about the way your parents raise you and all the things you absolutely hate. That way, when you're ready to have your own family, you'll remember what you found helpful and what kind of parent is just plain annoying!

**4. Start a travel log.** If you enjoy traveling—or even if you've never left your state—a travel log can be a great way to record your thoughts and feelings about new places. Take your log with you on vacation to pass time while in the car or on the plane. If you rarely travel, you can use your log to write about a cool new restaurant, book store, or even something new in your own backyard.

**5. Make a collage journal.** Cutting pictures from magazines, newspapers and postcards, or drawing them yourself, you can create a journal of your hopes, goals and fears. Use artwork and poetry to make a collage of who you are now, how you think others see you, or who you want to be one year from now. For example, if one of your goals is to get in shape, cut a picture of a fit body from a magazine, attach it to your journal, and paste your head onto the body. Wish to become more friendly? Draw a picture of yourself with a big smile surrounded by lots of things you love. You can add your favorite inspirational quotes or jokes for a special touch. Be creative! Whenever you feel lazy and unexcited about life, look back at your collages for motivation. Now that you have some great journaling ideas, get started! Journaling is something that can be done all your life, doesn't cost a dime, and can be a source of creative ideas to be used in all areas of existence.

—SARAH STILLMAN, 15

# The Girls' Life Guide to

## Your Body

# Whose Body Is This, Anyway?

"Mirror, mirror, on the wall, who's the fairest of them all?" You must have something to say about that. After all, you've been spending huge hunks of time in front of the ever-truthful looking glass.

Who is it you see staring back? Is it a girl who's—well, you hate to brag and all, but—darn good looking? Decent, but not about to grace any fashion magazine covers? Clearly uncomfortable even peeking into the mirror? While we're at it, is the girl you're seeing the same one that other people see?

Well, sure, your eyes are probably picking up the same image. But how does your brain interpret the info? Is the image getting distorted in your brain? It all has to do with body image—the way we perceive and judge our appearance. Part of forming your body image comes from comparing the vision you see in the mirror with the way you think you should look. Most of us have fairly strong opinions about which features are ideal; unfortunately, few of us think we possess these features. It's no wonder so many girls look into the mirror—and sprint away in sheer frustration.

When's the last time you heard a pal say, "You know, I'm happy just the way I am."? Have you ever heard anyone say it? It almost never fails: If you think your friend's freckles are cute, chances are, she sees them as revolting. Petite girls long to be tall. Brunettes think redheads are great looking. Busty girls would kill for a lanky bod. And so on.

Some of it we can blame on human nature. We want what we can't have. But feeling good about yourself has to be based on more than having a certain look. What makes someone attractive cannot be pinned down to eye color, hair color, or height. It's about how a girl carries herself, her attitude, her sense of style. So why is it so hard to believe that—dare we say it—we might be beautiful?

## SAY HI TO THE MEDIA

Here's a quick way to mess with your self-image. Sit through one or two shampoo commercials, take in a romantic comedy, or flip through a fashion magazine. "Yikes," your mind reels, "am I supposed to look like that? Because if that's normal, then I'm not even on the charts."

Like it or not, the media—TV, magazines, movies—constantly shape our ideas about "perfect" looks. Why else would companies spend 650 million dollars every year on advertising? Ads tell us what companies want us to believe: If we just use their products, we'll be prettier, richer, slimmer, happier. Then, in an effort to find this promised land, women spend 20 billion dollars per year on cosmetics! Obviously—and much to our disadvantage—ads work.

Girls dole out heaps of cash on conditioners, mousse, razors, wax, deodorant, mouthwash, and sprays. According to Wendy, 12, "For a year, I was petrified that someone would say I had b.o.

Some days, I'd sniff my armpits every hour just to make sure my deodorant was working."

Says Maggie, 12, "It's so depressing seeing girls my age in magazines. Their skin is rosy, their hair is just right, their bodies are amazing. I know I'll never look like them." Maggie is also the first to say that she spends the bulk of her allowance on beauty products.

The worst thing about ads (other than the bucks we shell out because of them) is that we believe their messages. We believe we're too hairy, our teeth are too yellow, and our faces too round. How's a girl supposed to feel okay? There's only one thing you can do: Ground yourself in reality. The next time you find yourself envying girls in magazines, ask yourself, "Who looks like these women, other than the women on the pages next to them?" Then, ask yourself if you really want to set your beauty standards based on the way top models (less than five percent of our population!) look. It's like comparing your bank account to Bill Gates'.

Here's something else to ask yourself: If there really were a perfect look, why would the media keep changing it? What's "in" changes in the blink of an eye. Dying your hair ultra blond is all the rage. Then red hair is "it." Next, glossy black. Hope you didn't dye it, because then skunk stripes are the look.

Hey, just think of how models' body shapes have changed in a few years. We saw tall and curvy (thanks, Cindy Crawford), followed by skinny "waif" (hi, Kate Moss), followed by the athletic, toned "*übergirl*" then back to skinny again. Who can possibly keep up?

The good news is that we don't have to let society—ads in particular—dictate what's acceptable. The more informed we stay about how advertisers rely on our inse curities, the better we can decide for ourselves what to think. We can determine how to look, what products we think are necessary, and how to spend our money wisely.

## HELP, MY BODY IS CHANGING

As if it weren't frustrating enough comparing ourselves to media beauties, here comes puberty. Your body is suddenly staging mutiny. Enter acne, body hair, growth spurts, hips, oily scalp—it's a nightmare.

**Q:** I wake up in the middle of the night with the worst leg cramps!

**A:** Cramps are common and often run in families. They can be associated with exercise or heat, but most often there doesn't seem to be any real cause. To decramp, stand and stretch your leg out, flexing the foot up as if you're pulling your toes toward your shin. While adult athletes sometimes cramp from lack of potassium (bananas help that), there isn't much you can do when it's your turn to ride the charley horse—sorry, aspirin or Advil won't help.

Bessie, 13, recalls, "My first pimple was horrible! My mom said she could hardly see it, but to me, it was a foot tall!" Says Terry, 10, "I wake up early every morning to wash and dry my hair, but by the time I get to school, it's flat and oily again." Alexis, 12, adds, "I can't wear my favorite sweater anymore. It clings to my chest and looks all weird."

And it's not like no one's going to notice. Girls can wreck each other's confidence without uttering a word. Karen, 11, was the first girl in fourth grade to wear a bra. "I put it off as long as I could, but my mom said I had to start wearing one. I felt like a freak," she admits. "Especially in gym. I could tell the other girls were staring at me."

Morgan, 12, describes similar humiliation. "The boys didn't even try to hide it, they looked constantly at my chest. I wore sweatshirts all the time, even on hot days." It's tough being the first or the last to experience body changes. Alicia, 14, is coping with the latter. "Everyone in my class has a chest, even if it's small. I've got nothing. All my friends say, 'Don't worry about it.' Easy for them to say!"

Truth is, just about everyone around you believes she looks freaky. Standard thinking is "Everyone must be looking at me and thinking how skinny (or squat or pimply or unattractive) I am."

Marion, 13, says, "Last year, I was the only girl in my group who didn't make cheerleading. I thought it was because I was the ugliest one." This year, she sees things differently. "I wasn't ugly. I was really shy and quiet."

"Yeah," some of you are thinking, "but attractive people never have to deal with this." Think again. Aileen, 12, is nothing short of exotic with her jet black hair and green eyes. She is forever receiving compliments and admiring stares and has even done some national modeling. According to Aileen, being exceptionally pretty is not all it's cracked up to be. "I moved to a new school recently, and the girls were so unfriendly," she says. "I had no idea why. Later on, I found out they thought I was going to be snobby before even saying hello. It happens all the time."

Andrea, voted Best Looking in junior high, says, "All anybody thinks about me is that I have this great body. No one sees me as the girl who plays flute or made honor roll." She also complains that people always treat her as if she were older. "They expect me to know things I don't. It's not my fault I look older," she says. "I just want to be normal."

## NO NEED TO BE RUDE!

At some point, most girls get teased about something in their appearance. There's not a lot we can say to make it better. Just remember that rude comments usually come from those who don't feel okay about themselves.

When girls make fun of you for being "too something," it's often out of jealousy. Think about it. Girls who are content with themselves don't need to put down others to feel good. When boys make fun, it's often because they're dealing with their own confusing feelings. Seeing your physical changes may spark feelings in them they probably aren't ready to handle, so they just go on the attack.

No matter who's doing it, it stinks to be the butt of someone else's joke. You're torn between pretending you didn't hear the person and strangling him. Ignoring might work, since kids usually get bored and give up when they see they can't get to you. But if you've had it, feel free to take a stand. Look him in the eye and say, "You're being obnoxious." And then walk away. There's not a reason in the world to stand there and listen to anyone who's making you feel badly.

Then there are the relatives. We're talking about family members who constantly poke fun and then nudge us with an elbow as they whisper, "Lighten up! It's a joke." Few of us forget the "just-a-jokes" about our huge feet, klutziness, chest size, or Dumbo ears.

Anna, 12, reports, "Last year our whole family got together during spring vacation and again after school ended. At the first party, my cousin Wendy looked like me. At the second party, she looked all curvy like my mom. Some of my aunts and uncles made jokes about what kinds of vitamins her parents must be giving her. Wendy didn't think it was too funny." Anna, on the other hand, has to deal with cousins who call her "surfboard," "sunken chest" and other annoying names, thanks to her curve-free body. For a while she put up with it. But when it got on her last nerve, she told them enough was enough.

You do not have to grin and bear it when relatives make fun. As soon as it starts, tell them firmly to stop. They need to know their comments are hurtful.

## WHEN THE FAMILY FREAKS

One more giant annoyance is when family members (usually Mom and Dad) refuse to admit you're growing up. Meghan, 12, says, "In my family, we don't talk about these things. I'm the youngest and only girl. When I talked to my mom about buying a bra, she said *I* wasn't ready. *She* wasn't ready."

Parents aren't blind, but some have a hard time with the fact that their daughter is growing up. By ignoring your changes, they're probably just trying to postpone your becoming a teen. Or, parents may have had a tough time with puberty themselves. By refusing to see you as you are, they may wish to forget their own painful memories or spare you from having similar experiences. It's not easy, but if you talk openly to them about your feelings, it'll help open their eyes.

## WHAT'S RIGHT FOR YOU

What's important is that when you look in the mirror, you're happy with what you see. Maybe you're not the "fairest of them all" and won't be strutting the catwalk, but who cares? What you look like doesn't guarantee happiness anyway. Many girls with average looks lead adventurous and exciting lives, while supermodels can be downright miserable. So, for those who recognize your beauty despite a flaw or two, hat's off!

If you see a reflection of a girl that's attractive but could stand a change or two, go ahead and make them. It may be as simple as getting a new haircut. Or buying an outfit in a color that best brings out your eyes. Or standing a little straighter. Have fun experimenting with styles and accessories. Just because you try out a new look doesn't mean you're stuck with it. Decide what you like about your looks, and compliment yourself freely. Hey, while you're at it, compliment your friends. It's a sure bet they're dealing with the same self doubts and could use the boost.

## DON'T FORGET TO ASK

Some changes might call for parental permission, such as buying your first bra or shaving your legs. When you decide you're ready, ask your mom or dad if they can spare a few minutes. Tell them what you think you need to do and why it's important to you. They may surprise you and say yes. If not, ask them to think about it before insisting no. They may need time to accept the fact that you're growing up. If they still say no, try enlisting another trusted adult.

Paula, 12, sought her aunt's help. "I wasn't getting anywhere with Mom," Paula says. "I was the only one in gym with hairy legs, but she said I was too young to shave. Finally, I talked to my aunt, her younger sister. She talked to my mom and helped my mom see how important shaving was to me. She finally okayed it."

**Q:** What's mononucleo-sis? Is it really from kissing?

**A:** Infectious *mononucleosis* (better known as "mono") is a viral disease...and, yes, you can get it from kissing because mono can be spread through saliva. What are some symptoms? Mono usually brings on a fever, sore throat, swollen glands, and extreme fatigue. Usually, the only treatment necessary is lots of rest. Mono is pretty rare, so don't worry about kids all over school being infected. But here's the real bummer—the virus can hang in the throat up to a year after symptoms clear. Hey, holding hands is nice!

Last, learn to accept that there are limits to what you can alter. Wishing for things you can't have (an extra five inches or new eye color) is a waste of time.

As Shelly, 13, puts it, "It's the only body you're going to get, so you might as well live peacefully with it." And remember, you do have control over the important things—like being the kind of person you are. Granted, being attractive looking can make life easier, but girls who feel good about themselves are the ones who end up with the truly fulfilling lives.

# Are You a Klutz?

Show us a girl who says she never makes a spectacle of herself, and we'll show you a liar. All of us (even Miss Almighty Popular who never seems to lose her cool) stumble over carpets, drop our utensils, and walk into telephone poles. However, there is a difference between suffering the occasional mishap and—hmmm, how shall we put this?—being a *total klutz*. How do you know if you fall into the "klutz" category? The quiz below should take care of that. But first, a word of hope: If you don't score as well as you'd like, don't despair. We'll give you the scoop on why this is going on and what you can do to survive your klutzy phase (two words, friends—protective gear).

*Circle the answer that sounds most like the one you might give.*

1. When your friend asks where you keep the Band-Aids, you answer:
    a) "Last time I nabbed one, they were in the medicine cabinet somewhere."
    b) "Uhh, I don't think I have that CD."
    c) "There's a couple on my left knee. I named 'em 'Itchy' and 'Scratchy.'"

2. The last time you took a header into a school locker was:
    a) Probably before *Toy Story* came out.
    b) You mean before lunch or after?
    c) Last week, after I hyperventilated during band practice.

3. Could you recognize a splint?
    c) Recognize one? I could design one.
    b) A what?
    c) Yeah, I had to wear one once after my bro left his skateboard on the stairs.

4. Have you ever seen the school nurse?
    a) Sure, I stopped in there one time to get a Q-Tip.
    b) A nurse goes to school here?
    c) Puh-lease! The nurse keeps a bed on reserve just for me.

5. The last time you bowled:
    a) I broke a league record.
    b) I dropped a bowling ball on my foot.
    c) I dropped a bowling bowl on someone else's foot.

6. You are often asked, "How many fingers am I holding up?" T / F

7. You find yourself face-to-face with the floor at least once a week.  T / F

8. Everyone takes cover when you enter the room.  T / F

9. You've been booted off the ice rink for "reckless skating."  T / F

10. You've considered wearing a helmet while playing Monopoly.  T / F

## SCORING
*Give yourself the correct number of points for each question, and then add them up for a total.*

1. a) 2  b) 1  c) 3
2. a) 1  b) 3  c) 2
3. a) 3  b) 1  c) 2
4. a) 2  b) 1  c) 3
5. a) 1  b) 2  c) 3
For 6 through 10, give yourself 1 point for each True, 0 points for False.

**5 to 9 points:** Prima ballerina, figure skating champion, Olympic gymnast—the world is your oyster. You have the balance of Dominique Moceanu, the grace of Michelle Kwan. Sure, you might suffer the humiliation of falling off your chair once in a while. But all in all, you've been blessed... enjoy. If nothing else, the survival tactics that follow hopefully will help you sympathize with less fortunate peers as opposed to busting a gut laughing at them.

**10 to 15 points:** You've pulled your fair share of mortifying moments, and you're no stranger at the pediatrician's office. Maybe you've been known to trip over a sidewalk crack or two, bang your head on a door frame, or get entangled in the phone cord. You know what it's like to be the butt of the joke, but you're in no excessive danger. Check out the tactics on the next page to help you survive your occasional foibles.

**16 to 20 points:** Okay, look around to make sure there's nothing breakable or pointy near you, and then sit down *very carefully*. Do not get up, or even move, until you finish reading every word of our survival tactics. These survival tips are created especially for you, and all we ask is that you heed our advice and take it easy for the next few years. Watch where you're going, and please, remember to wear protective gear.

## SO, YOU'RE A KLUTZ. NOW WHAT?
So you just found out you are an official klutz (no surprise, you have the battle scars to prove it). What's the deal? Just a year ago, you had the balance of a cat. Now you're lucky if you can make it down a flight of stairs without being hospitalized. What's up?

For one thing, your bones are growing more quickly than usual. The average girl begins major growth spurts at ten and a half years old, and the fastest growth spurt tends to hit between eleven and twelve. (For some, it starts earlier, and later for others. So don't panic if you're not scraping the ceiling yet.)

As your body grows, proportions change. Maybe you're putting some weight on around your hips, chest and thighs. Some girls put on as much as fifteen to twenty pounds in a single year as they (ugh) go through puberty. Your feet get bigger, and it may seem they're never ever going to stop. They will.

Says Allison, 13, "Sometimes I feel like I'm wearing clown shoes, and I want to scream, 'How can I walk in these?'" Adds Julie, 14, "I can barely walk these days, much less clear the kitchen table. If I drop one more dish, my mom is totally going to kill me."

You used to be able to squeeze between tiny areas, but your hips are now taking up extra space. Your chest knocks over store displays (or maybe you have no chest at all) and your feet kick over anything not nailed down. It takes time for your brain to adjust to your new proportions. So it's no surprise you're clumsier.

## 10 EXTRA SURVIVAL TIPS FOR KLUTZES

1. Avoid sports that involve movement.
2. Remember: Glass is your enemy.
3. Stay clear of batting cages.
4. Tape whiskers to your nose; hey, it works for cats.
5. When walking onto a stage, don't be afraid to ask for help.
6. Avoid any recreational activity with a "downhill" version.
7. Only carry unsharpened pencils.
8. Invest in a large bib.
9. Remind yourself ice is slippery.
10. Always keep a spare tourniquet in your locker.

Also, you are probably more preoccupied. Suddenly, you're dealing with a bunch of firsts—bras, zits, guys, periods, locker combos. As your brain gets more crowded, it gets harder to focus on other incoming info—like the glass door you're about to walk into.

The good news is your exasperating condition goes away—or at least eases up. (Some of us do wind up on the higher end of the klutz scale.) And, as your body catches up with your foot size, your coordination tends to resurface. The bad news is that, like a pesky little brother, there's not much you can do to remedy things right now. You just have to wait for harsh times to pass. Stock up on gauze and keep your head up. Other than that, the best survival tip: Keep exercising something you can't break—your sense of humor.

One of the worst parts of becoming a klutz is the daily ridicule you're forced to endure. As if nursing scraped elbows and bumped knees wasn't bad enough, now you must tend to your battered ego as well. Nothing makes a kid snicker more than seeing another kid take a header into a soccer net.

If you burst into tears or freak out, you're positively doomed. The trick to making a speedy recovery is this: Make the joke before anyone else does. Say you drop your lunch tray in the middle of a crowded cafeteria. Instead of fleeing for the exit, find a friend sitting across the caf and yell, "Sara, you're right. Tater-tots don't bounce!" Sure, you might get a weird look or two, but you will no doubt get some giggles too. And at least now you have people laughing with you, not at you. Hey, it beats spending the afternoon crouched silently in the bathroom stalls.

So make jokes and laugh often. Keep reminding yourself this too shall pass, and take the elevator instead of the stairs wherever humanly possible. Other than that, stay chill, avoid hammering and never let 'em see ya sweat!

# "Ideal Bods"

## Wishes vs. Realities

Think changing your body type would make life a breeze? Maybe you've thought, "I wish I were curvier," "I wish I had more muscular legs," or "I wish I were taller."

Perhaps you've wished for the opposite features—a waif-like figure, thin thighs or a chest that barely needs a training bra. It would seem to be the answer to all your problems. Even though we've all been told to accept the features we were born with, a secret part of us continually longs for a spontaneous physical transformation. Well, it's time to hear the truth from the mouths of "the perfect."

### 1. THE WISH: "I WANT TO BE REALLY SKINNY!"

**The Assumptions:**

★ You can eat as much as you want.

★ You'll look like a glamorous model.

★ You can wear anything, even string bikinis.

★ You'll get all the drop-dead cute guys.

### The Reality: Caroline's Story

What could possibly stink about being naturally slender? Caroline, 12, is happy to tell you. She's been rail-thin since she can remember. "It hasn't been a plus," Caroline says, "believe me." She says she eats all the time, but because she never gained weight and filled out like her older sister, her mother thinks something must be wrong with Caroline. So her mother obsesses about feeding her.

Caroline is sometimes forced to sit and finish meals while her sisters go do fun stuff after taking only a few bites. She feels pressured to eat, knowing how nervous her mom gets if she doesn't. And, no, she doesn't get to eat ice cream sundaes for every meal. Because she's so thin, her mother makes extra sure Caroline eats nutritious, balanced meals and doesn't fill up on junk food. "Sometimes, she makes me drink these gross shakes—the ones for old people."

Caroline gets picked on, too, for being super-skinny. Kids call her everything from "Skin-and-Bones" to "Twiggy." "People think they're so funny," she says, "like this boy in fourth grade who kept saying, 'Turn sideways and stick out your tongue—you'll look like a zipper.'"

But perhaps most annoying is constant teasing from relatives who, Caroline feels, should be more sensitive: "I never get through a family occasion without somebody asking me if my mother feeds me." During holiday dinners, aunts and uncles give her heaping portions of stuffing or pie, saying it will "put meat on your bones." Sometimes, Caroline confesses, she wants to scream, "Leave me alone!"

Now that she's in middle school, Caroline's even more self-conscious about her figure. She wants to look more like her friends, who've developed curves. Boys don't help by treating her as one of the guys. "They act like I'm their little sister and drool over girls who have chests." And the insinuation that Caroline has an eating disorder hurts even more. "People think I'm anorexic," she says. "I'm not, but I feel like I have to prove it."

You're probably thinking, "So what's so bad about being able to down as many candy bars as you want without the worry of weight gain?" Caroline says, "Yeah, I guess that's an advantage. But how many candy bars can one person eat? They get disgusting after a while, and all that chocolate makes me feel sick."

The best thing about being skinny, Caroline thinks, is fitting easily into tight spots like airplane seats and movie aisles. Eventually, she will get a figure. And she's convinced her shape will be a bonus in the future. Her mom, who also was naturally thin as a teenager, has found it a piece of cake to keep trim as an adult. "That's pretty good, I guess," Caroline says, "something to look forward to."

**The Nicknames:** ★ Bones ★ Stick ★ Scarecrow
★ Chicken Legs ★ String Bean

## 2. THE WISH: "I WANT A LARGE CHEST!"
**The Assumptions:**

> ★ You'll look great in your Speedo.
> ★ Guys will tie up your call waiting.
> ★ You'll model for Victoria's Secret.
> ★ You'll be treated like an adult.

**The Reality: Nell's Story**

Nell, 14, is the first to admit she got more than she hoped for. "I used to pray for something to stretch my training bra," she confesses. "I was sick of people teasing me about my 'mosquito bites.'

But all of a sudden I grew about two bra sizes. And that's when the problems started." What could be bad about being voluptuous?

Well, for starters, Nell finds it hard to buy clothes that fit well. "Everything is made for small or average-sized girls," she says, "so on me, it pulls across the chest." She and her mom never used to argue about her wardrobe, but now shopping's an ordeal. "Whatever I think looks cool, my mom thinks looks sleazy. I hate to admit it, but things that look great on my friends do make me look trampy."

It's not hard to imagine the torture Nell goes through with guys. "They stare down at my chest all the time," she says, "which is so humiliating. Sometimes they make these weird noises or rude comments. Like I'm not supposed to notice!" So Nell has taken to wearing huge workshirts or sweatshirts to hide her chest. Although she knows the outfits aren't flattering, they are concealing. "And gym's a nightmare," she confides. "When we do the mile run, I'm always worrying about my chest bouncing."

When a guy talks to her, Nell wonders, "Is he interested in me or just my chest?" Recently she has discovered another sticky situation—guys think she's older than she is. Says Nell, "Some guys come onto me like I'm already in high school. Like I'm really gonna go to a senior party!" Since she's just entering high school, Nell doesn't want to have to deal with this stuff yet—it's way too uncomfortable. "Why can't I be normal?" she asks.

*Cantaloupes*

But the good news is her pals are catching up. "One of my friends told me about this place for bathing suits where I could get one size top and another size bottom. It's great!" Nell has found other stores with clothes that are stylish and fitting. "And I guess it's not so bad," she says, "because sometimes I like the fact that I look kind of curvy. I have a body kind of like my favorite actress, Winona Ryder."

**The Nicknames:** ★ Dolly Parton ★ Twin Peaks ★ Hooters ★ Cantaloupes

### 3. THE WISH: "I WANT TO BE PETITE."
**The Assumptions:**
   ★ You'll always be cute.
   ★ People (especially guys) will always take care of you.
   ★ You'll have awesome clothes and adorable shoes.
   ★ You'll be a great gymnast or ice skater or dancer.

## The Reality: Ari's Story

"The worst thing about being 4-foot-10 is being the butt of really annoying short jokes," says Ari, 13. Aside from the usual nicknames, Ari has heard more than her share of wisecracks like, "Hey, how's the weather down there?"

Asked about the pros and cons of her height, Ari finds it easier to list the disadvantages. When she was younger, she found it hard to go to carnivals with friends. "You have to be a certain height to go on some rides," she says. "I was too short and felt stupid." People often treat her as if she were younger than she really is. "At camp," she describes, "some girls were talking about a scary movie and said, 'Don't say that around Ari. She's too little, and you might spook her.'"

*You must be this tall to go on this ride.*

**Munchkin**

Ari also finds it hard to keep up in athletics. When playing lacrosse, for example, her friends assure her that the only reason she can't run as fast as they can is because her legs are shorter. And (is this starting to sound familiar?) it's hard to find clothes. As Ari says, "The junior clothes are too long. I don't like clothes in the children's department. But the things I like aren't proportioned right for me."

It wasn't easy for Ari to think of the good parts about being short. But she did confess to using her height as an advantage from time to time. "I occasionally save money—they'll charge me the child rate for movie tickets and never even ask." Like Caroline, she can weave her way through tight spots. "I'm able to push my way to the front at general admissions concerts," she says, "but I have to be careful because I can get smushed."

**The Nicknames:** ★ Shrimp Cocktail ★ Little Bitty ★ Short Stuff ★ Munchkin

## 4. THE WISH: "I WANT TO BE MUSCULAR."
### The Assumptions:

★ You'll be a sports star.
★ You'll have a washboard stomach a la Madonna.
★ You're the picture of good health.
★ Not an ounce of flab is visible on your entire body.
★ Nobody will pick fights with you.

### The Reality: Morgan's Story

"I don't get why people want to be muscular," says Morgan, 12. "It's so annoying." She credits being on swim team with building up her muscles, but she comes from a long line of muscular people. In other words, she was pretty much born this way. One of the hardest things, she believes, is people assuming she's a jock. "Then they get mad when I don't score in basketball or I let the puck get by me in hockey." Truth is, Morgan's a great swimmer—but just okay in other sports.

Ever since she was little, Morgan looked a bit different from other girls. "I never had stick legs," she says. "My calf muscles were always big." But Morgan still struggles with being "bulkier," as she puts it, than her pals. Morgan has to remind herself that her contours are muscles rather than fat.

And there's the issue of weight. Even though she knows muscle weighs more than fat, "I still feel awful whenever some girl talks about how much she weighs. It's always like twenty pounds less than what I weigh. It makes me feel like a giant." The comments she gets, of course, are less than kind. "Boys are always saying stuff, and that makes me mad," Morgan complains. "Like asking me if I can bench press fifty pounds. And once some guys dared each other to challenge me in arm wrestling. Sometimes I feel like just showing them, but then they'll treat me like a boy. I want to be like every other girl."

Morgan is starting to realize that boys tease her for one reason—they're jealous! She's strong, she's in shape, she's everything they want to be. But girls often assume the same thing. As Morgan says, "During the summer, my friends all went to the lake, and we were talking about doing sit-ups for stomach flab. Katie asked me why I would even worry about stuff like that. But just because I'm muscular doesn't mean I don't have to work to stay in shape." Morgan takes comfort in reading about models and athletes who sport muscular bodies and exercise to stay in top form.

**The Nicknames:** ★ Incredible Hulk ★ Popeye ★ Sumo Queen ★ Arnold ★ Bulky

So, maybe you're surprised to learn that these supposedly fantastic figures are actually a royal pain for those who have 'em. If you've been using up your birthday wishes, throwing all your pennies in the pond, or hoping like mad for a certain must-have look, maybe you've been wasting your time. Trust us—it's better to accept the body you've been given and make the most of it.

Whether you're tall or short, muscular or wiry, you'll look and feel better if your body is toned by exercise and nourished by nutritious food. But no matter what, it's truly your attitude that counts most. Girls who give off vibes of not being proud of themselves (eyes peering downward, slouched-over posture) make people uneasy—a total turn-off. A cheery personality and great smile can transcend any body type. You only look your best when you feel awesome.

# Your Period

## Questions & Answers

Some girls would pay money to get their periods. They long to catch up to friends and get on with growing up. For others, "that time of the month" means cramps, counting cycles and zit cream. Either way, you probably have questions about this somewhat taboo subject. And since asking can be embarrassing, we've rounded up answers to commonly asked questions.

### How frequently will I get it?

Plan on getting your period approximately every twenty-eight days. However, while your body is still adjusting the first year or two, don't be surprised if your cycle is out of whack. That's perfectly normal.

### How long will my period last?

It's hard to say. It could be only two days but might be up to eight. Lots of times, a girl will have a light period one month and a long, heavy one the next. This variation is especially noticeable when you first start getting your period.

### How much blood will I actually lose?

Although it may seem like a lot, it's probably just a few spoonfuls—a cup at the very most.

### What does it feel like?

Some hardly notice, while others experience a slight ache in the belly. Also, most girls get clear body signals it's coming: Your chest may feel swollen, and you may feel bloated since your body is retaining water. Many also have a tendency to break out big time.

### Can I exercise and play sports?

Yes, yes, yes!

### Don't some girls get cranky or sad?

No doubt. Many feel emotional before and at the beginning of their periods. For some, this means being cranky (like yelling at your brother for being a boy). For others, it means being on the verge of crying over microscopic things (like bawling because half of the darn bag of popcorn wouldn't pop). It's all related to hormone changes and is part of PMS (premenstrual syndrome).

### What should I do?

If you feel blue, remind yourself there's good reason. Spend time alone—walking, reading, listening to music. Exercise can also help lift your mood. Or hang out with understanding buds. Do not go around acting like a lunatic, blaming it on PMS.

### Will I crave chocolate?

When *don't* you? Lots of females say their cravings for chocolate or salt do skyrocket just before and during their periods. Some curb the craving with raisins or pretzels—others find that a forty-two-pound box of bonbons does the trick.

### What about cramps?

It's a rare woman who hasn't dealt with cramps at least once. While they can be uncomfortable, they usually taper off after day one or two. For most, cramps are noticeable—but not enough to ruin the day.

### What if mine are severe?

For relief, soak in a warm bath. Some say raspberry tea helps or rubbing your belly lightly. Also, there are over-the-counter medications, such as Midol, for this very purpose. If you're having monster cramps every month, you may want to have a gynecologist prescribe something stronger.

### What should I wear when I get it?

There are only two choices: a pad or tampon. Pads fit on top of the crotch of your underpants. They're soft and absorbent, and usually have a plastic covering on the bottom to prevent leaking. There is also a sticky strip that keeps the pad attached to your underpants. They come in different thickness sizes, depending on how heavy your flow is.

Tampons, made of a cotton and rayon blend, are shaped like a lipstick tube so they will fit inside you. Many come with a throwaway cardboard or plastic applicator to make inserting it easy (directions are in the box). All have a string at one end for easy removal, and come in different sizes depending on your flow.

## Which is better?

It's up to you. Some prefer pads, which are easier to use and don't require insertion. Tampons are less bulky, however, and invisible when you wear a leotard or swimsuit. Also, you'll definitely need a tampon if you plan on swimming. By the way, tampons may seem confusing to use at first, but they do get easier—and, no, they do not hurt.

## What if I never ever get my period?

You will.

## What if I get my period at school?

Every nurse has a supply of pads in her office for this situation. It's no big deal—nothing to be embarrassed about. If you've bled a lot, call your mom (if she's home) and have her bring you some clean clothes.

## What if I bleed through the back of my pants and all of the kids in my school see it?

If you're wearing a sweater or sweatshirt, take it off and tie it around your waist to cover the spot. If you're wearing a skirt, turn it around so the spot is in front, and hold your bag or books in front of it until you get to the bathroom. If all else fails, try the oldest trick in the book: Ask another girl to walk behind you until you get to the bathroom.

Once you're safely inside, rinse out the spot, let it dry and then put your skirt or pants back on again. In the future, you may want to keep a spare pair of underwear or jeans in your locker, just in case. Finally, try to wear dark-colored skirts or pants when you're having a heavy flow. That way, it's harder for others to see if you do stain them.

## What if I'm in a place where I just can't get a pad or tampon?

No biggie, just ask a fellow female for one. If that's a bust, fold a thick layer of toilet paper to form a pad, and place it in your underpants. Be sure to wrap it around the crotch of the underwear to keep it in place. Worse comes to worse, think socks and bandannas.

## What if I go to buy pads or tampons and I know the check-out guy?

Of course, if you have a choice of stores, you can shop elsewhere. If that's not an option, ask your mom or older sister if she'll pick up the supplies. Or, decide to not be embarrassed. After all, most of the teenage and adult women in town buy these products, so chances are, the boy deals with this all the time. If he's cool, he won't say a thing about it. If he's a jerk about it, who cares what he thinks?

# The ABCs (and Ds) of Bras

When it comes to getting breasts, there are two camps of girls. One group smiles, "Hallelujah, I'm a woman! Would you look at my beautiful curves!" The other freaks, "Ick, I look like a woman! Would you look at my disgusting curves?" Seeing your upper bod totally grow before your very eyes can bring out some mighty strong feelings—and a whole slew of new wonders and worries. How do you know when you're officially ready for a bra? What if you don't want one? What if you wish you had more to fill it out? We know you've got lots and lots of questions. The good news is that we've got the answers.

### I want a bra but I don't really need it. I just want it! Everyone else has one.

A lot of girls don't want to be first or last for anything, and you may feel that wearing a bra would help you feel like you fit in with the crowd. Check out the options at the store and approach your mom, explaining that you would like to buy a bra. You can even suggest a training bra, which is a first-timer's bra for those who don't necessarily need one yet.

However, for those of you who don't need a bra and are happiest in cotton tees, don't worry about doing the bra thing. You'll have plenty of time to wear one later.

**Q:** I have sweaty hands even when I'm cold. I tried powders and lotions, but nothing works.

**A:** Excessive sweating, called *hyperhidrosis* in the medical world, usually doesn't pose serious health problems...but it can be embarrassing when holding hands with Captain Crusho. Since powders and lotions don't work, you should see a doctor about getting a special antiperspirant for the palms of your hands. This medication is applied weekly, covered by plastic wrap and left on overnight.

### I want a bra but I don't know how to approach my mom about it.

The best approach? Be straightforward. Talk about how you feel. If you want a bra so you can feel like part of the crowd, admit it. You might want to drop a hint such as, "I noticed that Meg and Taylor are wearing bras now. I was thinking that maybe I should too." If talking it over with your mom feels truly impossible, try approaching a grandmom, aunt, even your older sister. They've all been there, too. If you're totally stuck, talk to your doctor on your next visit. She can help you sort things out and possibly even approach your mom for you. And give it time. This is a transition for both you and your mom. She is used to thinking of you as a little girl and it may be overwhelming for her to realize you're becoming a young woman.

**Do I need a bra even if I don't have my period?**

It depends, really. Although it's true that your chest development is linked to the same hormonal surge that brings on your period, it's quite possible that you'll start to grow before you get your period—or vice versa.

**My mom wants to buy me a bra but I don't want one and don't think I need one. I'm happy with undershirts.**

Has your mom noticed some changes that you might not have? While many girls wait anxiously for any signs of puberty, some girls just have other stuff on their minds. So take an honest look and see if your mom might be right. Are you bouncing around? Are your clothes still fitting right? Chances are you aren't alone. Look around your school and you'll probably see that quite a few girls are going through changes, too. If you still want another opinion, ask a friend what she thinks. And then give bras a try.

## BRA FITNESS
### *How to Tell You've Got the Right Stuff*

You're fairly sure you have the right frame and cup size but something doesn't feel quite right. There is one word that should describe any bra no matter what your chest size—*comfortable*. You have to wear one every day and you better make sure each and every one of them fits so well you'll forget it's even there. Well, almost.

**Fit problem #1: I'm spilling out.** Cups that are too small need to be larger (and vice versa) but changing the cup size can also change the band size. The C cup on a size 36 is the same as a B cup on a 38. If you go down a band size, you'll go up a cup size. So try going a step up and down on the band and cup size to get your perfect fit. And don't forget about half sizes and "nearly" sizes from makers like Playtex.

**Fit problem #2: My band is riding up in back.** Your bra band is too loose, your cups are too small, or both. Try going up a cup size or down a band size. Don't forget, a large bust needs a wider, closer fitting band than smaller busts to provide proper support.

**Fit problem #3: My straps are sliding off my shoulders.** The easiest thing to do is tighten them up using the adjustment on each shoulder strap. If you have very narrow shoulders or if they slope, look for more sports bra type cuts that have wider straps placed closer to your neck.

**Fit Problem #4: My straps are digging into my shoulders.** Your band is too loose or your cups are too small. If your bust is larger, you also might want to look for a bra with wider straps.

**Okay, I'll get a bra, but I'm not going to buy one in public.**

First off, you have nothing to be embarrassed about. Just about every woman you know wears a bra, and bra shopping is a normal part of life. Also, if you run into girls from school, you can console yourself with the knowledge that they're there for the exact same reason you are. That said, some girls would rather not have a salesclerk screaming for a price check while half the drama club is in the next line.

One way to go is to shop at places where you know you won't run the risk of seeing anyone else. Says Pam, 13, "Once I knew how to pick my size, I would go to someplace I don't ordinarily shop and get whatever I wanted, knowing no one would see me running in and out of the dressing room with ten bras in my hand."

Emily, 14, makes it a point to get fitted for her growing bra size when she is on family trips. "There is a fancy mall where we go on weekends and my Mom and I tell my dad and my brother we'll meet 'em in an hour and I can go get fit again. No one knows who I am out there so I can buy whatever."

If you truly can't deal, ask your mom to buy a few bras on her next run to the mall; then try them on and have her return those that don't fit. Or, better yet, order by phone from catalogs like J. Crew or check out Victoria's Secret online.

**Victoria's Secret! I don't want a lacy bra with all the wire and stuff!**

No problem. You don't need to jump right in and do the lace and underwire thing. Try a sports style bra. It will give you the support you need without looking too frilly. There are tons of different styles out there. There are bras without straps, bras that hook low in the front or back, and bras that have straps placed either really wide or really close to your neck. It's all about what makes you feel most comfortable and confident.

**My breasts are two different sizes, I'm not kidding! Nothing fits.**

This is totally normal and nothing to panic about. Many girls and women have breasts that are different sizes. It's not unhealthy or freaky or even worrisome. Styles that have cups made out of stretch fabric can give you a better fit. But to get a true fit, you need a half size, something not a lot of bra makers have. One who does is Playtex. They offer Thank Goodness It Fits bras in Nearly A, Perfectly A, Nearly B, and Perfectly B sizes.

**I can see my bra right through my shirt, what gives?**

If your bra is white and so is your shirt, it can show through. If summer is around the corner, you also might notice that some of your shirts and dresses won't always work with the bras you have. Fortunately, bras come in all kinds of styles and colors, and lack of choice should never be a reason not to get dressed in clothes that make you feel good. Lots of bra styles come in nude colors that match your skin. With a little smart shopping, there shouldn't be anything in your closet that you can't wear.

**All my friends are so much bigger than I am.**

And, they'll be the first to tell you, that's not always such a good thing. Girls with big breasts often feel just as shy and awkward as you do. Just like some girls are way taller than you, everyone develops at a different rate. What you have now won't necessarily be what you have forever. In the meantime, appreciate how great your new body looks now and make the most of what you have.

**I want to stuff. Do you think it's a good idea?**

Stuffing horror stories abound. It never seems to fail that the day you break out the box of Kleenex is the day your crush falls on top of you in a freak cafeteria accident and a winter cold's worth of tissues goes flying out in front of the entire school. Your best choice is to make peace with the figure you have. Realize that there are lots of styles you can wear that bustier girls can't. You're also able to run and jump without tons of extra support. If you really want to pump up the volume a bit, look for a lightly-lined style that will provide a bit more shape.

**Do those bust-enhancing creams work? What about exercises?**

Do those bust-enhancing creams really work? If they did, our fingers would be too greasy to type. No, they don't. What they do, according to one beauty insider, is temporarily plump the skin with heavy moisturizers or make it tingle by adding refreshing ingredients. As for boosting your bust, most of the exercises you are referring to actually build up your back muscles or the muscles that lie underneath the chest, called the pectorals. Exercise is a great thing to do for your body but it won't do a darn thing for your cup size. The easiest way to make the most of what you've got is to stand up straight, walk tall, and stop toe-gazing when you're headed down the hall. Good posture makes everyone, and everything, look better.

## SIZING THINGS UP

Your bra size is made up of two parts. The first is a number—your frame size (30, 32, 34, etc.). The second is a letter—your cup size (A, B, C, etc.). To figure out yours, take a tape measure and measure snugly around your ribs, just under your bustline. If the measurement is on an odd number, add 5. If it's an even number, add 6 (for example, if you measure 26 around, that's 26 plus 6, so you're a size 32). Total them up and that's your frame size. Next, wrap the tape around your body again, this time measuring at the fullest part of your chest. Do this standing up straight, checking in a mirror that the tape is level. Subtract your original frame size from this measurement. Then check the chart below to figure out your cup size:

| Measurement Difference | Cup Size |
| --- | --- |
| The same as your frame size: | AA |
| up to 1" larger than frame size | A |
| up to 2" larger than frame size | B |
| up to 3" larger than frame size | C |
| up to 4" larger than frame size | D |

**This guy who sits behind me in English thinks It's totally funny to snap my bra. How do I make him stop?**

Next time he does it, turn around and give him a wedgie. Okay, just kidding, sort of. This guy is an immature loser. Cate, 12, found this retort effective, "Do that again and those fingers are going to be gone." Janie, 14, says, "I've learned just to say, 'Cut it out' in a firm tone of voice. That usually stops them." If you feel comfortable with your teacher, you can always threaten to get her involved. Worse comes to worse, ask to have your seat changed or wear a sports style bra. But this creep needs to change his behavior, not you.

# The Straight Talk on Braces

"Brace Face," "Metal Mouth," "Bird Cage"…not so funny when these terms of torment apply to you, huh? You just found out you're about to get wired, or maybe you're bracing yourself (sorry, couldn't resist) for the future possibility. You have tons of questions. But first, we'll tell you this: Most girls say braces really "aren't so bad"—and they're definitely worth grinning and bearing. And now some answers to the rest of your questions:

**Why do I need braces?** Well, your teeth are crooked and need straightening. But there are several possibilities. You may have 1) buck teeth: your upper front teeth stick out farther than your lower ones 2) an overbite: your upper front teeth cover your lower ones more than halfway 3) an underbite: your lower front teeth overlap your upper front teeth when you bite down 4) over-crowded teeth 5) too much space between your teeth.

**How do I know if I need braces?** See an orthodontist (an "ortho," as girls call them), a dental specialist whose job is to check out your teeth to prevent and treat the problems listed above. During your visit, the doc will do a full scale exam with X-rays.

**When should I go to an ortho?** Many girls have their first visit when they're about seven, when permanent front teeth come in. At that point, the ortho can start predicting problems you may have with your jaw and teeth. The quicker you address the problem, the less time you'll have to wear braces. The average age girls get braces is ten or eleven.

**How long will I have to wear them?** There's no definite answer, because everyone's teeth are different. However, the average amount of time is eighteen to thirty months.

**Do they hurt?** Okay, we won't lie to you. Your teeth will probably feel sore for a few days after you get them. As Lindsey, 15, says, "They hurt at first, but after three days, it gets much better. Just take some Tylenol." Orthos also recommend you rinse with warm salty water and stick a bit of wax over any trouble spots where the braces wreak havoc with your gums (you'll get a free sample of wax). And, except for occasional soreness after tightenings, you'll hardly notice your braces after a week or so.

**Tightenings?!?** Don't panic. The braces are training your teeth to position themselves a certain way. Every so often, your ortho needs to tighten the brackets to make sure they're still doing their job. It's all pretty quick—and, again, fellow braces wearers recommend post-tightening Tylenol and soft foods like applesauce, pudding, oatmeal, pasta and soup.

**Is my social life going to be over?** Hardly, especially since so many other girls wear braces. Says Christina, "After a while, you forget you have braces. They just become a part of who you are." Many readers say braces must be cool if Gwen Stefani sports them. As for getting teased, you have little to worry about. As one veteran said, "Who cares? I'm going to have awesome straight teeth when they're off!"

**How much are these brackets going to set back the 'rents?** You may have to wear them, but your folks are bearing the bucks burden. The whole ordeal, including all the visits, is approximately three to seven thousand dollars. So don't forget to smile at your parents—a lot!

**Do I have to get silver braces?** No. In fact, the coolest thing about braces is the choice of colors. "Some people just pick metal," says Amy, "but I pick a different combo of colors each time I go." Kayla picked "purple, my favorite color," and Mary Kay "got clear, so they aren't so obvious." You could get yellow, orange, pink, gold, sapphire, bright purple, or green. If you want to get festive, you can even add sparkles to braces. The price does go up with color, especially sapphire, made of the real gem, which costs one to two hundred dollars more.

*Grin and Bear It!*

**Is there anything I won't be able to eat?** There are definitely some no-no's. Orthos recommend staying clear of foods that are hard, sticky, or chewy, since they tend to snap the wires or loosen the brackets. In other words, say buh-bye to caramel, taffy, peanut brittle, hard candy, and the like. As for gum? "I had gum one day, and the bracket fell right off," says Casey. Also, be careful with carrots, apples, and other crunchy fruits and veggies.

**What about the nightmare of food getting stuck in them?** It happens. Aukey, 13, and Skittles, 14, say, "Getting food stuck in your braces is the only really embarrassing thing." They say it's especially gross to see "green broccoli and red tomatoes mixed together." What can you do about it? Carry around a toothbrush, and use it after every meal. Ask one good friend to clue you in when there's a particle on your braces. A small pocket mirror doesn't hurt either.

**What is headgear?** Headgear, or a "night brace," is a brace that connects to your braces with a strap that goes around your head. It's used to correct a jaw that sticks out too much or not enough. The bad news is that you'll basically look like Saturn (the planet with the rings, not the car). The good news is that it's usually only worn at night.

**Q:** Can I gain weight in a way that is healthy? I look like a toothpick.

**A:** Eating a balanced diet and leading an active lifestyle are key. But the secret to winning at weight gain is to take in more calories than you burn. You may need to add to those "three square meals." Eat substantial snacks between meals—crackers and cheese, veggies and dip, peanut butter and celery. During meals, pick calorie-rich foods that provide protein, vitamins and minerals—breads, beans, milk, cheese and yogurt. You can also add fats, oils and sweets, but be moderate.

Here are some tips on "maximizing each mouthful." First, use milk in place of water in hot cereal, soups and sauces. When brown-bagging it, add avocado, cheese and dressing to sandwiches. At dinner, mix extra cooked meat, wheat germ, nuts or cheese into casseroles and pasta. Unlike your slimming-down sisters, don't shy away from calorie-dense drinks like milkshakes, appetizers like brie, creamy soups and mayo-based salads, and sides like mashed potatoes. Oh, and don't skip dessert!

**How about a retainer?** The retainer is a plastic appliance made to fit your teeth. Some girls only have to wear one on their top teeth, but others have to wear retainers on both top and bottom. They have a single wire that crosses in front of your teeth. Most kids wear them after having their braces removed, just to make sure their new straight teeth stay in place. The best part is that you can master the "360 degree", a technical skill in which you use your tongue to flip that baby around in your mouth.

**What's the good news about having braces?** What else? The gorgeous pearly whites you'll have for the rest of your life. Just be sure to wear those retainers.

# Seeing the World

## Through Rose-Colored Glasses

My Autograph? Of course, dahling.

So you just found out you need glasses, or maybe you simply suspect your face will need frames sometime soon. One obvious clue: Your face is so close to this page you could lick the ink. If you do need glasses, there's no reason to freak out. Being a four-eyes can be fashionable since there are loads of cool styles. Think of them as an accessory for your face. Some of you may be considering making the switch from glasses to contact lenses but fear sticking foreign objects in your eyes. You have questions. We have answers. Read on—with adequate lighting, of course.

### How do I know if I need glasses?

Well, obviously your best bet is to get a proper eye exam from a trained professional, if you're not having your eyes checked regularly at school. If any of the symptoms below feel familiar, you may want to ask mom or dad to make you an appointment with an eye doctor.

★ Trying to read the blackboard is like trying to read a fortune cookie message at the bottom of a pool from the high-dive board.

★ Objects you see are blurry, as if you were running by them at top speed.

★ You're nicknamed "Mr. Magoo" because of all the squinting you do.

★ If you cover one of your eyes with your hand, you actually see better.

★ You keep mistaking your boots for your cat, Blackie.

### How can I tell if I'm nearsighted or farsighted?

If you are nearsighted, reading this book is no problem, but everything gets blurry when you try to look at something far away, like a scoreboard at a sporting event. If you are farsighted, it's the opposite. The words on this page may be swimming before your eyes, but you can easily make out the words on a poster all the way across the room.

**I know doctors check for 20/20 vision, but what does that mean?**

It means your eye sees at twenty feet what a normal eye can see at twenty feet. If your eye can see much less than what the normal eye catches from twenty feet away, you'll probably get hooked up with glasses.

**I was told I should see an eye doctor. But one person told me to go to an ophthalmologist and another suggested an optometrist. What's the diff?**

We know they all sound the same, but there are major differences. An ophthalmologist is a medical doctor (M.D.) who is trained to diagnose and treat all disorders of the eye. An optometrist is a licensed professional who examines eyes for vision problems and eye disorders and prescribes corrective lenses. Then there's an optician, who makes or sells eyeglasses and contact lenses according to an ophthalmologist's or optometrist's prescription.

**Say I find out I do need glasses—will I look like a dork?**

Do you think Lisa Loeb looks like a geek? Jodie Foster? Jennifer Aniston? Janet Jackson? These are just some of the celebs who have turned eyeglasses into fashion over the past couple of years. We're not sure which of these women even needs glasses to see better, and which simply bought them to look cool. But looking smart today means looking glamorous—and it's about time!

**But I'm not a celeb!**

When girls find out that they're going to wear glasses, their very first fear is being labeled "four eyes." But the reality is that most girls today have no problems with teasing. There are so many styles and color choices, you can pick ones that bring out your best features! According to Ashley, 13, "Sometimes my friends even try to fake that they need glasses just to look cool!" Jenna, 15, says, "I have really cool black glasses with pink tints, and now all of my friends want them."

**Will I have to quit playing sports?**

Absolutely not. If you look around, you'll see all sorts of hockey, football, and basketball players donning sports glasses. The frames of these lenses are made of a stronger, more durable material to protect your eyes against injury. The last thing you need in a game of Around the World is a basketball smashing your eyeglasses, so look into these or contact lenses if you're an athlete.

**Are glasses expensive?**

There's a huge range in cost, from ten bucks to three hundred dollars. At the high end, you're getting ultra thin lenses and better vision quality. If your prescription is extremely high, you might want to consider shelling out bucks for quality lenses. Those ten dollar ones you see at the drug store are basically nothing more than magnifying glasses surrounded by plastic frames (fine, if your prescription is way low).

**What if I want colored glasses?**

There are prescriptive lenses that come in all sorts of funky colors such as blue, pink, green, yellow, rose, and brown. But according to one ophthalmologist we spoke with, tints cannot be added to glass lenses. The color must be part of the material itself when you buy the glasses. Also, plastic lenses which have been tinted tend to fade over a period of years.

**How do I take care of my glasses?**

First of all, keep them in a protective case when you're not wearing them. This does not mean at the bottom of your backpack with loose Skittles and lint. They should have their very own case. If you're just taking them off for a quick second, make sure you don't put them face down on any surface or they might get scratched. To clean them, use water or lens cleaner and a soft cloth. No paper towels or tissues, which are too rough on glass. If you get dust or other strange particles on your lenses, blow them off instead of trying to wipe them off with your fingers.

**What if I want to switch to contact lenses?**

Well, a lot of girls love contact lenses because as Kristen, 15, puts it, "I love my eyes and I want people to see them." Or they don't want to have to deal with scratching, breaking, or misplacing their glasses. On the other hand, many girls, such as Kimberly, 14, "can't stand the thought of sticking something in my eye" and other girls said they didn't want to be bothered with the responsibility of cleaning, disinfecting and storing contacts properly. If you do want to give them a go, talk to your parents first and, if they give you the thumbs up, have them take you to an ophthalmologist. Most doctors will only prescribe contacts after a certain age (around 13), so keep that in mind before you bother begging.

**Do lenses hurt?**

Nope, once you get used to putting contacts in, you'll never know they're there. Says one wearer, "The first week you have them, they are hard to get in, but once you get the hang of it, it's really easy. Do not listen to people who say they hurt!"

**Can I wear those cool color lenses?**

That's up to you, your parents, and your doctor. The color lenses have definitely become a lot more sophisticated over the last ten years. Thankfully, gone are those prototype bright green demonic lenses. Today, we are seeing much more natural, realistic blues and greens. Some girls have different contact lenses for different outfits. Says Mica, 13, "I like wearing blue contacts when I wear my blue sweaters. I think it looks great."

# How Do You Eat?

## There's More to It Than Being Hungry

It's 6 P.M. and Brittany Fisher, 12, has been home from school over an hour. She's starving, as usual. Standing in front of an open fridge, she tries to decide what to eat. The choices are not exactly appealing—a few apples, some salad, half a roasted chicken, leftover pasta.

What about the pantry? Ah-ha! So this is where Mom is hiding all the good stuff. Brittany grabs a bag of chocolate fudge cookies and plops down in front of the tube to watch Baywatch reruns.

"Look at all these girls in their skimpy suits," Brittany says to her friend Emma, "I mean, these TV babes must eat nothing but salads and water to look like that. I'd rather die than eat like that." After ten minutes, Brittany gets up, passes the fridge, and heads to the pantry for some chips.

So what's wrong with having cookies and chips with your afternoon tube watching? Well, if you feel in the mood for a few cookies after school, nothing. Many of us crave a little something after a hard day. The problem lies in *why* you eat what you eat. Why you might choose cookies over chicken. Chips over apples. In a lot of ways, these choices were made when you were little. How? As little kids, our parents give us messages about food. We get these messages in lots of ways. See if you recognize any of these common situations...

**I Hate Veggies.** When you were little, you hated veggies. To get you to eat them, your parents told you that if you finished, you would get dessert as a reward.

**The Clean Plate Club.** If you ate all your dinner, you could be in the "Clean Plate Club." Girls who didn't finish would either not be allowed to have dessert or were punished for being "bad" and left at the table until every scrap disappeared.

**Starving Children.** Your parents told endless stories about kids with nothing to eat. Kids who, unlike you, would be thankful for even one piece of spinach.

**Insulting Mom.** Not finishing something was regarded as a major insult. Mom spent lots of time on that meatloaf. Her job was to cook it, yours to eat it and like it.

**Q:** I can't fall asleep at night. I just lie there while my mind races, thinking about everything I have to do. I wish I could just get up and have it be morning. When I finally fall asleep and morning does come, I am exhausted.

**A:** The best thing you can do is keep your schedule regular. That means no sleeping until noon on weekends. Keep your sleep and waking times constant every day, within one hour.

Fact is, everything from fluctuating hormone levels during your menstrual cycle to what and when you eat and drink play major parts in how well you sleep. A #1 sleep helper is a balanced diet. Your best night's rest starts in the morning with a big breakfast. Then have a good lunch, a healthy snack, and a light dinner with protein (which takes longer to digest, helping you avoid the hungries). And watch the raw veggies. They can leave you gassy, bloated, and uncomfortable. Dieting is a huge sleep enemy. When you don't feed your body enough, it sends a constant hunger signal to your brain, keeping you awake.

Caffeine is another culprit. Avoid coffee, tea, cola, chocolate, orange soda, and even coffee desserts. And check for sneaky sources of caffeine in pain relievers like Excedrin and Maximum Strength Midol.

What more can you do? Get exercise (afternoon or early evening is best), avoid naps, take a steamy ten-minute bath (twenty drops of lavender oil can help) and before bed, try to clear your mind by preparing yourself for the next day. Lay out your clothes, pack your lunch, put your homework in your backpack, and your backpack by the door. Then, turn off the tunes, kill the nightlight, and you should be on your way to sweet dreams.

**Eat Now or Not at All.** At dinnertime, everyone ate—hungry or not. If you weren't famished, something must be wrong.

So what's wrong with these pictures? On the surface, they seem like harmless ways to get a finicky kid to eat. But deep down, there's a lot wrong. As you read this list, you may think we are reading a lot into a few harmless comments. But it's not the words your ears hear that are the problem, it's the message your mind gets over and over. Think hard about what these situations are really saying....

**Hating Veggies.** By setting up the dessert as a trade for eating the vegetables, your parents give you the message that veggies are "yucky" and sweets are "yummy." As you grow, you see eating vegetables as something you must do, not something you want to do. Even though you may learn to like them and know that they are good for you, dessert almost always is the preferred choice. The even more dangerous message is that sweet stuff is a reward— something to be turned to when you've done something "good."

**The Clean Plate Club.** By encouraging you to eat all your food, your parents are telling you that "good" kids eat everything on their plates no matter what (heck, you even get to belong to a club). There are two dangers here. Not only do you think that "good" equals an empty plate but by telling you how much to eat, you don't learn to listen to your body. Appetites come in different sizes, and our bodies know when to stop taking in food—much like how a gas pump stops when the car tank is full. Many girls who belong to the Clean Plate Club never learn to stop when their stomachs say they are full.

**Starving Children.** Girls have been hearing about starving kids in other countries for about as long as international borders have been around. But the message your brain gets is not to appreciate what you're eating, but that if you don't finish it all, you're ungrateful. Instead of being full, you're again being "bad."

**Insulting Mom.** It takes a lot of effort for parents to do the food shopping and prepare a good meal for the family. And some families have limited budgets for groceries. When someone makes an effort, he or she expects something—a compliment, the sense that you enjoyed the effort, whatever. When you don't finish, some parents take that to mean you don't appreciate all they do for you and that you don't know how hard it may be for them to "put food on the table."

Some girls learn that to honor their parents and show their love and appreciation they must eat it all. Some eat out of the terror that there may be a fight if they don't finish or that they may just disappoint a parent. The message then is that eating food equals showing love or feeling loved. And again, eating it all means you are being a "good" daughter.

**Eat Now or Not at All.** Dinnertime is—and should be—a special family time. How many times have we all sat down and eaten, to be part of the group, even though we were not hungry? But eating a full meal on a threat or the need to be part of the group sends the message that eating means acceptance. Again, you never learn to watch your body's food clock, just the clock on the wall.

Certainly not all girls have these problems. But many do. If you're one of those girls, now's the time to change the messages and to change how you see food, how you feel about it, and how you eat it. Whether or not you think you eat with these messages in mind, there are smart things that every girl should know about eating.

Remember, you have reached a point in your life where it is important to put good food (and good amounts of it) into your body. For some girls, that means cutting back on how much they eat or making smarter choices about what they feed themselves. For others it may mean that they stop resisting the natural shape of their bodies and give themselves what they need to grow. Proper nutrition is vital to everyone's body, no matter what shape or size. Your body is developing and it is relying on you to feed it right. Now is the time for you, not your parents, not your friends, to decide what goes into your mouth.

What follows are some common sense ways for you to start a healthy, happy way of eating that will satisfy both your stomach and your soul.

**Try it, you'll like it—nutritious foods can also be tasty.**

Not to start off sounding like the 'rents, but trust us on this. Things that make you yak as a kid can turn tasty as you get older. Just because you hated spinach or lima beans don't assume you'll find all vegetables gross. Give all kinds and ethnic types of foods a try. You might be surprised. And don't hesitate to try steaks, lobster or other grown-up foods that gave you the willies as a little kid. You may find you actually like pigs' feet—or maybe not.

**Listen to your body (not other people) and stop eating when you feel full.**

It's not a crime to leave food on your plate, despite what your parents might tell you about the poor starving children in Africa. When someone puts a guilt trip on you to eat more than you want, or when a relative pushes second helpings in your direction because "you're so skinny," this person isn't doing you any favors. Just politely say, "No thanks, I'm full."

**Don't equate food with love.**

Love is an emotion. Love is not an ingredient in any recipe. While someone cooking for you shows that they care, you can show love to them by voicing appreciation for their efforts, not by eating when you're full. There will always be exceptions, like when Grandma bakes you a cake for your birthday or you are a guest in someone's home. Then it might be rude to say, "No thanks." Just make a big fuss over the fact that Granny made you a   special cake, and then sample a few forkfuls.

Stores are filled with books on people who eat to fill an empty heart. Abusing food is a complex issue but tattoo onto your brain that the only thing food does is allow your body to function. It can't resolve a fight, make you realize how special you are, or be a friend when you need one. Only people can do this. Instead of shopping for food that fills you, shop for people who do.

**Eat only when you're hungry.**

When you're depressed, nervous, lonely, or bored, shoving food in your mouth only makes you feel worse. Instead of raiding the fridge when you're worried about a math test, call a friend. When you feel like eating but aren't really hungry, get busy. Don't let lifting a fork to your mouth become your favorite form of exercise.

When you come home from school to an empty house, the absolute worst thing you can do is flip on the tube and munch down a large bag of Doritos. Instead, grab something filling and nutritious like a sandwich, a handful of pretzels, or some fruit. Then get off your tail and exercise, play, or go for a walk.

**Don't revolve your social life around food.**

Yeah, it's fun to meet your friends for lunch or stop for a slice of pizza after school, if it's an occasional treat. Just be careful not to center all your activities around eating, because studies show people tend to eat more in groups, in restaurants, and in fast-food joints than when they're alone and at home.

And just because all your friends order double cheeseburgers with fries doesn't mean you should too. No matter where you are, no matter what the menu, you can always make choices that are right for you. But that said...

**Don't deny yourself a taste of the foods you like.**

If you crave Mickey D fries, go for it. Remember, the key to a balanced diet is moderation, not denial. If you love fries but forbid yourself to eat them they only get more desirable. Give your body a nice mix of foods; don't make yourself insane.

**Ask yourself often how you are feeling about your body and about food.**

Consuming huge amounts of food can lead to obesity, just like restricting yourself to tiny amounts of food can lead to bulimia or anorexia nervosa. Some kids use food to relieve loneliness, depression, anger, boredom, or other emotions. It's important to monitor yourself and question anything about your eating that seems unhealthy.

Have you ever tried to diet? Do you wish you could lose a few pounds? If you answer yes, you may be imitating something your mother or friends are doing. If you really do need to shed a few pounds, ask a doctor to supervise a healthy diet.

If you're at a perfectly normal weight but are still unhappy with the way your stomach or thighs look, your doctor or parents can help you determine the reasons you feel badly about your body. Thinking that your friends or boys will like you more if you were slimmer may indicate low self esteem. Because such negative attitudes often lead to eating disorders, it's really important to discuss with an adult your feelings about dieting.

**Know the changes your body is going through.**

The first change in girls before puberty is the rounding of the lower abdomen— your stomach. Because of this natural process, the desired image of a flat stomach is physically impossible as you mature. That is, unless you halt your normal development by starvation. Girls who don't eat right will pay a stiff price later for stunting the natural growth of breasts, abdomen, and hormones. Many girls who don't eat enough don't produce normal hormones or get their periods. If you don't feel comfortable with the way your body is developing, talk to an adult you trust.

**Take down every picture of every model on your wall.**

Did you ever wonder why you hardly ever see girls on the street who look like the ones on TV, on billboards, and in magazines? It's because they don't really exist except on TV, on billboards, and in magazines. Let us say it—these people are genetic rarities, freaks of nature! They are taller than normal; they weigh less than normal. They are teenage mutant European models. They can mostly thank makeup artists, wardrobe assistants, and photographers for that uncommon look. Models are there to sell you something, not set a standard for how we should all look in our jeans. Surface beauty fades quickly, a healthy body does not.

# The Girls' Life Guide to The Tough Stuff

# You're Moving!

## How to Survive

Every summer you say an ecstatic farewell to homework, boring teachers, and nasty cafeteria meat. Life is simple. You have killer plans for parties, beaches, and cookouts with your pals. Your only worry is applying the correct SPF to your skin.

That is, until the announcement. One night at dinner, your parents tell you they have something important to talk to you about. Cousin Suzie ran off with a Frenchman? Weird Aunt Lil is coming to visit? No such luck. "We're moving," they announce, smiling. At first, the words don't sink in. "Can't be," you think.

Suddenly your world is crumbling, and you have no say in the matter. There's just no way to avoid the complete and utter shock of it. The good news is this: It can be a much better deal than you figured, especially once you know the secrets of surviving.

### FACING THE FEAR

One of the toughest parts about moving is feeling the rug has been pulled right out from under you. All your plans for the summer are history—the parties, beach days, and trips to the local amusement park.

When Pam, 12, heard the news she was horrified: "Every single thing I was looking forward to is suddenly gone. All my friends will just disappear, and I couldn't even say a word about it."

It makes you feel pretty out of control. But there are some decisions you will soon be making: how you'll decorate your room, what places you'll hang out at, which after-school activities you'll join.

For some kids, the moving jitters are mixed with excitement. After all, moving is a chance to say farewell to a crabby teacher and hello to a brand new bedroom. But for others, change and fear of the unknown are downright terrifying.

When Amy, 13, found out she was moving across the country, she said, "I kept wondering what it would be like, if the kids would be friendly, if they would include me or be mean." It's normal to feel sad about leaving friends, a familiar school, and a home you like.

According to 11-year-old Lauren, "I'm moving and it's not like I don't know I'll make lots of new friends, but it's still really hard to say good-bye to all my friends now." The longer you've lived in one place, the more connected you feel and the more special memories you have—and the less you want to move.

The toughest part about moving—whether you're a novice or an old pro—is dealing with change. No matter how much you may like things stirred up, change is stressful. But you can handle it. Think about all the difficult experiences you've dealt with before. Maybe you had to deal with a new brother or sister. Or you went to summer camp and were forced to meet all new friends. Whatever it was, you coped. And you'll deal with this. Even though you feel shaky now, let the fact that you coped before give you confidence now.

## FIRST REACTIONS

The first thought that probably enters your mind: "Hey, what about my friends?" You've built incredibly close relationships with girls who know almost everything about you, and now you have to start over. Alex, 9, lived in the same town since she was born. "My best friend Jen and I did everything together," she says. "We met on the bus the first day of kindergarten, and we've been friends ever since. I couldn't imagine living without her."

Your very first instinct may be to share the dreaded news. The bursting need to tell at least your best friend is understandable, but it's best to wait until the idea of moving settles a bit. That way, you can decide how you feel about it, and be prepared to handle friends' reactions.

And be prepared for some strange ones. After all, they'll probably be almost as shocked as you were. Melanie, 13, says, "I expected my best friend to be upset, maybe even cry, when I told her. But she just got this weird, angry look and walked away! I couldn't believe it."

**Dear Carol:** My parents said we are going to move. I'm upset about it and so is my best friend. What if I don't make any friends at the new school?
—MAD ABOUT MOVING

**Dear Mad:** Moving is not easy for kids, parents, or left-behind friends. But I can absolutely promise you that just as you made friends in your old school, you'll do it in your new school. Be friendly, introduce yourself often, join a sport or afterschool activity, and do not regale the new kids with stories about how cool your old school was. Then keep an open mind. You may really like the girls—and the guys—in your new school. As for old friends, stay close by writing letters, emailing each other, phone calls, and planning visits. Good luck!

Angie, 10, remembers some girls in her class became more weepy than she could handle: "At first, I was thinking it would be kind of fun to move. But when I told my friends, they kept saying it was the worst possible thing. It made me wonder if I was wrong about it being fun, and I got upset too." How your friends react depends on lots of stuff, like their own feelings about moving, how things are going for them, or even their mood

that day. Give them time to get used to the idea. The fact that you're leaving may be especially hard to handle for some friends—particularly those who, because of death or divorce, have said a lot of painful good-byes before. Sometimes, these girls avoid good-byes by shutting you out or even seeking new friendships right away to counter the loss. Watching your buds get close to others can be almost unbearable—you feel as if they've replaced you in a heartbeat. As cliché as this sounds, remember you've done nothing wrong. It's nearly impossible not to take it personally, but these friends are just trying to cope as best they can.

If you have time, have a full-out, fun good-bye party. Angie's friends, who eventually calmed down about her move, planned a "good-luck barbecue." She says, "It was a lot of fun. We told stories of funny things that happened to us, and they gave me a scrapbook filled with pictures." If your friends don't think of throwing you a party, plan one yourself. Take pictures so you can share them with your friends and take them to your new home.

## A CHANCE TO START OVER

After you've had a chance to digest the news, it's time to open your mind to the new possibilities. The best part may be the chance to start over. You might live in a new climate, play in snow for the first time, experience a new accent, or try a new sport. Even if you're perfectly happy where you live now, you might actually prefer living in a different location. This is your chance to find out.

For Susan, 12, the chance to begin anew was perfect: "I got good grades when I was younger, but they started to slip once I got to middle school. I got off on the wrong foot and, pretty soon, teachers expected me to forget my homework or talk too much during class. It was hard to change that." When Susan found out she was moving, she decided to turn over a new leaf and hit the books. "Maybe I could have done it at my old school," she says, "but it's easier here because the teachers don't know how I used to be."

Similarly, Pam was having friend troubles when she heard the news about an upcoming move. Fifth grade was a tough year that seemed to go on forever. She says, "At first I was upset we had to move. But then I thought about how sick I was of fighting with people. When we fought, I got really nasty and said mean things I later regretted." Moving to a new town gave Pam a chance to meet a different group of girls and change her ways. "I got to start fresh," she says. "I don't have to see the girls I had problems with, and nobody here knows about it. I learned to walk away when I'm ticked off."

## ADJUSTING TO YOUR NEW HOME

Your parents can help you learn about your new area. If you can't go along when your parents are house hunting, ask them to take pictures of your new home—especially your room, school and neighborhood so they'll look a little more familiar, less overwhelming. And check out your new hometown on the web—many cities have sites and so do local newspapers.

When it comes to packing, set aside some favorite things to carry with you instead of shipping them in cardboard boxes. Leave out photos of friends, a diary, a CD player, and your beat-up teddy with one missing ear. Your room may get packed up and shipped out before you leave, and you don't want to spend your last days in an empty, dreary room. You also might arrive at your new home before the moving truck, and it helps to surround yourself with familiar sights and sounds.

As soon as you can, explore your new turf. Whether you hike or bike, get to know the area right away. Find out where the best pizza place and music store can be found. Check out where to go with your new friends, like the mall or movies. Want to meet people faster? Take your dog for a walk. People are more likely to stop and chat while they pet him.

Try to arrange a tour of your new school. Locate the cafeteria, library and office, so you won't feel lost on that first official day of school. If you have enough lead time, ask the principal if you can spend a day with someone from your grade so you'll know a familiar face. The more you learn about your school before it starts, the more comfortable you'll feel that first day.

According to many girls who've moved, the best survival strategy is to get involved as quickly as possible. When Alex moved, right away she joined a dance class, where she met several cool girls. She says, "I almost didn't take ballet after I moved because I didn't know if everyone would be better than me. But my mom convinced me it didn't matter, so I decided to try. I got to know one girl pretty well, and it turned out she was in my class when school started."

During the summer, when school's out, it's even more important to find ways to get into the swing of things. Look into activities offered by parks and recreation facilities, like swimming or plays. If going by yourself seems too awful, ask your family if they're up for trying a family program. Also consider volunteering somewhere. You'll be more likely to see other kids than if you just stay home—and your help will be much appreciated.

**Dear Carol:** My friend keeps pressuring me to try smoking. Should I give in? It's getting harder each day, and I really like her, but I don't want to smoke. Help!—NON-SMOKER

**Dear Non-smoker:** Definitely do not give in. Peer pressure is hard to resist, but there"s also such a thing as positive peer pressure, and maybe your friend will stop smoking once she realizes that many of her classmates (and crushes) think the habit is gross—not cool. For now, don't lecture her nonstop about lung cancer or smelly clothes, but do stay strong yourself. When she offers a puff, say no, and if it's easier for you, say that you're allergic or that smoke makes you cough or gives you a headache. Keep making new friends too. Girls change a lot during these years and friendships sometimes change too.

Youth programs are another great way to get involved. As Jessica, 14, says, "I joined a church group like my old one. We even sing the same songs. It makes me feel right at home." Join the local chapter of an organization you used to belong to, whether it was scouts, service clubs, whatever. Or join for the first time. It's best to contact organization leaders before you move so you can take part as soon as you arrive instead of waiting for registration.

### COMPARING FRIENDS

When meeting new girls, it's tempting to compare everything and everyone to how it was back home. Bad idea. How would you like it if a new friend kept comparing you to her old friend? As Jessica advises, "You're always thinking how your new school is different from your old one, or how some new girl reminds you of a friend. I found out it's best to stop doing that because it can really turn girls off."

 But don't forget your old friends either. It takes some work to keep long distance friends. You probably won't keep up with all of them, but it's worth the effort with your closest ones. Write tons of e-mails, telling them what cool things are going on and what you miss. Calling is fun, too, but can get costly if you're calling long distance. Why not arrange to be online at the same time and chat?

Planning a visit to your old home also eases the pangs. It may be possible for you and a friend to exchange summer visits. You could arrange to go to camp or volunteer somewhere together. Some find this difficult, but if you feel pretty good about the whole ordeal, go for it.

No matter how you feel about it, moving is overwhelming. But being a little nervous never stopped you before. Like the Muppets once said, just keep "movin' right along."

# Paws Off!

## What's Flirting, What's Hurting?

"All year, the boys have been chasing us in the hall. This guy Dave is always after me, which I figured meant he liked me. But whenever he caught up to me, he tried to look down my shirt or grab my skirt. I told him to quit it, but he won't. It's not funny anymore. I don't know why he won't stop." —BRITTNEY, 10

"I've kind of been going out with Mike, who's really cute, but sometimes he's so weird when his friends are around. Like once they made these stupid kissy noises, which I didn't like. I ignored it, but it's only gotten worse. One of his friends says Mike told him I had great boobs. Now I don't know what to think. He says he likes me, but am I supposed to think that's a wonderful compliment? I feel so weird when I'm around him or his friends." —FILONA, 12

"There's this Derek guy on my bus, who sometimes pulls out my ponytail as I go by his seat. He's just kidding around. Last week, though, he reached out and snapped my bra in the back. It hurt, but the worst part was that it was really loud and everybody laughed. I was so humiliated! The bus driver didn't say a word, and now this jerk is pulling some so-called 'joke' every day." —LORIN, 11

Your stomach flip-flops whenever that gorgeous guy in homeroom beams his green eyes at you. And when the Goddesses of Romance hears your prayers and makes your crush whisper sweetly to you, you practically glow with happiness. In your most delightful daydream, your

## KNOW YOUR RIGHTS

In 1999 the U.S. Supreme Court drew the line between "schoolyard teasing" and sexual harassment. While the ruling is complex, it boils down to this: If sexual harassment interferes with a student's ability to learn, that's discrimination. And discrimination is against the law.

It also ruled that school systems could be held responsible if school personnel do nothing to stop the harassment. So if you're being harassed and your repeated requests for help from your teacher, principal or counselor don't end the problem, have your parents inform them that the next person you're going to talk to could well be a lawyer.

amour just happens to brush his hand against yours and, next thing you know, it's the start of a beautiful friendship.

Unfortunately, the real world of girl-boy relations doesn't always turn out happily Ever After. Instead of gazing admiringly, some guys stare at territory much lower than eye level. Walking by a crowd of boys, you may hear crass comments about you. Male acquaintances might tease or make rude gestures. If this has ever happened to you, you've probably thought, "What's going on here? Are boys flirting with me or—what?"

These kinds of comments, contacts, and come-ons happen much more often than many people realize. According to one survey, eight out of ten girls have been touched, pinched, or grabbed by guys they know. Even more have been on the receiving end of suggestive jokes, comments, gestures, or leers. Let's put it this way—very few girls are fortunate enough to escape unwanted, inappropriate attention from the opposite sex. That's why we're giving you the lowdown on recognizing harassing behavior and advice for how to deal with it .

## WHAT'S GOING ON?

Situations such as those described are confusing for lots of reasons. Like, maybe you liked a guy and wanted him to notice you—at least, at one point you did—but not in the way he's doing it. Having him look at you like you're a pork chop isn't exactly what you had in mind. Or say a male pal starts out being nice, and then says or does something offensive that totally throws you. Maybe he gets way too close—beyond your comfort zone, that is. Or his teasing—which you once considered all in fun—has taken a totally nasty turn. Now, it just makes you feel bad about yourself. Perhaps you hear he's been spreading sick rumors about you—is that liking you, or what?

Another reason it's confusing is that the guy may tickle, pinch, or grab under the guise of "all in good fun"—despite your shooting him dirty looks and yelling "STOP!" As Marla, 12, puts it, "When Jimmy came up to me in line and was rubbing his hands in my hair and saying it was pretty, he acted like this was supposed to be a major compliment. So I was like, 'Why doesn't this feel right?'"

And so much of the time, this stuff happens right out in the open, like in the cafeteria, during gym, or even in class. Tons of other people are around—your friends, his friends, even teachers. As Caroline, 13, says, "So if he's being so horrible, how come other people don't even notice?"

The fact is, even if people do see what's going on, they don't always react the way they should. They might even tell you to chill out and stop making a big deal—as if it's your problem. This makes many girls wonder if they're losing their minds. But, whatever you do, don't second-guess your gut reaction. Feeling out of sorts, uneasy, uncertain, or upset by someone's aggressiveness is perfectly normal.

## WHAT'S THE DIFF?

How can you tell what's innocent flirting and what's not? Simple. If it makes you feel okay, it's flirting. If it makes you feel uncomfortable, it's not flirting—it's hurting. Whether a boy talks to you, touches you, or teases you, if you don't want him to, it's not okay. You have a right to say how someone's behavior makes you feel. If you consider the attention unwanted, unwelcome, and inappropriate, by definition it's considered harassment. Some girls describe this as being pestered, bothered, annoyed, hassled, bugged, dissed, insulted, or teased.

It doesn't matter how your BFF sees it or what your favorite teacher says. Even if they think what a boy says or does is hilarious, if you don't, then it's not. No matter what anyone else in the universe says, trust how you feel inside.

Pay attention to uneasy feelings. They can signal that something's not right in how someone treats you. Be aware of your emotions. If you're not sure how you feel, talk to someone, maybe a friend or sib who's had a similar experience. Writing about it in your diary could help you realize you're upset, scared, or sad.

## WHAT IF SOMEONE ELSE IS BEING HARASSED?

Sometimes you're not the one who's being harassed, but you're watching the goings-on from a front row seat. Maybe you were in the lunch room, on the field or on the bus when someone started hassling a girl and wouldn't stop. Even if you acted breezy, it may have made you uncomfortable, scared, or upset.

Some girls say they didn't speak up after seeing such incidents because they didn't want to start trouble or get in trouble themselves. But then they've felt guilty afterward about leaving girls who've suffered in the lurch.

Others have told adults, sometimes with disappointing results. Amanda, 13, says, "After a bunch of girls and I went to the office, the school did absolutely nothing. The boys were out there the next day, doing the same annoying things." It seemed to Amanda that nobody cared and that school was no longer a safe place.

That's why it's important to take action not only when you've experienced inappropriate behavior, but also when you've witnessed it. Plus, when you follow through, you learn how to protest injustices and make positive changes. The more girls who speak up about these issues, the more likely the voice will be heard.

Lorin, the girl whose bra was snapped by a boy on her bus, says, "I got so embarrassed that I didn't even want to go to school anymore. My mom started driving me." Filona, the girl whose figure is the topic of discussion among her boyfriend's friends, says, "Even though I know I didn't do a single thing wrong to deserve their rude comments, I still feel cheap somehow."

If you find yourself changing your routine, avoiding situations or people, or feeling low, it's likely someone has crossed the line of what's comfortable for you. The next step is taking action. What can you do? Plenty.

## SEND A CLEAR MESSAGE

Think you're helpless to change what's going on? Wrong! About one third of girls in these situations are too scared to utter a word, but the worst thing you can do is laugh along with the "joke" or ignore your so-called friend's behavior. Guys rarely stop on their own—especially if they've been made to feel they haven't offended you. And, girls feel worse and worse about themselves when they feel powerless.

About two out of three girls in such instances tell the guy to stop doing whatever he's doing. They may say it using polite words ("Please stop that right now!") or, more rarely, they transmit the message via a universal physical language. As Melinda, 12, puts it, "I punched that jerk as hard as possible."

Regardless of how you say stop, say it like you mean business. Try, "Stop! I don't want you to do that one more time!" Often it is necessary to say it again, as in, "I'm telling you for the second and last time. I won't tolerate you doing that again."

And while we urge you to be assertive, some approaches are not exactly recommended. Even though you might be seething and cooking up furious revenge fantasies, acting on impulse usually backfires by causing the situation to escalate. As tempting as it might be to start a rumor about a boy who wronged you, please resist. Harmonious boy-girl relations are a two way street—make that, hallway. Will saying "stop" work? Sometimes. Other times, no.

## WHEN AND WHY TO "TELL"

If all else fails, you need to think seriously about turning in a boy who won't heed your clear messages to cease and desist. Even if you can think of two zillion reasons not to. For example, you may still doubt you have a legitimate reason to be upset. Maybe you're too embarrassed to report what happened. Or you worry that adults won't believe you. Or like the girls described above, you may have tried to tell people who merely respond, "He just likes you," or "It's no big deal." Roberta, 13, reports, "When I got up the courage and finally told my principal what had been going on, he said I should work it out on my own. But how? I already tried that, and it didn't work." Some girls dread ratting on guys because they figure they will retaliate or won't even be punished for their actions.

In truth, these are all possibilities. But there are many good reasons to try to get adult help. It's often hard to get boys to stop inappropriate behavior on your own. You may need extra support. If you don't put a lid on the problem, boys think it's okay to treat girls inappropriately. The behavior could continue or even get worse. It can do a number on your pride, your confidence and even your grades.

So if you tell an adult who doesn't listen patiently enough or take you seriously, don't be discouraged. It doesn't mean you've done anything wrong or that your problem isn't important. Tell another adult. Keep on telling people until someone realizes these aren't just kid pranks, that it's upsetting you, and that steps should be taken to stop it. Try your parents or other relatives, a family doctor, teacher, school nurse, religious leader, or guidance counselor.

The bottom line? Know your boy-comment barometer. Every girl has one. If someone says something that makes you hopping mad, don't just grin and bear it. Speak up, for goodness sake, or seek help. Many states now have harassment laws to protect women and girls from the offhand comments that come a little too often. Does this mean that the next time Billy calls you Benedict Arnold from across the room, you should stand up and start quoting the Constitution?

Well, no. When you feel uncomfortable, and act on that gut reaction, your instincts are pretty reliable. After all, it's your right to feel safe and secure, sister.

# BILL & DAVE CLUE YOU IN ON:
## *Why Guys Sometimes Don't Know the Difference*

In no way do we condone inappropriate behavior toward girls. But by understanding what motivates some guys to act like jerks, you'll be better prepared to deal with sticky situations. And we're all for slamming smarmy, forward guys so shy, unassuming boys like us will get all your attention. Several factors play in when it comes to aggressive guys.

**Girls, for one.** Gals, you're a confusing lot! Think about the thought process that goes into picking out a great skirt or top. Your girlfriend might comment, "Wow! That'll get their attention!" Revealing outfits are never an invitation for a guy to be crude, but be ready if some wisecracker reacts to your sartorial splendor with something a bit more graphic than, "That's a really great shirt. Banana Republic?"

**Guys.** Obviously, no one's more to blame than guys themselves when it comes to dog like behavior. Dogs smell fear, and so do guys. If a guy's antics get you riled up, you're giving him exactly what he wants. But if you're self confident and appear unimpressed, he'll usually back off and find other prey.

Let's take the dog analogy a little farther—as in the way guys bark out rude comments when they are in a pack. Teen guys feel a need to belong to a group and often think insulting the opposite sex is the way to prove ourselves to our buds. Unfortunately, this kind of boorish behavior is hard to control, but a well placed, "Would you allow someone to talk about your sister or mother that way?" can sometimes make a pretty succinct point.

And don't forget to pay a little attention to the quiet "nice" guy in the group. After all, when you ignore Mr. Polite, you encourage Mr. Nasty.

**The media.** We can blame almost anything on mass media. But guys are inundated with images of aggressive, swaggering men portrayed as chick magnets. Why shouldn't guys see this as proper conduct? Rarely does the sensitive, caring guy get the girl. Nope, it's the pumped-up lout that walks off with the babe.

All in all, it can be disorienting for a guy trying to catch the eye of a girl. Sometimes, it's like taking a trip with no map. And when you finally see a sign, it points you in the wrong direction. But there's a distinction between harassment and simple flirting.

If you feel you're being harassed, remedy the situation. If a guy is just making a sorry attempt at harmless flirting, imagine how it feels to be in his shoes. Have you, without realizing it, let this guy's subtle signs that he likes you fly over your head? Perhaps he's taking it to another level to get a response. The key is to differentiate an innocent, well-intentioned appeal for female attention from actions that cross the line into unacceptable behavior.

You can get along for a while without a boy. And you can get along for a lifetime without a harassing slob. Put that jerk in his place—nowhere.

# Saying Good-bye

## The Real Deal on Grieving

You may have thought you've known real grief. Maybe a friend has backstabbed you, your crush has zero interest in you, or you've woken up with a mountainous zit on the tip of your nose. You want to crawl into a hole and hibernate. But the first time someone we care about dies (DIES!), we get a whole new perspective on grief. The very topic of death is scary, confusing, and unbearably sad. And what's really terrible is realizing the situation is forever.

At some point, we all have to deal with losing someone. This is one of life's toughest blows. Whether it's a pet, family friend or grandparent who dies, some mighty powerful feelings get triggered. Many complex questions might run through your mind: Why did it happen? Why do people die? Why is life so unfair? Meanwhile, everyday life turns upside down—the phone rings off the hook, a major school project is pushed aside, plans are canceled. We're suddenly left to figure out how to say good-bye to the person who died, all while comforting others.

For many girls, it's a challenge determining the correct behavior in such circumstances. They ask themselves, "How do I act without making a fool of myself? Are my feelings normal? What can I possibly say to make my friend/aunt/father feel better? Is there anything I should *not* do?" While we can't provide a magic formula for grieving, we can assure you that the pain does ease up, and you will find yourself in normal everyday life again. While you're grieving, however, here's some advice on getting yourself or a friend through the process.

## THE BIG SECRET

Why is the topic of death so hush-hush? Terminally ill uncles and hospital visiting hours are hardly cafeteria table conversation. Funerals are often mentioned in near whispers. Why are some people so afraid to talk about it? To put it bluntly, death is scary because it's the great unknown. It's hard to accept that we can't control this huge, important event. Of course, it's also terribly difficult to think of saying good-bye to those we love.

Some adults try to "protect" girls by avoiding the D word. But when adults clam up every time the subject is brought up, girls might wonder what there is to fear. Death is scary, but it's a part of life we all will deal with sooner or later.

## WHAT TO EXPECT

No two people grieve the same way. Psychologists believe there are some likely reactions to death that all people go through, but not everybody experiences each of them—and certainly not in any specific order. If your cat is hit by a reckless driver, your initial feeling might be sadness—or fury. There are no such things as wrong feelings. The only questionable reaction is pretending the death didn't happen. Accept your emotions. It's helpful to know the possible responses, so you feel more prepared about what to expect.

**Disbelief.** Sure, you know the person (or pet) isn't going to walk through the door ever again. Yet, your first thought after news of a death might be, "I can't believe it." It's unreal. Serena, 14, says, "After my grandfather died, the family got together for Thanksgiving and it was weird that he wasn't at his usual spot at the table. I kept waiting for him to yell, 'Got any sweets?' to Grandma, like he always did."

**Anger.** Death often seems unfair. Even when we know deep down no one is at fault, it feels better to blame someone. Doctors, nurses, pesky sibs, or divine beings make great targets when there's nobody else to resent. You might even get angry at the deceased person for leaving. Anyone who's still enjoying the same kind of relationship you lost can also become the object of your rage. Greta, 10, says, "When my dog got hit by a car, I couldn't stop crying. One day, I saw this boy walking a black lab that looked just like mine, and I wanted to hit him."

**Bargaining.** When people we care about are injured or ill, we'd do anything to make them recover. Since there usually isn't much we can do, we fool ourselves into thinking we can bargain for the person's survival. Even if you're not religious, you might beg a higher power to strike a deal with you.

Monica, 13, reports, "I swore that if my horse got better, I'd never be mean to my sister again." The trouble is, sometimes the sick person or animal dies anyway. That doesn't make it your fault.

**Loneliness.** Ever since the death occurred, you may have had trouble shaking a worried mood or getting the person's image out of your mind. Looming thoughts and feelings can make us feel removed from reality, as if we're there but not quite. Believing that others can't possibly comprehend what we're going through can make us feel lonely. Maggie, 14, says, "After my granddad died, I felt like nobody could imagine how I was feeling. I felt so alone."

**Feelings of craziness.** Being preoccupied also makes us forget things. You're so busy concentrating on the big issues that everyday stuff seems to evaporate from your mind. Forgotten locker combinations, missed book reports and canceled dates with friends are common. Some girls may even imagine things.

Emotions that change as often as the weather can also make you feel like you're going crazy. One minute you're crying; the next you're laughing. These experiences are not only normal but, thankfully, temporary.

**Sadness and depression.** It's practically impossible not to think about people or pets we loved without becoming sad that they're gone. Depression can prevent us from enjoying usual activities.

Anna, 11, was not as psyched for gymnastics as she used to be. "My parrot got sick and died right before a big tournament. I didn't even want to go. Even though I love gymnastics, I couldn't have cared less about it for a while."

**Guilt and regrets.** It's easy to slip into such thoughts as, "I wish I had spent more time with her and told her how much I loved her." But torturing yourself with what-ifs and should-haves isn't worthwhile. Chances are, you did the best you could to show you cared. But even if you said you hated the person, or wished he'd disappear, you did not cause the death! What is said in a moment of anger does not magically occur.

**Questioning.** Some people deal with death by trying to make sense of it. Girls ask, "Why did this have to happen to such a good person?" or, "What is the meaning behind his death?" If this is your way, you're not alone. You could seek out a religious leader to help you sort through your beliefs. But you should know that few people ever find definite answers to such colossal questions.

Plus, research shows that those who mull it over and over are the most distressed. After a few mental go-arounds, focus on other ways of coping.

**Acceptance.** It may seem impossible, but your feelings—whatever they are—will gradually subside, becoming less sharp. At various times, especially birthdays, anniversaries and holidays, the pain may come back. But, in general, you'll realize life must go on without the person who died. Your world won't ever be the same, but the person or pet will live on through your memories.

## PARENTS AND GRIEF

Parents, too, struggle with grief. Their coping styles have an impact on yours. Two girls describe their experiences with parents' extreme reactions.

Nancy, 13, says, "When we got the phone call saying Granddad had died, it was like they heard about some random car accident. My dad said, 'Oh, really?' in the same voice he'd say, 'Pass the potatoes.'" Because Nancy was confused by her parents' ho hum reaction, she was afraid to talk to them about her sadness. Says Nancy, "I didn't know what else to do, so I called my aunt. She told me this is the way my parents handle stuff—they keep it inside them. She said she's more like me, which made me feel better."

Vicky, 12, had the opposite happen: "When Grandma died, my mom cried in her room all day. I was really worried about her." What did Vicky do? "I went in and told her she was scaring me," she explains. "That snapped her out of it. We talked about grandmother and had a good cry together. That was better than crying outside her bedroom door."

## CEREMONIES

Every family and culture has its own customs to deal with death. There may be a memorial service, funeral, or cemetery burial. There may be a time to visit the bereaved family beforehand, such as with an Irish wake, or afterward, such as the week of sitting Jewish shivah.

You need to decide which events you're comfortable attending. This should be a personal decision you make with your parents. Whether or not you attend a funeral says nothing about your feelings for the deceased.

Catey, 10, says, "My family always has open caskets. Thinking about it gives me nightmares." She and her parents decided she'd only go to her grandfather's memorial service, where the coffin would be closed.

Sometimes, parents make such decisions without considering their daughters' feelings. Many parents forbid their kids to attend funerals. Girls may or may not agree with this decision. Although you may not change your parents' minds, it is okay to speak out.

Evie, 9, says, "I told my parents I'd be upset if I was left out. I knew I could handle it, and I did." Evie found it hugely comforting to be with relatives.

Don't be afraid to ask questions. Robin, 12, remembers her agony before her grandfather's funeral: "I needed to talk to Mom about what to wear. I was so worried I'd show up looking overdressed or disrespectful."

## COMFORTING OTHERS

There's no perfect phrase to recite when someone is grieving. It's okay to tell the person, "I'm sorry to hear your relative died. Are you okay?"

Many girls wonder if they'll cause more hurt if they speak of the deceased. Usually, the opposite is true. Most mourners feel better talking about their loved ones. Just listening is probably the most comforting thing you can do.

## POWER TO YOU

Here are some coping skills to help when you or someone else is grieving.

**Write a speech or obituary.** You might feel tons better if you write a story about what the person meant to you. Read it at the funeral or family gathering, have someone else read it for you, or stick it in a diary for your eyes only.

**Get a keepsake.** Memories comfort. They allow us to keep people alive in our minds. Keepsakes we can look at and touch help maintain vivid memories. If you can, ask to have something that belonged to your loved one. Photos, clothes or whimsical items (Grandma's egg timer, a baseball cap, coffee mug) make great physical reminders.

**Make a scrapbook.** Collect pictures and mementos from the occasions you shared with the pet or person who died, and paste them into a scrapbook. Write captions or stories to remember the good times you had together.

**Have a ceremony.** When you can't attend a funeral or if a pet dies, it helps to have your own ceremony. Give a speech, sing a song or say a prayer. You might pick your pup's favorite spot in the yard, and place a marker with wood or stone. If you can't bury your pet (some states prohibit this), dig a hole for his food dish or favorite toy instead.

## BEING THERE

If you know someone who is gravely ill, you may now have a better idea what feelings to anticipate. However, there is no way to truly prepare yourself for how you will react when the time comes.

Don't hesitate to tell the person what you feel and how much you care. If visiting is hard, make a card or write a poem. Although you may feel uncomfortable, try not to avoid a person who's sick or dying. A quick phone call or loving squeeze of the hand can make a world of difference. Your

**Dear Carol:** A friend of our family died of AIDS last year and I really loved him. My friends at school constantly make fun of people who are gay. I know they are wrong, but I don't know what to say. And I can't seem to get over this death.
—STILL SAD

**Dear Still Sad:** t's hard to get over the death of someone you love. You lost a friend, and your grief is a tribute to how much you cared for him. Talk to your parents about your feelings, because they are probably sad too and it's nicer to feel sad together than to feel sad separately. If your classmates make ignorant or mean-spirited remarks about people, they need to learn about tolerance and kindness. Maybe you can help. Tell them you lost a friend to AIDS, and that they are too smart to make fun of people and to be prejudiced and disrespectful.

compassion will go a long way in comforting someone who's suffering—and will make you feel good about yourself.

## WHAT WE LEARN

Hopefully, all your friends, relatives and pets will live to be positively ancient. But, as you know, death is an inevitable part of the life cycle. There's a beginning and an end to everything. Although we can't prevent or control death, we sure can avoid unnecessary risks. We can take good care of ourselves and our health, paying attention to safety (such as wearing seat belts and bike helmets) at all times. We can make a conscious commitment to fully enjoy life, taking advantage of all the opportunities that come our way. Most of all, we can remember to treasure our loved ones and tell them how we feel while they're still with us.

# More Tough Stuff

Okay, sometimes girls have to deal with situations that leave them feeling powerless, scared, and out of control. If you find yourself stuck in a bad situation, the best thing to do is confide in a trusted adult (parent, favorite aunt, teacher, minister, rabbi, someone) as soon as possible. These are not problems you can solve on your own, so don't feel pressured to even try!

Here are answers to some common, but tough, questions. Also check out our resources section on page 253 for more detailed advice and a list of hotlines, web sites and recommended reading. More than anything, we hope that if you or someone you know is suffering, you will gather your courage and get help now. We promise you'll be livin' la vida loca again, even if you are marching to the beat of the doldrums right now. You'll see.

## EATING DISORDERS

**Q:** About a year ago, I ate way too much at a holiday party because I felt sad and lonely. When I got sick to my stomach my friend told me I should go into the bathroom and make myself throw up by sticking my finger down my throat. I did it, and it was easy. I started doing it more and more—eating as much as I could and then throwing it up. It makes me feel better to get rid of the food. Now, I feel like I can't stop doing it. I do it most when I'm depressed.

**A:** You are right to be worried. Millions of girls suffer from *bulimia nervosa*, the disorder you describe. People with the disorder eat in large quantities in a short period of time and then take laxatives or self-induce vomiting to rid the food from their bodies. The bulimic often carries out this behavior as a way to punish herself for something she feels she should be blamed for or to let out feelings of anger, depression, stress, or anxiety. Bulimics typically hide or "store" food for later eating binges and often eat secretly so no one can watch them.

It may seem easy enough — food in, food out. But this process takes a severe toll on your body. When you get rid of the food, you deny your body the necessary vitamins, minerals, and proteins that fuel it. You also put your body at risk for dehydration, which can lead to kidney failure, heart failure, and tearing of the esophagus. These are just a few medical problems you may face. We beg you to stop immediately. If you can't, tell your parents what's going on so they can get you professional help right away.

**Q:** I am very worried about my friend. I think she's starving herself. She and I used to pig out all the time on sundaes and pizza. Now she hardly eats anything—just cut-up vegetables, which she spends more time moving around her plate than eating. She's getting skinnier and skinnier, and all she talks about are fat grams and calories. Why is she doing this?!

**A:** It sounds as if your friend may suffer from anorexia nervosa, a disorder that is pretty difficult to understand. An anorexic may be abnormally sensitive about being perceived as fat and/or scared of losing control over food she eats. Likely, she is driven by a desire to control her emotions and suffers from low self esteem. She may feel she deserves no pleasure out of life, and therefore denies herself food. Other symptoms are obsessive exercise, calorie and fat gram counting, use of diet pills and laxatives, and a constant hang-up about her body image.

Anorexia is an incredibly dangerous disorder, one that can lead to severe health risks, including respiratory infection, kidney failure, blindness, heart attack and even death. So it's important that your friend gets help soon. You can tell your friend you are very worried about her but, unfortunately, there is a good chance she will deny she even has a problem. If this is the case, tell her that if she doesn't talk to her parents, you will. Then follow through. Or if that feels too much like tattling, talk to your parents and ask them to step in.

## PARENT PROBLEMS

**Q:** My father is cheating on my mother. I found out because I caught him kissing some strange woman. He has no idea that I saw him. I wasn't going to tell him, but I couldn't stop thinking about it. So I wrote him a letter saying that I saw him kissing her and that if he didn't tell my mother, I would. He hasn't said anything to me or even acknowledged the letter, and now I don't know what's going on. I don't want my parents to get divorced. I keep getting stomachaches over this.

**A:** You are understandably hurt, upset, worried and scared. It stinks that you had to see your father kissing someone other than your mother. But what we have to realize that this is between your father and mother. Whether they work things through, go to therapy together, or even divorce, it is totally out of your hands—as it should be. The best thing you can do right now is remember that they both love you. They are the adults, and it is up to them to figure out what choices they make.

Meanwhile, it's important that you take care of yourself. You don't have to keep this all bottled up inside. Perhaps you could talk to your father about your feelings, especially since he has presumably read your letter. Rather than telling him what you think he should or should not do, tell him what you feel. If you cannot talk to him or he won't respond, find someone else to talk to—a close friend, guidance counselor, someone you feel safe confiding in.

**Q:** You have to help me. My parents were fighting recently, and my father threw a bottle at my mother. It missed her, but he threw it hard so if it had hit her, she would have been really hurt. They have made up since then, but I'm kind of freaking out. This happened once before. What if he tries to hurt her again? Or hurt me? Plus, I don't want to get him in trouble.

**Dear Carol:** I have asthma and my friends get all worried about me every time I get out my inhaler. To me, it's not that big a deal. How can I tell them to calm down?
—I HAVE ASTHMA BUT I'M FINE

**Dear I.H.A.B.I.F.:** Asthma is very, very common, but many people don't know much about it. Why not tell your friends what you know and how you feel? Say, "I appreciate your concern, I really do, but relax, I know how to take care of myself." It's natural for your friends to have questions, and if you have questions, you can call 1-800-560-0300. The more your friends see that you are comfortable with yourself, the more comfortable they will be with you. Meantime, it is nice that they care, right?

**A:** It sounds like your father is already in trouble, given his behavior. If he doesn't get help, he could do some real damage to you or your mother. This is no time to sit back and see what happens. Tell your mother you are scared and upset over your father's behavior and fear what will come next. If she is unwilling to do anything, talk to another adult, anyone who will listen and take this problem seriously. This is not squealing. This is protecting the entire family and hopefully leading your father to get help.

**Q:** My mother is an alcoholic and makes my life miserable. She says embarrassing things to me while my friends are over. One minute she is laughing and up, and the next she is saying the meanest stuff in the world to me. Some days she's normal; other days she's a mess. My stepfather is helpful when he's around, but he's at work all day. I hate her, which makes me feel guilty. What can I do?

**A:** First, realize that alcoholism is a disease your mother suffers from. It's the disease you most likely hate and understandably so. You have every right to feel ticked off, embarrassed, confused, anxious, guilty, and any other way you feel. Remember: you have absolutely no control over your mother's behavior, and that it is in no way your fault. You might feel that if you were only a better daughter or got better grades or whatever, this wouldn't happen. But that's not true. You are not accountable for your mother's drinking problem.

Also, remind yourself that you are not alone. An estimated 6.6 million children live in households with at least one alcoholic parent. That means millions of kids know exactly what you are going through.

And there are things you can do. Talk to someone you trust about the way you feel. Sharing your secrets is not being disloyal to your family, and it will help you feel less alone. Your stepfather might be a good choice, since you say he's helpful. Get involved with fun things at school to offer you good times. Sign up for drama club or that sports team you've been considering. Groups such as Alateen (www.al-anon.alateen.org), for teens whose lives have been affected by someone else's drinking. In these groups, young people come together in schools, libraries and other places to share experiences, discuss difficulties and encourage one another.

## WHEN A PARENT IS ILL

**Q:** My mother told me she is taking my father to the hospital for some tests but that it's nothing to worry about. I hear them whispering to each other when I'm around, and they look sad a lot. I don't know what is going on, but I'm starting to imagine the worst!

**A:** When we don't get the information we need, it's human nature to imagine the worst. Your parents surely think they are protecting you by keeping you in the dark, but you need to explain to them that hearing bits and pieces makes you crazy. You must be feeling very scared and alone right now, in addition to frustrated. Assure your parents that you know something is going on and would like to at least know the basics. Don't yell or accuse them, as they are doing what they think is best. Instead, explain as calmly as you can that not knowing is scaring you. Most likely, they will open up to you. But you have to respect their choice to keep some of the information private for now.

**Q:** My mother was just diagnosed with cancer, and my world has stopped. The doctor says she may only have a few years left, and I can't even look at her. I am afraid to spend any time with her, but I am scared I will run out of time with her without having said and done all the things I want to. I feel angry, and I don't understand why this is happening to me!

**A:** Your feelings are very normal. It's terrible to have no control or ability to make this better for your mother or for yourself. And you're right—it's totally unfair and should not be happening to you. It's even tempting during times like this to blame yourself for her sickness, but know that it has nothing to do with your behavior—no matter what you've done.

What's important is that you realize she is still your mother and she loves you just as much as always. Talk to her. You don't have to talk about the illness during every conversation. Bring up anything you want to, but also don't be afraid to ask questions and tell her how you feel. There are no rules or codes here. You just have to feel it out with each other. If something makes her uncomfortable, she'll tell you. You do the same if she tells you things that make you feel uneasy.

Talk to other people about your feelings too, rather than keeping it all inside. In addition to friends and relatives, there are hotlines and Web sites created specifically for people with ill parents. It also might be a good time for you to keep a journal, since your feelings may be changing all the time. You don't ever have to apologize or defend your raw outbursts in a journal.

## DEPRESSION

**Q:** I'm fifteen, and sometimes I get incredibly sad for no reason. Not a little bit sad. I sit in my bedroom and cry for hours. I feel like I can't stop. It's weird because I don't really have any reason to feel this way. I have good friends, a loving family, and I'm pretty popular. I don't know if this is normal, and I'm too scared to tell anyone because I don't want to be put away.

**A:** You are not going to be put away. In fact, we don't know many teens who *haven't* sat in their rooms and cried for no reason. This may be partially due to new hormones coursing through your body (thanks, puberty) and setting your brain slightly off kilter. Puberty is notorious for making teens cry over lost earrings, Hallmark cards, and even spilled milk. If this is the case, it will simply run its course.

However, it is possible something else is causing your sadness. Are you certain something isn't eating at you? Sometimes letting your feelings pour out in a journal can help. You may find something is making you sad that you didn't realize. It's also possible you suffer from a medical condition. Many people have clinical depression—approximately fifteen million in fact—and it's on the rise in young people.

Talk to a trusted adult as soon as possible so you can find out where your depression is coming from and how to get rid of it. No matter the cause, it's treatable. According to the American Psychiatric Association, when diagnosed accurately and with some combination of antidepressant medication and other non-drug therapies, "There is virtually no one who cannot be helped."

**Q:** My mother has been depressed for months. I have no idea why. She just sits in her room all day long and barely speaks to anyone. My father says it is not my fault. He also tells me she doesn't always take her medication and that's why she's sad. I don't know what to do.

**A:** Your father is exactly right—this is not your fault. It may sound glib to say, "Don't take it personally," but that is our best advice. You are not to blame for her de-pression, nor is there anything you can do to get rid of it. It is up to your father to insist she get back on her medication or talk to her doctor about a new prescription if the current one isn't working. It is your job to take care of you. It may be helpful to get more information about depression (log on to http://www.depression.com).

Also, try not to absorb the tension from your mother's moods. Instead, go out with friends, pursue new hobbies, go for walks, take bike rides. If you're struggling, ask your father if you can see a professional counselor to talk to about the problem. The counselor will listen and help you sort through your feelings.

## SUICIDE

**Q:** My friend has told me several times that she wants to kill herself. She has shown me her suicide letters and even how she'll do it. This friend exaggerates everything and loves drama. So I don't know whether I should take her threats seriously. Plus, I've been sworn to secrecy.

**A:** Definitely take her threats seriously because you can't afford to be wrong on this one. Statistics show over seventy percent of people who threaten suicide either attempt it or complete the act.

We also know that most people who plan to commit suicide usually give warning signs or try to tell others. So please step in and get your friend help. Talk to her parents or older family friend of hers or her teacher. Tell them exactly what she's told you. While you can listen to your friend's feelings and encourage her to talk about her problems, you are not trained to handle this difficult situation.

If you can't think of anyone to tell or no one will take you seriously, encourage your friend to call a suicide hotline or call the number yourself. This is no time to be concerned with secrecy—your friend's well being is far too important.

**Q:** Sometimes, I have fantasies of just swallowing a bottle of pills and being done with life. But then I picture my mom, dad, or little sister finding me. I couldn't hurt them like that. I feel guilty, but sometimes I just don't want to be here anymore.

**A:** You are obviously going through a really hard time right now, and it's a horrible feeling when you can't see a way out. You probably think no one understands what you are going through and that you will always feel this way. But, there are ways to feel better.

The first step is to acknowledge that this is not something you can handle on your own. You need to find some professional help, which may seem overwhelming at first. Trust that this can get better, gather your courage (think again about how much your family cares for you), and tell a trusted adult—parent, teacher, guidance coun-selor, aunt, anyone—how you feel. He or she will be able to help you find someone trained to help you. Do not give up!

## INAPPROPRIATE TOUCHING

**Q:** A year ago, my oldest cousin told me he wanted to show me something. We went up to my bed-room and he shut the door. When I asked him what he wanted to show me, he pushed me onto the bed and put his hand under my shirt. I kicked him as hard as I could and ran out. Before he left our house, he told me he was going to do it again. I haven't told anyone, and I don't know what I am going to do the next time he visits. I feel humiliated.

**A:** This is not your fault! Nobody has the right to touch your body in a way that makes you uncomfortable. What your cousin did was totally off-limits and one hundred percent wrong. As scary as it may sound, you must tell an adult. Can you talk to your parents? If not, tell another relative or even a friend's parent. Someone needs to step in and let your cousin know his behavior is completely inappropriate and get him help so he won't harm you or anybody else again.

The best thing you can do is be totally straightforward. Tell the adult exactly what your cousin did and how it made you feel. If it helps, write it down on paper and hand that to the adult. Do not feel weird about needing protection. That is the responsibility of your parents and other adults. Nor should you feel bad about busting your cousin as you did nothing wrong—he did.

## RUNNING AWAY

**Q:** I am sixteen and thinking of running away. I hate my parents. They treat me like a little baby and never, ever listen to anything I have to say. At least if I run away I can get a job somewhere and make my own decisions and live how I want to live.

**A:** Hold up. What kind of job are you going to get that pays for your health insurance, clothes, food, and a place to live?

Every year, 1 million to 1.5 million kids run away from home. Many, like you, are looking for freedom from their parents and the ability to make their own decisions. The problem is that the choices out there are not the kind of choices any teen should have to make: Where can I get food when my money is gone? Who will put me up? What will I do with my life? It's even scarier for a girl on the run, since way too many male predators are waiting to strike. You will have all your adult years to be free and make choices. For now, why not take advantage of your warm bed, free food, and education?

If you are planning on running away because you feel alone, afraid or confused, it's important that you get help. Talk to a trusted adult—parent, friend's parent, religious leader, aunt, anyone who will take you seriously. If you are in an abusive situation and there is no one you feel safe talking to, call the police and ask for juvenile affairs or call an abuse hotline (the number is on page 254).

**Q:** My best friend told me she's going to run away but made me swear not to tell anyone. I don't want to betray her, but I don't want her to be in danger either. What do I do?

**A:** Tell someone, and fast. This is not the kind of secret a friend should ask you to keep, and all bets are off when it might mean danger for her. Talk to her parents and tell them what is going on. If you can't talk to them, talk to your parents.

# RESOURCES

You can call the following numbers or log on to the Web sites day or night, whenever you need someone to talk to or to evaluate your options. The 800 numbers are all free.

**IF YOU OR A FRIEND HAS AN EATING DISORDER:**
Eating Disorders Information and Referrals: http://www.edap.org or call 1-800-931-2237

*Bulimia Nervosa: The Secret Cycle of Bingeing and Purging* by Liza N. Burby (Rosen Publishing, 1998)

*Anorexia Nervosa: When Food is the Enemy* by Erica Smith (Hazelden Educational Materials, 1999)

**IF YOU ARE FEELING SERIOUSLY DEPRESSED OR SUICIDAL:**
Covenant House: http://www.covenanthouse.org

Depression.com: http://www.Depression.com

National Youth Crisis Hotline: 1-800-999-9999

National Runaway Hotline: 1-800-231-6946

*Depression* by Cathie Cush (Raintree Steck-Vaughn Publishers, 1993). Deals with suicide, running away, how to get help and develop coping skills.

**IF YOUR PARENT IS AN ALCOHOLIC:**
Alateen—Hope for Children of Alcoholics: www.al-anon.alateen.org

*Something's Wrong in My House* by Katherine Leiner (Franklin Watts, 1988). Deals with domestic violence and alcoholism, and how they affect children.

*My Dad Loves Me, My Dad Has a Disease* by Claudia Black (M.A.C. Publishing, 1997). A workbook designed to help children learn about themselves, their feelings, and the disease of alcoholism in their families.

**IF YOU ARE BEING ABUSED:**

CHILDHELP USA Child Abuse Hotline: 1-800-422-4453

**IF YOU HAVE A LONG-TERM ILLNESS:**

Band-Aides and Blackboards: When Chronic Illness or Some Other Medical Problem Goes to School: http://funrsc.fairfield.edu/~jfleitas/contents.html

**IF YOU HAVE LOST SOMEONE CLOSE TO YOU:**

KIDSAID: http://www.rivendell.org/KIDSAID

# CREDITS

This book would not have been possible without the incredibly talented people listed below. We'd also like to thank our own Dear Carol, Carol Weston, who is the author of *Private and Personal*, *For Girls Only*, and *Girlstalk* (both from HarperCollins). And special thanks to Jodi Bryson for our "Do Anything Better" ideas and to our Guy Q & A columnists Bill and Dave for giving us great guy point of views.

### The Girls' Life Guide to Friends
*F-R-I-E-N-D-S* by Roni Cohen-Sandler
*Quiz: Best Bud Challenge* by Michelle Silver
*Peace on Planet Friendship* by Michelle Silver
*I Just Got Dumped!* by Michelle Silver
*After the Blow Up* by Roni Cohen-Sandler
*Bad News Buds* by Roni Cohen-Sandler
*Branching Out* by Karen Bokram
*How to Be a Happy Camper* by Michelle Silver

### The Girls' Life Guide to Family
*Battle of the Sibs* by Roni Cohen-Sandler
*Superstar Sibs* by Roni Cohen-Sandler
*You Say Potato, I Say…* by Roni Cohen-Sandler
*Mom Envy* by Roni Cohen-Sandler
*Daddy's Little Girl?* by Jules Spotts
*'Fess Up to the Folks* by Jodi Bryson
*The Big "D"* by Roni Cohen-Sandler
*Wedding Bell Blues* by Kelly White
*The Evil Stepmother* by Roni Cohen-Sandler

### The Girls' Life Guide to Crushes
*You're Not Sick, You're Not Crazy… You're Crushed!* by Roni Cohen-Sandler
*Quiz: Is He Crushworthy?* by Kelly White
*Controlling the "Crush Crazies"* by Karen Bokram
*To Date or Not to Date?* by Michelle Silver
*Waiting for Dating* by Michelle Silver
*Where the Boys Are* by Roni Cohen-Sandler
*Boy Friend or Boyfriend?* by Karen Bokram
*Quiz: Cracking the Crush Code* by Gabrielle L. Gabrielle
*Dance Fever* by Michelle Silver